THIRD FORCE POLITICS

THIRD FORCE POLITICS

Liberal Democrats at the Grassroots

PAUL WHITELEY
PATRICK SEYD
ANTONY BILLINGHURST

OXFORD
UNIVERSITY PRESS

OXFORD
UNIVERSITY PRESS

Great Clarendon Street, Oxford OX2 6DP

Oxford University Press is a department of the University of Oxford.
It furthers the University's objective of excellence in research, scholarship,
and education by publishing worldwide in

Oxford New York

Auckland Cape Town Dar es Salaam Hong Kong Karachi
Kuala Lumpur Madrid Melbourne Mexico City Nairobi
New Delhi Shanghai Taipei Toronto

With offices in

Argentina Austria Brazil Chile Czech Republic France Greece
Guatemala Hungary Italy Japan Poland Portugal Singapore
South Korea Switzerland Thailand Turkey Ukraine Vietnam

Oxford is a registered trade mark of Oxford University Press
in the UK and in certain other countries

Published in the United States
by Oxford University Press Inc., New York

British Library Cataloguing in Publication Data
Data available

Library of Congress Cataloging in Publication Data
Data available

Typeset by SPI Publisher Services, Pondicherry, India
Printed in Great Britain on acid-free paper by
Biddles Ltd, King's Lynn, Norfolk

ISBN 0-19-924282–8 978-0-19-924282–5

1 3 5 7 9 10 8 6 4 2

Acknowledgements

We are extremely grateful to the Economic and Social Research Council for the grant (R000237789), which enabled us to carry out the survey of Liberal Democrat party members. Since 1989, the ESRC has provided us with the financial support to conduct studies of Labour, Conservative, and, now, Liberal Democrat party members. Its willingness to fund these studies has enabled a previously unknown area of British party politics to be opened up to scrutiny. We would like to acknowledge the consistent goodwill and encouragement that we have received from ESRC staff.

The research would not have been possible without the cooperation of Liberal Democrats. On behalf of the party, Chris Rennard agreed to our research proposal and then negotiated our access to the party's central membership records. He also wrote a letter to the individual Liberal Democrat members who had been selected for the survey encouraging them to respond. Without the support of the individual members of the party, this research would not have been possible. To the more than 4,000 members who took the time to respond to our questionnaire (and often then added comments at the end of the survey, many of which were extremely valuable and interesting) we are very grateful. We trust that while your anonymity has been guaranteed, you will recognize something of yourselves and your colleagues in the following pages. We also thank the members of the Sheffield Hallam and Hillsborough constituency parties who gave up some of their time to attend evening sessions at the University of Sheffield, where we piloted various versions of the questionnaire.

Janet Allaker was the project Research Officer. She did an excellent job in managing the various stages of the project, from questionnaire piloting through to liaison with Data Research Services, who were responsible for the administration and the scanning of the questionnaires. At the same time Janet was managing the Liberal Democrat survey, she was also running another survey of Labour party members. The successful completion of both of these surveys is a testament to her skills and commitment.

Acknowledgements

We would like to thank Oxford University Press, and particularly Claire Croft, for their encouragement and support in writing this book. Claire was extremely patient in the face of numerous delays, which arose principally from our other research commitments. Shortly after the Liberal Democrat survey was completed, both PW and PS took on heavy research and administrative duties associated with the ESRC's Democracy and Participation programme, and these delayed the writing of the book.

From the moment that PW and PS first embarked on these party membership studies in the late 1980s, Sue and Ros have provided enthusiastic support. They have perhaps had their fill of discussions of party members around the breakfast and dinner tables. We do not guarantee that we have finished with the subject of party members. We are threatening more surveys! But we know that they will continue to be our sharpest supporters and critics!

We are solely responsible for the contents.

Paul Whiteley, Patrick Seyd, Antony Billinghurst.
Colchester, Lezat-sur-Leze, France and Sheffield.

September, 2005.

Contents

List of Figures

List of Figures

List of Tables

1

'Introduction and Overview'

The British Liberal Democrat Party is a mystery. It is a vacuum round a void inside a hole. No one can describe a distinctive feature of Liberal Democracy. It has no cause, theme, culture or strategy, beyond a yearning for the eternal coalition of proportional representation.

(Simon Jenkins, *The Times*, 17 May 2002)

As a party, we now have some of the most long-established policies in British politics. And that can be good. We have been a party ahead of our time. Many of our most long-standing policies are actually being implemented.

(Paddy Ashdown's farewell speech as leader, Liberal Democrat conference, 21 September 1999)

We are being seen more and more as a party which does win elections, which does exercise responsible representation, which has become increasingly comfortable with the duties and the disciplines of power.

(Charles Kennedy speaking at the party's annual conference, 23 September 2004)

1.1 Introduction

In the 1951 general election, the Liberal Party secured only 2.5 per cent of the popular vote and returned just six Members of Parliament (MPs) to the House of Commons. This once powerful governing party was on the fringes rather than in the mainstream of British politics, and it looked like it was moving towards extinction. In contrast, the Liberal Democrat Party emerged from the 2005 general election with 22 per cent of the popular vote and sixty-two MPs, the largest number of seats the party had captured since 1923. Unlike the Liberals, whose seat share went into sharp decline after the 1923 general election, the Liberal Democrats have increased their representation in Parliament at each successive election since they were founded in 1988. Furthermore, Liberal Democrats have made steady progress in local elections since the 1950s. In the 1994 English Metropolitan Borough and Shire County elections the party overtook the Conservatives both in the share of the vote and in seats won (Rallings and Thrasher 1997: 112–13). Liberal Democrats have shared power with the Labour Party in the devolved Scottish and Welsh executives and have governed some of England's major cities, such as Liverpool, Sheffield, Newcastle, and Southampton. For a party facing oblivion in the 1950s, it has been a remarkable recovery of fortunes. Charles Kennedy's comment, quoted above, does look like an accurate description of the contemporary party.

However, success was by no means inevitable. The last independent Liberal Government ended in disarray during the First World War, although the party continued to play a role in coalition government until after the war. At its nadir in the 1950s, the Liberals were reduced to a rump of five MPs. On a couple of occasions, it looked like the party would disappear altogether and be absorbed into one of the other major parties. However, this did not happen, and for the last half century it has been climbing slowly back towards power. For four decades, the ascent was a very slow process with numerous false dawns. At times during the 1970s and 1980s, the Liberals won famous parliamentary by-election victories such as Torrington (1958) and Orpington (1962), which were hailed as the start of a revival. But these successes were temporary, and for a long time the party remained resolutely stuck on the launching pad.

The aim of this book is to explain why the party has recovered, paying particular attention to the role of the grassroots party members in shaping this recovery. A number of factors have contributed to the party's resurgence, including the performances of its main rivals, the Conservative and Labour parties, and the decline in partisan attachments throughout the entire electorate, but the evidence in this book should convince the reader that the grassroots party has played the decisive role in bringing this about. It is the men and women who joined the party as members, and then actively worked on its behalf by campaigning or standing in local and national elections when the political climate was cold, who are the key players. Thus, a major focus of the book is to examine these people, and in this respect it follows a similar template to our earlier studies of the Labour and Conservative parties (Seyd and Whiteley 1992, 2002; Whiteley, Seyd, and Richardson 1994; Whiteley and Seyd 2002). Through the text, we examine the attitudes and beliefs, the political experiences, and rates of activism of a representative sample of Liberal Democrat party members. However, there is a different emphasis in this book compared with the earlier studies. There is a greater concentration on the role of the grass-roots party in mobilizing and sustaining electoral support. Grassroots campaigning is important for all three major parties, but it is particularly important for the Liberal Democrats. In fact, the party could not have recovered from the electoral desert of the 1950s without the work of its activist base. It is no exaggeration to say that, in the case of the Liberal Democrats, the grassroots party has made the difference between recovery and disappearance.

This chapter is designed to set the scene for the later analysis. We start by providing a brief outline of the history of the party, before going on to examine the evolution of its policy goals over time. It is a piece of conventional wisdom that the Liberal Democrats are the centre party of British politics, wedged between their two great rivals in the middle of the political spectrum. Centre parties always have difficulty defining themselves separately from their rivals, and by implication this has always been a problem for the Liberal Democrats. This is the reasoning behind the quote from Simon Jenkins at the head of this chapter. However, as we shall see, this is an oversimplification. In a number of key policy areas, the Liberal Democrats are not the centre party of British politics. Moreover, if we examine their position on a whole series of policy issues combined into a single left-right scale, there have been times when the party has been more right wing than the Conservatives, and other times when it has been more left wing than Labour. So it is a considerable oversimplification to say that they are an ill-defined centre party. We return to this issue below in a discussion of the party's policy goals after we have outlined the origins and development of the Liberal Democrat Party.

1.2 The Origins of the Liberal Democrats

The Liberal Democrat Party was founded in 1988 from a merger of two hitherto independent but allied parties, the Liberal Party and the Social Democratic Party (SDP). The former had existed in different forms for more than 300 years, whereas the latter emerged from a split in the Labour Party in 1981. Therefore, a starting point for an analysis of the history of the Liberal Democrats is to understand the origins of the two founding parties.

From the perspective of the dominant two-party politics of the 1950s, the odds were against the survival of the Liberal Party as an independent political force. Historians have debated the 'Strange Death of Liberal England' (Dangerfield 1935), and disagree about the precise causes of the Liberal Party's decline in the early part of the twentieth century. Some attribute it to the rise of class politics, which gradually squeezed the party between the Conservatives, the party of the middle class, and Labour, the party of the working classes (McKibbin 1983). Others argue that the shift to class politics had largely taken place by the start of the First World War, and since the Liberal government was still in power at that time, it could not be the explanation for the decline (Wilson 1966; Clarke 1971). Whatever one's views about this debate, there can be little doubt that the First World War played a decisive role in the decline of the party. Victorian Liberalism was a creed ill-suited to coping with the mass slaughter of the First World War. As Kenneth Morgan perceptively argues: 'It was their principles, which the very fact of total war with the unbridled collectivism and the "jingo" passions which it unleashed appeared to undermine' (Morgan 1978: 58).

A bitter civil war in the party erupted when Lloyd-George ousted Asquith as Prime Minister from the coalition government in 1916. The resulting conflict persisted intermittently until 1935 (Dutton 2004: 68–136). The historical details of the split are of lesser concern than the consequences. The party that emerged from this prolonged struggle was a pale shadow of the party that had been in government before the First World War.

Once it had been pushed into third place, the party began to feel the full force of Duverger's law—the idea introduced by the French political sociologist—that third parties are unlikely to survive and certainly cannot aspire to power in a single member plurality electoral system of the type we have in Britain. Duverger explains why in the following passage:

Every policy implies a choice between two kinds of solution: the so-called compromise solutions lean one way or the other. This is equivalent to saying the centre does not exist in politics: there may well be a Centre party but there is no centre tendency, no centre doctrine. (Duverger 1964: 215)

In this view, a centre party will be squeezed between its two main rivals, and since it lacks the distinctive political space to define itself, it will become very vulnerable to collapse or to a takeover bid. Such a party rapidly becomes the victim of the 'wasted vote' argument, since it is never likely to achieve power. People who are sympathetic to the party will nonetheless refuse to vote for it on the grounds that such a vote would be wasted. This can set off a dynamic interaction between third party status and a loss of votes, which then turns into a self-fulfilling prophecy.

The pioneering study of electoral behaviour in Britain by Butler and Stokes (1969) stressed the importance of social class as the foundation of British electoral politics. Although there were always exceptions, Butler and Stokes argued that the middle class largely identified with, and voted for, the Conservative Party, and the working class did the same for Labour. In their analysis of electoral behaviour, there was little room for a centre party like the Liberals.[1] Other scholars took a very similar view. In his classic study of the British party system published at the height of two-party politics in the 1950s, for example, McKenzie paid little or no attention to the Liberals (McKenzie 1955).

1.3 Why Did the Liberal Democrats Survive?

So why did the party survive and eventually prosper? There are a number of factors that contribute to an explanation of the party's survival. One important point was the fact that the party was always able to keep a presence in Parliament. Although it was a small group of MPs, it nonetheless clung on as a distinctive grouping in the House of Commons. This gave it a national platform, something which the great majority of the 250 or more minor parties that have existed in Britain over the last century lacked.

Survival was enhanced by the fact that the party has existed in some form or another for more than 300 years, making it the oldest party in Parliament. It was founded as a loose group of parliamentarians who wanted to exclude the Duke of York from the succession to the throne in 1679 on the grounds that he was a Roman Catholic (Boothroyd 2001: 151). The group actually lost this battle, since the Duke became King James II. They acquired the name 'Whig' in the course of time, a term that originally referred to Scottish horse thieves. By the 1830s, the Whigs began to be described by their opponents as Liberals, a name originally intended to denote their laxity of morals. As often happens, the recipients of this insult began to proudly identify with the name

---

[1] They ignored the Liberal Party altogether in their discussion of the relationship between class and party. See Butler and Stokes (1969: 74).

and used it to describe themselves. During the nineteenth and early twentieth centuries, the Liberals were the alternative party of government to the Conservatives. Following the introduction of the mass franchise in the late nineteenth century, Joseph Chamberlain and his 'Birmingham Caucus' pioneered the mass party organization, which is still recognizable today. Thus, the Liberals were the pioneers of modern party organization in Britain. Clearly, a party with such a long pedigree acquired roots, which helped it to survive subsequently in a very cold climate.

A second factor in the party's survival was that it has always had a distinctive policy agenda. Traditional Liberalism stood for free trade, religious tolerance, internationalism, and individual freedom. In the early twentieth century, the New Liberalism pioneered by Lloyd-George took on board the idea that the state should provide welfare for all its citizens. Their opponents have adopted a number of these policies at different times, but not always consistently. For example, from time to time the Conservatives have been opponents of free trade. This was true in the early nineteenth century when they supported the Corn Laws, and also in the 1930s when they advocated tariffs in response to the economic crisis of the time. Similarly, while supporting internationalism in general terms, Labour was nonetheless a strong opponent of British membership of the European Economic Community in the 1970s. As we shall see later, the Liberal Democrats continue to advocate a number of distinct policies, which differentiate them from the other two parties, and this has helped to ensure their survival.

A third factor in their survival relates to the social base of the British party system. In a world of strong class politics, with Labour representing the working class and the Conservatives the middle class, there is little room for a relatively classless party of the centre. However, recent work has shown that the importance of class as the basis of British electoral politics has been exaggerated (see Clarke et al. 2004). The social class base of British political parties has always played a minor, albeit important, role in explaining Conservative and Labour electoral success. The fact that the Liberals, and subsequently the Liberal Democrats, have not really had a distinctive class base has not therefore been an insuperable barrier to their electoral success. A related point is that although the party lacked a class base, it did have a distinctive geographical base. Some two-thirds of the six Liberal MPs elected in 1951 represented seats in the Celtic fringes of Scotland and Wales. This geographical base persists to this day. For example, Liberal Democrat representation has grown in the West Country over the last twenty years. After the 2005 general election, the party took more than 30 per cent of the seats in the south-west compared with less than 10 per cent elsewhere. So geography helps to explain both the survival and the subsequent recovery of the party.

A fourth factor that sustained the party was its leadership. Ironically, while the civil war triggered by the dispute between Lloyd-George and Asquith almost destroyed the party, it was subsequently fortunate in having leaders who were determined to protect its distinct identity. Two relatively little-known politicians, Archibald Sinclair and Clement Davies, led the party in the bleak years between 1935 and 1956. The National Liberals, who had been in coalition with the Conservatives since 1931, made overtures to Sinclair in 1943 with a view to a merger aimed at constructing a post-war anti-socialist alliance. Talks were held, but Sinclair made it clear that his prime concern was to ensure the survival of the Liberal Party as an independent political force, and so nothing came of the initiative (Dutton 2004: 146). Similarly, an offer of a merger with the Conservatives came in 1951, and on this occasion Clement Davies resisted Churchill's embrace by turning down his invitation to become Minister of Education in the newly elected Conservative government (Dutton 2004: 177). If these leaders had put personal ambition before party, the Liberal Democrats would probably not exist today.

We have already referred to what, in our view, is the single most important reason for the survival and subsequent recovery of the third force party–the existence of a grassroots voluntary party organization, which kept things going during the bleak years. There were enough men and women, often working in small groups up and down the country, who were determined to keep the party alive. Without these people, it would not have survived. The evidence for this will be set out in the rest of this book. But an idea of the importance of grass-roots organization can be obtained by comparing the Liberal Party with the SDP, its ally during the early 1980s.

The SDP was launched with a fanfare of national publicity following Labour's split in 1981 and was joined by a number of prominent politicians. Among the party's founders were four former Labour cabinet ministers: Roy Jenkins, Shirley Williams, Bill Rodgers, and David Owen. Its roots lay in the conflicts between the left and the right in the Labour Party, which manifested over a number of issues such as the European Union, nationalization, the role of markets in the modern economy, and unilateral nuclear disarmament (Crewe and King 1996). The new party was met with an upsurge of enthusiasm, which briefly saw it achieving higher levels of support in the polls than all of its rivals.[2] Despite some initial successes, the party suffered from the key defect of being a top-down party with a very limited grassroots organization (Whiteley and Pridham 1986). When the inevitable decline in popularity occurred after the 1983 general election, the party lacked a voluntary organization to sustain it. The imbalance between the Liberals and the SDP, the two members of the Alliance,[3] was revealed fairly early on following the 1983 general election when the Liberals returned seventeen MPs and the Social Democrats only six MPs to the House of Commons. Moreover, an analysis of local council by-elections between 1983 and 1985 showed that Liberal candidates won four times as many contests as SDP candidates (Rallings and Thrasher 1997: 130). One of the main reasons for this was that the Liberals had the volunteers to campaign on behalf of their candidates, whereas the Social Democrats did not. The lack of an SDP activist base was one of the key reasons why the party was, in effect, 'taken over' by the Liberals in 1988.

As well as an imbalance in the activists, there was also an imbalance in the membership of the two Alliance parties. This was revealed in the membership ballot conducted by the two parties over the merger in early 1988. Some 52,741 Liberal party members voted in the ballot on the merger, whereas only 28,651 Social Democrats did so (Butler and Butler 1994: 156). Thus, the Liberals had nearly twice as many members who participated in the ballot as the Social Democrats. Over time this imbalance grew, as shown by a survey of Liberal Democrat party members conducted in 1993, some five years after the foundation of the merged party. Only 13 per cent of the respondents to this survey described themselves as former Social Democrats, compared with 48 per cent who were former Liberals (Bennie, Curtice, and Rudig, 1996: 151). Thus, four times as many members of the new party were ex-Liberals as were former Social Democrats, suggesting that many of the latter simply dropped out of politics altogether.

The grassroots organization has played a vital role in the growth of the Liberal Democrats' representation at Westminster. The Liberal Party was the pioneer of 'community politics', an approach to local campaigning introduced at the party conference in 1970 (Webb 2000: 104). Community politics arises from a traditional Liberal appeal to localism and decentralization in government, coupled with an emphasis on the importance of

---

[2] See Chapter 6.
[3] The Alliance was an electoral agreement between the two party leaders David Steel and David Owen not to challenge each other's parties in the same constituencies.

campaigning in the community on local issues as the eventual road to power. It became the basis of an effective strategy for winning power in local government, and ultimately became a means of capturing seats in Westminster in the 1997 general election. It is discussed more fully in Chapters 5 and 6.

Finally, the fifth aspect of Liberal Democrat survival and growth relates to the fact that the third party 'squeeze' predicted by Duverger never fully happened, because the party has managed to maintain a distinct policy identity throughout the long years of competition with Labour and the Conservatives, a point referred to earlier. It has taken distinctive policy positions on a number of issues and we examine this next.

1.4 Liberal Democrat Policy Goals

Judging the policy goals of a political party is not an easy task, since a party is a coalition of actors, many of whom directly or indirectly contribute to its overall policy stance. One approach might be to judge the party's policy goals from the speeches of the leader, but that produces a number of problems. Leaders' speeches are often fairly broad-brush in nature, and particularly at party conferences, they are more concerned with rallying the troops and getting coverage in the media than with setting out policy agendas. An alternative is to widen the scope, and look at the speeches of frontbenchers who speak on behalf of the party on certain policy areas. However, such speeches are often orientated towards specific parliamentary debates, rather than wider policy agendas. A third source are party publications, such as the 'Orange Book' (Marshall and Laws 2004), that clearly provide important input into the policymaking process. However, such publications usually involve floating speculative ideas that may never become party policies.

Probably the best source of information about party policy goals comes from manifestoes, which are published at each general election. They are read in their entirety by only a handful of people, but they are nonetheless the nearest thing to a broad statement of objectives, often qualified by specific details, that exist for defining party policy goals. The manifesto research group has analysed party manifestoes in Britain and other countries, using a common coding framework designed to apply both across countries and over time (see Budge et al. 2001). This provides an excellent source of information about Liberal Democrat policy goals. The manifesto data are coded into more than thirty policy categories, many of which are not really mainstream issues. We shall examine trends in Liberal/Alliance and Liberal Democrat policy goals as set out in the manifesto data for six major policy issues that are important for the political agenda. The issues are the role of the market in the modern economy; the importance of welfare policies and redistribution; internationalism with a special reference to Europe; the environment; law and order; and individual freedom and human rights.

Figure 1.1 contains the codes from the manifestoes of all three major parties for their proposals relating to the role of the market in the modern economy. The manifestoes extend from 1945 to 1997, which is more than half a century. To receive a positive score on this scale, a party must include statements in its manifesto that make favourable references to free enterprise, suggest that individual enterprise is superior to state control, or argue the need for traditional financial discipline.[4] It is interesting to see that in the early part of the 1950s, the Liberals were more in favour of free enterprise and traditional economic orthodoxy than the Conservatives. As Dutton argues: 'On balance, by the time that Grimond became leader, the party had become a largely right-leaning body, an anti-socialist rather than an anti-Conservative force in British politics' (Dutton 2004: 189).

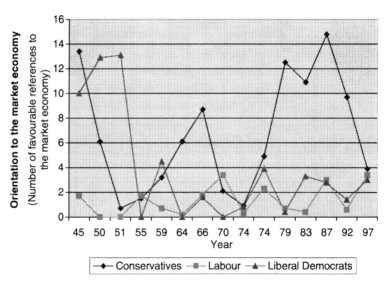

Figure 1.1 Party orientations to the market economy 1945–97
Source: Budge et al. (2001)

---

[4] This includes per401 and per414 in the manifesto project data-set (see Budge et al. 2001).

This situation changed fairly rapidly after Jo Grimond became leader in 1956. He believed that the Liberals needed to be a radical, though non-socialist party, and he positioned them to the left of the Conservatives and in direct competition with Labour on the issue of the role of markets and free enterprise. As Figure 1.1 shows, the party remained close to where Labour was located in relation to this issue from 1955 onwards. When the Conservatives went radically to the right on the issue following Mrs Thatcher's election as leader in 1975, the Liberals continued to remain close to Labour.

Party manifesto positions on the issues of welfare and redistribution appear in Figure 1.2. In this figure, a positive score on welfare means that a party makes references to the need for equality and social justice, as well as favourably mentioning the desirability of generous social benefits.[5] Figure 1.2 shows that the Liberal Party closely resembled the Conservatives on welfare until the 1960s, since it downplayed the importance of this issue before that time. During the 1960s and early 1970s, the party had difficulty working out a coherent position, since it fluctuated widely between a

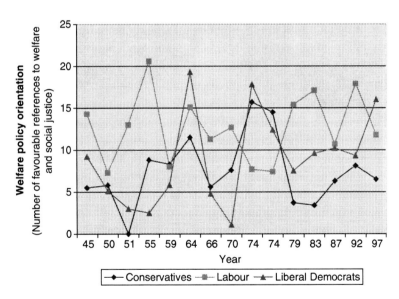

Figure 1.2 Party orientations towards welfare and social justice 1945–97
Source: Budge et al. (2001)

[5] The welfare orientation scale is made up of per503 and per504 from the manifesto data.

strong pro-welfare position in 1964 and a relative neglect of the issue in 1970. Only with the arrival of Mrs Thatcher did it start to trace out a more stable position roughly equidistant from Labour and the Conservatives. This is an example of a policy in which the party was 'squeezed' in the middle.

Figure 1.3 shows that the Liberal Democrats, like the Liberals before them, have taken a strong positive position on internationalism, particularly in relation to Europe. Internationalism stresses the importance of international cooperation between countries, the need for aid to developing countries, and the desirability of having a positive attitude to European integration.[6] With the single exception of the Conservatives in 1955, the party has always been more internationalist and pro-European than its two main rivals. It has not sought to emulate Labour or even to 'split the difference' between Labour and the Conservatives on the issue, and it remains radical on this policy to the present day. On this issue, it is not in the centre ground of politics.

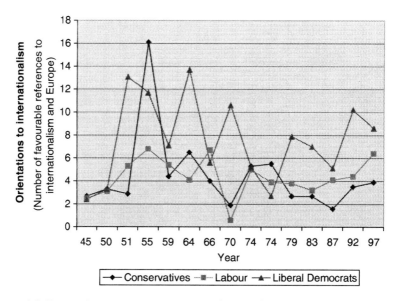

Figure 1.3 Party orientations to internationalism and Europe 1945–97
Source: Budge et al. (2001)

---

[6] This scale is made up of per107 and per108 from the manifesto data.

Figure 1.4 measures the positions taken up by the three major parties on the issue of the environment. Favourable references in manifestoes to the environment include phrases about the importance of preserving natural resources, the proper use of the countryside and national parks, as well as criticisms of selfish interests that despoil the natural world.[7] Figure 1.4 shows how environmental protection really only became an issue on the party agendas after about 1970, since before that time the parties made few references to it. However, from that time onwards, the Liberals and subsequently the Liberal Democrats have carved out a distinctive position on the issue. With the sole exception of 1983, the party has been generally more radical than its rivals on the issue of the environment. Again, there is no suggestion of the party trying to find a middle ground between Labour and the Conservatives. Rather, it is mapping out a distinctive position as the party that strongly advocates environmental protection.

Figure 1.5 measures party manifesto commitments in relation to law and order and crime. In the party manifestoes this refers to statements that stress the importance of taking action against crime and also the need to

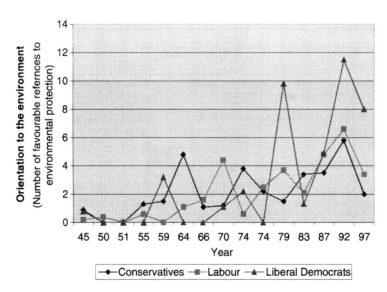

Figure 1.4 Party orientations to environmental protection 1945–97
Source: Budge et al. (2001)

[7] This is per501 in the manifesto data.

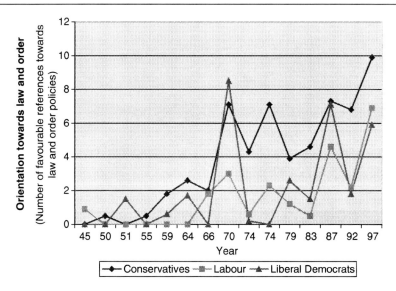

Figure 1.5 Party orientations towards law and order 1945–97

Source: Budge et al. (2001)

enforce laws effectively.[8] Since the 1970s, the parties in general have paid more attention to this issue as the fear of crime has moved up the political agenda. The Liberal Democrats joined in this general trend towards emphasizing the importance of law and order, but they have generally been closer to Labour on this issue than the Conservatives. The latter have made much of the running on the issue of law and order, and there is a sense that the other two parties are following their agenda.

Figure 1.6 plots trends in manifesto commitments in relation to individual freedom and human rights. Appeals for individual freedom to be respected and human rights safeguarded are the hallmarks of this particular issue dimension.[9] It can be seen that the Liberals and Liberal Democrats have been at the forefront of references to these issues over time, although there was a period in the 1960s when they were low on the party's agenda. But in most other elections, the Liberals and Liberal Democrats have been more concerned about human rights and individual freedom than their rivals. The Conservative profile is curious since their highest manifesto score on this issue occurred in 1987, when Mrs Thatcher was Prime Minister. However, much of this was Cold War rhetoric echoing the views of

---

[8] This is per605 in the manifesto data.   [9] This is per201 in the manifesto data.

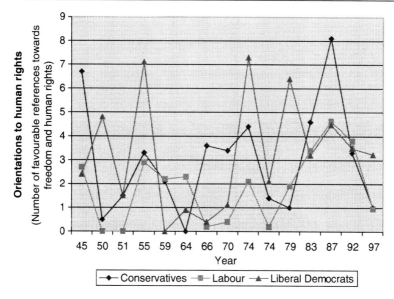

Figure 1.6 Party orientations towards human rights 1945–97
Source: Budge et al. (2001)

the Reagan administration in the United States. Once the Soviet Union disappeared in 1990, the Conservatives rapidly lost interest in these issues.

The evidence from these six policy areas suggests that the view that Liberal Democrats are simply in the centre of the political spectrum wedged between Labour and the Conservatives is inaccurate. On the issues of internationalism, the environment, and human rights, they are for the most part more radical than either of the other two parties. On the issue of welfare, they have only been in the centre of the political spectrum on some occasions, and on the market economy, they tend to track the Labour Party. To get an overall picture of their position in the political spectrum, it is useful to combine the policy positions of the parties over a wide range of issues into a single left-right scale. This is done in Figure 1.7, which includes scores for all the elections between 1945 and 2005.[10]

Figure 1.7 supplies a political map of the electoral agenda of British politics over a sixty-year period. It confirms the point that the Liberal Democrats were on the right of both of their rival parties during the

[10] The details of this scale appear in Budge et al. (2001). We are grateful to the manifesto team for supplying the unpublished data for 2005.

1950s. When Labour shifted sharply to the left in 1974, and the Conservatives shifted sharply to the right in 1979, the Liberal Democrats were left in the centre ground of politics. Thus, their location resulted from changes in the policy goals of their rivals, rather than through their own actions. During the 1960s and 1970s, Liberal policy goals fluctuated rather widely between successive elections, and it was not until the Liberal Democrat Party was formed and the 1992 election was over that these fluctuations damped down and the party settled into a fairly stable centre ground position. In 1997, when New Labour came to power, the Liberal Democrats became the party of the centre-left as New Labour located itself on the centre-right. The Conservatives moved gradually back to the centre following their sharp shift to the right in 1979, and this trend clearly accelerated after their defeat in 1997. Labour has finally returned to being the party of the left in the 2005 general election, and currently the Liberal Democrats are very much the party of the centre.

This evidence suggests that the view that the Liberal Democrats and the Liberals before them have always been in the political centre is simplistic.

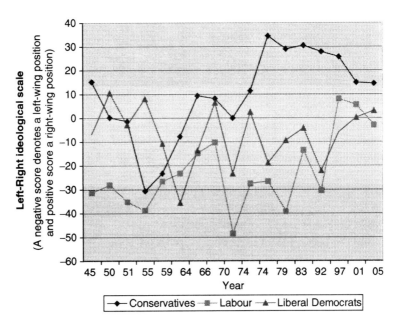

Figure 1.7 Party policy positions on the left-right scale 1945–2005

Source: Budge et al. (2001) and private communication

In the elections of 1955 and 1959, they were the party of the right, and in the elections of 1997 and 2001, the party of the left. In addition, the whole agenda of British party politics has swung to the right since the 1980s, and they have joined in this along with the other parties. The British electoral agenda is dynamic and the policy positions of the Liberal Democrats have reflected this fact. This explains in part why the two-party squeeze predicted by Duverger has not occurred and prevented liberal Democrats from winning seats.

Overall, there are a number of distinct reasons why the Liberals, and subsequently the Liberal Democrats, survived as a party and have gradually begun to pick up support, both in terms of vote shares and in terms of seats. We will focus extensively, though not exclusively, on the role of the grass-roots party in bringing this about in the remainder of this book. In Section 1.5, we review the broad research findings in this book.

1.5 An Overview of the Book

The analysis begins in Chapter 2 with a profile of the party members in terms of their social backgrounds and political attitudes. Part of this analysis involves making a comparison between the evidence from a survey of members conducted in 1993 with our own survey of 1999 to see what changes have occurred. Further comparisons are made between the social backgrounds of party members and those of Liberal Democrat voters in the 1997 general election. Finally, levels of attachment to the party and rates of activism among grass-roots members are explored at the end of the chapter. The evidence suggests that, while many party members are active, there has been a decline in party activism over time and a weakening of the ties between the party and its members. In this respect, the findings replicate those for Labour and the Conservatives in our earlier research (Seyd and Whiteley 1992; Whiteley, Seyd, and Richardson 1994).

In each case, the aim is to see if there are significant differences between the groups being compared, particularly the members and the voters, with the idea of assessing what these might mean for the party's electoral support. There are striking differences between members of the Liberal Democrats, and voters. The former are older, more middle class and better educated than the latter. Despite this, party members and voters have many attitudes in common, although the members often feel more strongly about issues than do the voters. Significant conflicts between the views of the members and those of the voters are quite limited.

Chapter 3 probes more deeply into the attitudes of party members to explore their ideological beliefs. This addresses the basic issue raised in the quote by Simon Jenkins at the head of this chapter, namely, do the Liberal Democrats stand for distinctive policies that make them different? We have seen that, as far as party manifestoes are concerned, there are distinctive Liberal Democrat policies, but is there a distinctive Liberal Democratic ideology? The analysis shows that there is a distinctive set of principles underlying Liberal Democrat political ideology. The ideology centres around individual freedom and tolerance in relation to lifestyle issues, a belief in redistribution and social equality, a commitment to free markets and a positive attitude to internationalism, as exemplified by members' views of the European Union (EU). This distinctive set of ideological beliefs underpin Liberal Democrat policies and add a coherence to the party, which makes it different from its rivals in British politics.

Chapter 4 examines the pathways to party membership. After an initial description of ways in which people can join the party, we go on to examine what membership of the party actually means to the individuals concerned. There are rival theoretical explanations as to why some people join a party when others, with rather similar social backgrounds and attitudes, do not. We examine two of these, the civic voluntarism model and the general incentives model, and evaluate the extent to which they provide accurate explanations of why people join the party. The former stresses the importance of resources, and the latter the human choices that explain why some people participate. The possibilities for fully testing these rival models are limited in the absence of a comparable survey of supporters who have not joined the party. But some inferences can be made about the role of resources, as well as choices, when it comes to explaining why people join the party in the first place. These are made possible by comparing evidence from the membership survey, with evidence relating to Liberal Democrat voters from the British Election Study. The comparisons suggest that both resources and choices are important in explaining why people join the party. Certainly members have more resources in the sense of higher incomes, better educational attainments, and higher status class characteristics than voters. But additionally, incentives are also important for influencing the decision to join the party. Thus, both models appear to be relevant in explaining why people join.

Chapter 5 examines grassroots activism in the Liberal Democrat Party. It begins by defining what is meant by activism, including an examination of the role of members as community politicians. In this case, we are able to test the civic voluntarism and general incentives models more directly, since all the indicators needed for testing these models are available in the survey. After spelling out what variables are included in each model, they are tested towards the end of the chapter. Overall the results suggest that party activism can be explained by a combination of the individual's psychological engagement with both politics and the party, together with their judgements about the costs and benefits of political engagement. Resources play a role in this, but it appears that incentives, and the choices associated with them, are particularly important in influencing the individual's decision to be active.

Chapter 6 studies the role of the party members in influencing voting behaviour in the 1997 general election. It is at this point that we begin to assess the importance of local campaigning in influencing electoral support. There has been a debate in the literature about the relevance of local campaigns, with some writers arguing that local campaigns are irrelevant, while others argue that they are quite important in influencing electoral behaviour. To evaluate the impact of Liberal Democrat campaign activity on the election, it is important to take into account the campaign activities of its main rivals, Labour and the Conservatives. This is done using data from a survey of Labour party members conducted in 1997, together with local campaign spending data for all three parties. The results are fairly clear, and suggest that local campaigning plays a very important role in influencing the Liberal Democrat vote.

Chapter 7 builds on Chapter 6 by taking into account wider factors, other than campaigning, which influence the vote. In this way, the impact of local campaigning on the vote can be assessed more fully. The chapter looks at trends in Liberal Democrat voting intentions over a thirty-year period, with the aim of identifying how these relate to Labour and Conservative voting intentions. These time series models are particularly useful in identifying the causal sequences at work in explaining trends in electoral support. This long-term analysis shows that the competitive situation between the Conservatives and Liberal Democrats is significantly greater than the competitive situation between Labour and the Liberal Democrats. But it also shows that the party has to wait for its main rivals to make political mistakes and lose support before it can profit by winning over voters. We describe this as the political equivalent of 'waiting for Godot', and it means that the Liberal Democrats are not the masters of their own electoral fate. The remainder of Chapter 6 looks at a more complex model of Liberal Democrat voting support, using data from the 2001 and 2005 British Election Study surveys. A number of conclusions are drawn from these models, but the most important one is that the party needs an active grassroots campaigning organization to win votes, since local campaigns are more important for the Liberal Democrats than they are for Labour or the Conservatives.

Finally, chapter 8 addresses the issue of where the party goes from here. The big question is whether or not it can replace its rivals as the second, or even the first, party of British electoral politics. In the light of the earlier discussion, we examine the circumstances under which this is likely to occur, and draw conclusions about the future strategy of the party arising from these. The key point is that a breakthrough into second party status is likely to require a split in one or other of its main rivals, as well as the reform of the electoral system for Westminster elections. While the Liberal Democrats have done very well to win seats and to increase their vote share in recent years, the 62 seats they won in 2005 are a long way from the 324 needed to give them a majority in the House of Commons. To achieve the breakthrough into power is a difficult task, and the chapter examines the circumstances under which this is likely to take place. From a series of simulations, it concludes that these circumstances are quite likely to occur in the next general election in 2009 or 2010.

2

Who Are the Members?

For most people, their contact with the Liberal Democrats comes through the pages of *Focus*, the ubiquitous local party newsletter distributed to households. The paper celebrates local Liberal Democrat achievements in relation to often mundane and unglamorous issues, such as road repairs and street cleaning. These issues are important to people living in the locality, and they help to establish the party as a political force in local government. This street-level activity is often referred to as 'community politics'. Concentration on local level issues places high demands upon the active party members, however, since they have to become campaigners all year round, and not just at election times.

In this chapter, we ask who the Liberal Democrat party members are. We will examine their social and demographic profiles, along with their political attitudes. We will draw upon an earlier study of Liberal Democrat party members (Bennie, Curtice, and Rudig 1996) to examine changes in their profiles during the 1990s. Comparisons will also be made with Liberal Democrat voters in order to determine what differences, if any, exist between the two types of party supporter. Following this, we analyse activism within the party and examine whether there is any evidence of a decline in participation in recent years. This is a particularly interesting question, given the evidence of a decline in grassroots activism in both the Labour and Conservative parties (Seyd and Whiteley 1992, 2002; Whiteley, Seyd, and Richardson 1994; Whiteley and Seyd 2002).

2.1 The Social Backgrounds of Members

As we pointed out in Chapter 1, the Liberal Democrat Party was created out of the Liberal Party and the SDP. As a starting point, it is interesting to probe into the political origins of the current party members. Clearly, there are three alternatives: they were either members of the Liberal Party (43 per cent), members of the SDP (14 per cent), or recruited directly into the Liberal Democrat Party (42 per cent). Despite having a party leader, Charles Kennedy, who was formerly an SDP MP, it is clear that the ex-Social Democrats play a relatively minor role in the grass-roots party.

In 1997, the party returned just three women MPs to the House of Commons, as compared with forty-three men. In 2001, this increased to five women as against forty-seven men. The election of Sarah Teather, the youngest MP at the time, in a by-election in September 2003, increased the total to six women. In the 2005 general election, ten women Liberal Democrat MPs were elected as against fifty-two men. Thus, the gender imbalance at the top of the party remains great, even though the number of women MPs is growing slowly. As Table 2.1 shows, there is also a gender

Table 2.1. Socio-economic profile of the party membership: gender, age, education, and employment ($N = 2,866$)

Members	%
Gender	
Male	54
Female	46
Age	
18–25	2
26–35	5
36–45	11
46–55	23
56–65	22
65+	36
Mean	59
Education	
GCSE/School Certificate/Scottish Lower Certificate	56
'A' Level/(Scottish) Higher Certificate	45
Technical qualification	17
University or CNAA degree	42
Employment	
Full-time education	2
Employed	50
Unemployed	2
Retired	32
Looking after the home	6
Voluntary work	5
Graduate status	
Yes	42
No	58

Note: The figures in this table, and all the following ones, have been rounded and therefore the percentages may not always total 100.

imbalance amongst the members, which is skewed towards men: 54 per cent of the membership is male. Our studies of Labour and Conservative parties (Seyd and Whiteley 1992; Whiteley, Seyd, and Richardson 1994) revealed that males dominate Labour, but much less so the Conservatives. Thus, the gender composition among the members of Britain's first and third major parties is overwhelmingly male.

The average Liberal Democrat member is 59 years old, which is eight years older than the average Labour member, but three years younger than the average Conservative (Seyd and Whiteley 1992; Whiteley, Seyd, and Richardson 1994). Fifty-eight per cent of Liberal Democrat members are 56 or over, with 42 per cent aged between 18 and 55. The party may not be as antiquated as the Conservatives, but it is not a party of young people. An older membership has advantages in that it provides stability for the party in terms of continuity of membership, and the evidence shows that 90 per cent of the members continue to renew their subscription. On the other hand, the party has to recruit younger members if it is to avoid long-term decline.

This ageing membership belies the image of the Liberal Democrats as a party of new ideas and young activists. Of course, the problem of recruiting young members is not confined to the Liberal Democrats alone. In 1992, Labour could only boast of 5 per cent of its membership in the 18–25 age category, a figure which has not changed subsequently (Seyd and Whiteley 1992, 2002). The Conservatives are in a worse position, with only 1 per cent of the membership under the age of 25 (Whiteley, Seyd, and Richardson 1994).

Of the three main parties, the Liberal Democrats are the most highly educated. Forty-two per cent of members have a degree compared to 30 per cent of Labour members and 19 per cent of Conservatives (Seyd and Whiteley 1992; Whiteley, Seyd, and Richardson 1994). Of the total sample of Liberal Democrat members, 56 per cent are educated to General Certificate of Secondary Education (GCSE) level (or Scottish Lower Certificate) and 45 per cent to 'A' level (or Scottish Higher Certificate). Seventeen per cent of members have a technical qualification. A highly educated membership should result in a more efficient and effective party. For example, one of the important functions of members is to provide people to staff the party organization and to run for office at local and national levels (Scarrow 1996). However, highly educated members can also prove to be a burden for the party leadership. This is because they are likely to be more confident and less deferential in expressing an opinion. Achieving party unity under these circumstances is likely to be difficult, and party management requires a strategy of diplomacy and debate with the members.

Given the age profile of the membership, we might expect many of the members to be retired from work. In fact, one-third of the members are retired; just over one-third are in full-time employment; and a further 10 per cent are in part-time employment. Table 2.2 shows that the majority of members work, or have worked, in the non-profit sector of the economy. Forty-six per cent work in the civil service or in a nationalized industry, while 10 per cent work in the charity or voluntary sector; just under 4 in 10 work in the private sector. Given their high level of educational achievement, it is not surprising to find that 74 per cent of the members work, or have worked, in professional occupations and qualify as members of the salariat. The middle class dominates the party membership, as it does for both the Labour and Conservative parties. Working-class members make up only 5 per cent of the Liberal Democrats, compared to 26 per cent of

Table 2.2. Socio-economic characteristics of the party membership: work sector, class, and income

Members	%
Type of work organization	
Private company/firm	38
Nationalized industry	3
Other public sector (e.g. Central Government, Civil Service)	43
Charity/voluntary sector (e.g. charitable companies, trade unions)	10
Other	5
Socio-economic occupational classification	
Salariat	74
Routine non-manual	11
Petty bourgeoisie	7
Foreman and technician	4
Working class	5
Household income (£p.a.)	
Under 5000	5
5000–10000	11
10000–20000	27
20000–30000	22
30000–40000	13
40000–50000	9
50000–60000	6
60000 +	8
Subjective social class	
Middle class	53
Working class	12
Other	2
None	33

Labour and 8 per cent of Conservatives. Thus, grassroots party politics in Britain is dominated not only by men, but also by white-collar professionals.

In terms of class perceptions, just over half of the members think of themselves as middle class and only 12 per cent think of themselves as working class, with about a third not thinking of themselves in class terms at all. However, when asked about the class background of their family, some 37 per cent of members felt that their family was working class when they were young, so there has been a lot of subjective social mobility among the current members over time.

High educational qualifications can lead to well-paid jobs and high incomes. However, the fact that over 50 per cent of members are employed in the non–profit sector of the economy helps to explain their lower levels of income than might be expected. The average Liberal Democrat member has a household income in the £20,000–30,000 range. Forty-three per cent of members report a household income of less than £20,000, a third between £20,000 and £30,000, and a further one in four of £40,000 or above.

As Table 2.3 shows, a majority of the members (65 per cent) consider themselves to be religious. Of those who express a religious preference, 70 per cent are Church of England, 15 per cent Methodist, and a further 11 per cent Roman Catholic. The party is also dominated by members who classify themselves as white/European, with these members making up 99 per cent of the total, while the remaining 1 per cent are represented by Asian and black members.

Table 2.3. Socio-economic characteristics of the party membership: religion and ethnicity

Members	%
Religious	
Yes	65
No	15
No response	20
Denomination	
Roman Catholic	11
Church of England/Wales/Scotland/Anglican	70
Methodist	15
Muslim	1
Jewish	4
Ethnic origin	
White	99
Asian/Black	1

2.2 The Political Attitudes of Members

As the party's name suggests, Liberal Democrats combine two distinct and long-standing political traditions: liberalism and social democracy. The former emphasizes individual rights and limited government, and the latter stresses social justice and common welfare in a mixed economy. These traditions form the basis for members' political attitudes.

A sift through our data allows us to identify six broad categories of political attitudes, which align with the principled themes maintained by the party over a number of years. These attitudes can be labelled *institutional reform, European integration, markets and collectivism, redistribution and welfare, the environment*, and *morality, law, and order*. Not surprisingly, these echo the manifesto commitments discussed in Chapter 1, although the categories are not exactly the same. We shall now discuss each of these in turn.

2.2.1 Institutional Reform

Liberal Democrats are institutional reformers. The party favours the decentralization of state power, greater freedom of information, and the reform of Parliament, especially the House of Lords. Above all, the party has long campaigned for the reform of the electoral system, and replacement of the present simple majority system by the single transferable vote. As we see in Table 2.4, in response to the statement that 'the single transferable vote is the only acceptable electoral system for Britain', 48 per cent of members agree and 21 per cent disagree. However, the detailed technicalities of electoral systems would appear to baffle even Liberal Democrats, as one in three members neither agrees nor disagrees with the statement, even though it is party policy, suggesting some confusion about this particular voting system.

Table 2.4. Members' views on institutional reform (percentages)

	Strongly agree	Agree	Neither agree nor disagree	Disagree	Strongly disagree
A	12	36	31	19	2
B	5	32	35	24	3
C	21	35	12	27	4
D	8	13	16	35	28

A: The Single Transferable Vote is the only acceptable electoral system for Britain.
B: Coalition governments are the best form of government for Britain.
C: The reformed House of Lords should be a wholly elected chamber with no appointed members.
D: It would be a good thing to abolish the monarchy.

A likely consequence of proportional representation is coalition government. The membership is not overwhelmingly convinced of the benefits of this, even though it is likely to provide the party's best route to power. On this issue, members split into three blocs: 37 per cent agree with coalition government; 35 per cent have no preference; and 27 per cent are against. On another institutional issue of contemporary relevance, namely reform of the House of Lords, over 50 per cent of the members agree that the chamber should be wholly elected. While reform of this ancient institution wins approval, reform of another such institution does not win the support of the membership. Some two-thirds of the members disagree with abolition of the monarchy.

2.2.2 European Integration

The future of Europe has long been a defining issue for Liberal Democrats. The party has consistently supported European integration, while the Conservative and Labour parties have undergone numerous policy shifts and internal conflicts over the issue. Thus, it is not surprising to see in Table 2.5 that Liberal Democrats are strongly in favour of the EU. Sixty-nine per cent disagree with the statement that 'Britain should resist further moves to integrate the European Union'. The major symbol of increased integration with the EU is the single European currency. Two-thirds of the members believe that the Euro should be Britain's currency, underlining the Liberal Democrats' commitment to European integration. One in five would like to see a single European government, while nearly a quarter of the membership would like an increase in the powers of the EU. Taken together, we find nearly half of the membership expressing greater

Table 2.5. Members' views on European integration (percentages)

Britain should...	Strongly agree	Agree	Neither agree nor disagree	Disagree	Strongly disagree
Resist moves to integrate into the EU	6	11	13	41	28
Agree to a single European currency	28	38	13	12	9
Do you think that Britain's long-term policy should be to...?					
Leave the EU			5		
Stay in the EU and reduce its powers			37		
Leave things as they are			14		
Stay in the EU and try to increase its powers			24		
Work for a single European government			20		

European commitment. However, not all Liberal Democrats are convinced of integration. Just over one in three (37 per cent) would prefer that Britain remains part of the EU, but would like to see a reduction in EU powers. And 5 per cent of the membership would like Britain to withdraw from the EU.

2.2.3 Markets and Collectivism

The first part of Table 2.6 gives members' responses to some indicators of attitudes to the free market and collectivism. We see that a plurality of members are in favour of free markets in relation to the production of goods and services, and a large majority are in favour of individuals taking responsibility for themselves. This is an echo of the Liberals' historical concern with free markets and free trade referred to in Chapter 1. At the same time, members are not overwhelmingly in favour of private enterprise as the best way of solving economic problems. In fact, there is a near equal three-way split between those in favour, those against, and the

Table 2.6. Members' views on markets and collectivism (percentages)

	Strongly agree	Agree	Neither agree nor disagree	Disagree	Strongly disagree
A	5	38	24	29	4
B	7	51	26	15	1
C	3	28	34	31	4
D	4	31	30	30	6

A: The production of goods and services is best left to the free market.
B: Individuals should take responsibility for providing for themselves.
C: Private enterprise is the best way to solve Britain's economic problems.
D: The government should establish a prices and incomes policy as a means of controlling inflation.

	Definitely should	Probably should	Does not matter	Probably should not	Definitely should not
A	7	18	22	32	23
B	3	16	16	42	23
C	3	12	22	47	16
D	28	57	10	5	1

Government should
A: Get rid of private education.
B: Encourage the growth of private medicine.
C: Introduce stricter laws to regulate trade unions.
D: Give workers more say in the places where they work.

Are you generally in favour of	
More nationalization of companies by government	28
More privatization of companies by government	10
Things should be left as they are now	63

neutral respondents on this topic. Members are also equally divided on the issue of a prices and incomes policy, which is the touchstone indicator of corporatist approaches to economic policymaking.

A difficult issue for all parties today is the provision of health care and education, particularly whether or not these should be provided exclusively by the state. As the members are highly educated, this may help to explain why many of them disagree with the abolition of private education. By a margin of more than two to one, members oppose the abolition of private education. Private medicine touches upon the question of freedom of choice, but it also touches upon the National Health Service (NHS), which, as the second half of Table 2.6 shows, is a very popular cause among Liberal Democrats. The members are clear as to which side of the argument they favour, since those against the growth of private medicine outnumber those in favour by a margin of 3 to 1.

An important feature of Liberal Party policy in the post-war years has been a commitment to worker participation in industry. While the party has been less supportive of trade unionism than the Labour Party, it has had distinctive views on industrial relations. The Thatcher era opened the way for curbs on trade union activity. The members are heavily against the introduction of further laws to regulate trade union activity. Moreover, they believe there is a need for the trade unions to protect employees' working conditions and wages. On the issue of workers' rights, 85 per cent of members agree that workers should be given more say in the places where they work.

The final section of Table 2.6 shows that party members are not much in favour of nationalization, while at the same time they are largely against further privatization. In relation to this issue more than six in ten members favour the status quo. Overall, members have some sympathy for the private market, but they are far from being free marketeers who wish to roll back the state and promote private enterprise at all costs.

2.2.4 Redistribution and Welfare

A key policy commitment for Conservative governments in the 1980s and 1990s, which New Labour felt obliged to follow in its first two years of office, was the control of public spending. Thus, both of these parties have sought to curb public spending at times. In the case of Liberal Democrats, however, as can be seen in Table 2.7, an overwhelming majority of the members favour increasing government spending and taxation, with only 1 in 100 favouring cuts in taxation and spending.

Table 2.7. Members' views on redistribution and welfare (percentages)

Suppose the government had to choose between three options. Which do you think it should choose?

Reduce taxes and spend less on health, education, and social benefits	1	
Keep taxes and spending on these services at the same level as now	16	
Increase taxes and spend more on health, education, and social benefits	83	

	Strongly agree	Agree	Neither agree nor disagree	Disagree	Strongly disagree
A	7	39	32	19	3
B	33	54	5	7	1
C	17	45	21	14	4
D	10	47	24	18	2
E	11	50	19	18	1
F	8	27	18	41	7
G	9	28	18	42	3

A: Income and wealth should be redistributed to ordinary working people.
B: Government should spend more money to get rid of poverty.*
C: The government should give more aid to poor countries in Africa and Asia.
D: Everyone's taxes should go up to provide better old-age pensions for all.
E: The only way to deal with the funding crisis of in the NHS is to have a substantial increase in general taxation.
F: High income tax makes people less willing to work hard.
G: Prescription charges for medicines should be abolished even if this means higher taxes.

* Note that the response categories for this indicator are definitely should, probably should, does not matter, probably should not, and definitely should not.

In the second part of Table 2.7, we consider Liberal Democrat responses to additional questions about taxation and spending. It can be seen that members are in favour of the redistribution of income and wealth. Members also overwhelmingly want to see more money spent on getting rid of poverty. We saw in Table 2.6 that members do not want to see a growth in private medicine. This is because they support the NHS in overwhelming numbers and it is evident that they want to see more money spent on the service. It is also apparent that members are in favour of increased government spending on pensions, but they do not shy away from the tax consequences of this policy. Equally, the members are not persuaded that higher taxation has a deterrent effect on work incentives; half of them disagree with this proposition. However, members do see limits to government spending, as they are not in favour of using higher taxes to abolish prescription charges.

2.2.5 The Environment

The responses to our survey show that the party members tend to hold strong views on environmental issues. As Table 2.8 shows, a very large proportion of members (81 per cent) are opposed to an incursion into the green belt to build houses, and a similar high proportion (79 per cent)

Table 2.8. Members' views on the environment (percentages)

	Strongly agree	Agree	Neither agree nor disagree	Disagree	Strongly disagree
A	3	16	23	37	18
B	2	6	10	51	30
C	12	41	16	25	6
D	31	48	13	7	1
E	18	68	10	4	1

A: Further nuclear energy development is essential for the future prosperity of Britain.
B: The only way to solve the housing crisis is to build on greenfield sites as much as brownfield sites.
C: For the sake of the environment, car users should pay higher taxes.
D: Modern methods of farming have caused great damage to the countryside.
E: Ordinary people should do more to protect the environment, even if it means paying higher prices.

believe that modern farming methods harm the countryside. Over one-half of the party (55 per cent) is opposed to the development of nuclear energy, and believes that car users should pay higher taxes to protect the environment (53 per cent). As we shall see later, as far as car use is concerned, their views are very much at odds with the views of Liberal Democrat voters. The members' commitment to the environment extends to paying for a more determined environmental policy, with 86 per cent of them believing that more should be done to protect the environment, even if it results in higher prices.

2.2.6 Morality, Law, and Order

With its roots in the liberal tradition, we would expect the members of the Liberal Democrat Party to take a tolerant view on key moral issues. On some issues this is evident, as we see in Table 2.9, with just over half of the members being pro-choice in relation to the subject of abortion, and close to two-thirds disagreeing with the statement that homosexuality is always

Table 2.9. Members' views on morality, and law and order (percentages)

	Strongly agree	Agree	Neither agree nor disagree	Disagree	Strongly disagree
A	8	17	22	38	15
B	7	24	25	28	16
C	14	31	30	21	3
D	17	32	14	31	6
E	14	43	23	16	4
F	8	11	20	35	27

A: The government should make abortions more difficult to obtain.
B: The use of cannabis should be legal for all citizens.
C: People who break the law should be given stiffer sentences.
D: Life sentences should mean life.
E: The government should discourage the growth of one-parent families.
F: Homosexual relations are always wrong.

wrong. However, while the party leadership has supported the legalization of cannabis, only a third of the membership approve of this policy. One-quarter of the members have no view, while 44 per cent of the members are against such legalization. On law and order, members can be illiberal, with pluralities believing that stiffer sentences should be handed out to criminals and nearly half of them believing that a life sentence should mean life. Over half (57 per cent) of the members also favour discouraging the growth of one-parent families. Therefore, while the party has roots in the liberal tradition, the members often take a distinctly right of centre view on many of these moral and legal issues.

Given the pattern of responses to the wide range of issues evident in Tables 2.4–2.9, this raises the question of how flexible or inflexible Liberal Democrats are when it comes to the application of liberal principles. A traditional view of party members is that they get involved in party politics because they are extremists of one sort or another. This implies that their views are out of line with the views of the electorate, and we will examine this issue later. But it also implies that they may be inflexible and unwilling to compromise on principles or policies for electoral reasons. It is interesting to see if this view of the Liberal Democrat members is accurate.

Table 2.10 reveals that members strongly believe the party should stick to its principles, even at the cost of losing an election. Overall, 55 per cent would not compromise their principles in order to achieve electoral success. Some 70 per cent believe that their party is principled and is not merely concerned with its media image. Thus, there is support for the idea that party members can be rather inflexible when it comes to compromising on principles for electoral purposes.

In light of this discussion of Liberal Democrat grassroots characteristics and attitudes, it is interesting to see how these changed during the 1990s. On the face of it we might expect significant changes to have occurred, as this was the decade in which the Liberal Democrat Party became

Table 2.10. Members' views of political principles (percentages)

	Strongly agree	Agree	Neither agree nor disagree	Disagree	Strongly disagree
A	2	7	22	56	14
B	3	25	17	45	10
C	18	62	12	7	1

A: The Liberal Democrat Party places more emphasis on its media image than it does on its principles.
B: Party members should be willing to compromise their political principles if the party is to achieve electoral success.
C: The Liberal Democrat Party should always stand by its principles, even if this should lose an election.

consolidated after the merger of the Liberals and Social Democrats in 1988. We can get some insight into this question using a survey conducted in the early 1990s.

2.3 Changes in the Membership

In 1993, Lynn Bennie, John Curtice, and Wolfgang Rudig conducted a survey of Liberal Democrat party members. Using their data, we can see whether there has been any change in the profile of members in the intervening years. We find in Table 2.11 that the gender profile remains stubbornly male. As far as age is concerned, the mean age of members has increased from 56 to 59. Earlier, we remarked upon the high educational achievements of the members. However, while in 1993 49 per cent of them had a university degree, by the time of the later survey this figure had dropped to 42 per cent. This drop in the number of members with a university degree could be significant. If we assume that members with a better education are more likely to voice their opinions and be active within the party, the fall in the number of graduates could lead to a more passive party.

The class composition of the membership is very similar over time, with a slight increase in the percentage who are members of the salariat. One striking trend is the growth of public sector employment among the members, which increased from 30 per cent to 43 per cent during this period. From 1993 to 1999, both the numbers of public and private sector employees increased at the expense of employees in the nationalized industries. The latter declined considerably, due most obviously to the privatization programme of Conservative governments.

An examination of the attitudes of party members in 1993 and 1999 produces some interesting comparisons, as Table 2.12 shows. The table contains a sample of the indicators referred to earlier. Most attitudes did not change significantly over this period. This was true of members' attitudes to free markets, taxation, prices and incomes policy, abortion, private education, private medicine, and trade union rights. But in relation to attitudes to coalition governments and taxation on motoring, there were significant changes. Members became more favourably inclined to coalition governments, their attitudes no doubt being influenced by the Labour–Liberal Democrat coalition established in Scotland after the elections to the Scottish Assembly in May 1999. They also became more conservative on the issue of taxing the motorist for environmental reasons.

Table 2.11. A comparison of members in 1993 and 1999: social characteristics (percentages)

	1993	1999
Gender		
Male	53	54
Female	46	46
Age		
18–25	3	2
26–35	8	5
36–45	16	11
46–55	21	23
56–65	19	21
66+	33	36
Mean	56	59
Employment		
Full-time	39	50
Unemployed	3	2
Retired	32	32
Full-time education	3	2
Looking after home	9	6
Employment sector		
Private firm	34	38
Nationalized industry	11	3
Other public sector	30	43
Graduate status		
Yes	49	42
No	51	58
Socio-economic occupational classification		
Salariat	71	74
Routine non-manual	14	11
Petty bourgeoisie	4	7
Foreman and technician	2	4
Working class	10	5

Source: Bennie et al. survey of Liberal Democrats (1993) and Liberal Democrat membership survey (1999)

In relation to one of the key defining Liberal Democrat policy commitments, namely Europe, the proportion of Eurosceptics wanting to leave altogether, or to reduce the powers of the EU, has remained steady at just over 40 per cent. The proportion of Europhiles wanting a federal state has also remained steady at around 20 per cent. The shift has occurred among those wanting to remain in the EU while increasing its powers. The proportion of members taking this stance has fallen by 6 per cent.

Following with the comparison of Liberal Democrat party members to Liberal Democrat voters, would it be true to say that the former are 'extremists' in comparison with the latter? We examine this next.

Table 2.12. A comparison of members in 1993 and 1999: political attitudes (percentages)

		Strongly agree	Agree	Neither agree nor disagree	Disagree	Strongly disagree
A	1993	8	27	39	20	6
	1999	12	41	16	25	6
B	1993	8	37	27	23	4
	1999	5	38	24	29	4
C	1993	11	40	32	15	2
	1999	4	31	30	30	6
D	1993	9	26	23	36	6
	1999	11	50	19	18	1
E	1993	27	35	17	14	6
	1999	12	41	16	25	6
F	1993	10	14	21	35	20
	1999	8	17	22	38	15

A: Coalition governments are the best form of government for Britain.
B: The production of goods and services is best left to the free market.
C: The government should establish a prices and incomes policy as a means of controlling inflation.
D: High income tax makes people less willing to work hard.
E: For the sake of the environment, car users should pay higher taxes.
F: The government should make abortions more difficult to obtain.

		Definitely should	Probably should	Does not matter	Probably should not	Definitely should not
A	1993	6	15	25	32	21
	1999	7	18	22	32	23
B	1993	2	9	16	39	34
	1999	3	16	16	42	23
C	1993	4	16	21	38	22
	1999	3	12	22	47	16
D	1993	33	51	11	4	1
	1999	28	57	10	5	1

Government should
A: Get rid of private education.
B: Encourage the growth of private medicine.
C: Introduce stricter laws to regulate trade unions.
D: Give workers more say in the places where they work.

Europe		
Leave the EC/EU	7	5
Stay in and try to reduce EC/EU powers	36	37
Leave things as they are	9	14
Stay in EC/EU and increase powers	30	24
Work for single European government	18	20

Source: Bennie et al. survey of Liberal Democrats (1993) and Liberal Democrat membership survey (1999)

2.4 Liberal Democrat Members and Voters: Social Characteristics

Previous studies have found significant differences between the social characteristics of party members and party supporters in the electorate

(Seyd and Whiteley 1992; Whiteley, Seyd, and Richardson 1994). For example, the Labour Party attracts a greater proportion of women as voters than as members of the party. It also attracts a larger proportion of working-class supporters under the age of 25 among its voters than among its members (Seyd and Whiteley 1992: 39). Similar social disparities exist between the Conservative Party's members and voters. For example, the Conservatives have a much higher proportion of their voters under the age of 35 than their members. In addition, there are far fewer working-class members in all parties than there are voters (Whiteley, Seyd, and Richardson 1994: 50). We can repeat this comparison of party members and voters for the Liberal Democrats using data from the 1997 British Election Study.

In common with the earlier party membership studies, there are more female Liberal Democrat voters than members as Table 2.13 shows. There is also a substantial difference between the average age of the members and the voters. Liberal Democrat voters are on average twelve years younger (47) than the members. There is a significantly higher proportion of voters in the 18–45 age groups (52 per cent) than among the members (18 per cent). In addition, there are many more older members, with 81 per cent of them aged 46 or over, compared with 48 per cent of voters in the same age group. With five times more Liberal Democrat voters than members under the age of 35, party strategists may well want to target this group when they are recruiting new members. We saw earlier that the Liberal Democrat membership is highly educated, with 42 per cent of them having a university degree. The same point, however, cannot be made about Liberal Democrat voters, since only 16 per cent of them have degrees. Since higher education has expanded enormously over the last twenty years and Liberal Democrat voters are much younger than the members, this is not entirely expected.

In relation to employment and occupational status, there are two significant differences between the members and the voters. Firstly, one in three (32 per cent) members is retired, compared with one in five (19 per cent) voters. Secondly, the employment status of members and voters differs. Liberal Democrat voting support lies much more with the working class and in blue-collar occupations than is true of the membership. Only 5 per cent of the members are in working-class occupations, compared with 23 per cent of the voters. By contrast, almost twice as many party members are in professional occupations, or are members of the salariat, compared with voters.

Table 2.13. A comparison of members and voters: social characteristics (percentages)

	Members	Voters
Gender		
Male	54	47
Female	46	53
Age		
18–25	2	12
26–35	5	19
36–45	11	21
46–55	23	19
56–65	22	12
65+	36	17
Mean	59	47
Education		
GCSE/ School Certificate	56	54
'A' Level/ (Scottish) Higher Certificate	45	38
Technical qualification	17	13
University or CNAA degree	42	16
Employment		
Full-time education	2	4
Employed	50	59
Unemployed	2	2
Retired	32	19
Looking after the home	6	10
Income (£)		
< 10,000	16	24
10,000–20,000	27	30
20,000–40,000	35	33
40,000+	22	13
Occupational status		
Salariat	74	39
Routine non-manual	11	21
Petty bourgeoise	7	8
Foreman and supervisors	4	7
Working class	5	23

Source: Liberal Democrat Membership Data and 1997
British Election Study Survey Data

Not surprisingly, considering their employment and occupational profiles, the income levels of the members and voters also differ. Liberal Democrat voters are much more likely to be on modest household incomes in comparison with members. Fifty-four per cent of voters have an income of £20,000 or less, and 24 per cent have an income of less than £10,000. By contrast, members enjoy far higher incomes than the voters, with almost twice as many of them earning more than £40,000 per annum.

Our evidence suggests that there are significant differences between the voters and members, some of which may have electoral consequences. Generally, it is important for a party's membership not to be too different from its voters, otherwise its electoral prospects may be damaged (Seyd and Whiteley 1992: 52). This is true, firstly because members acting as 'ambassadors' in the community may present a restricted and potentially unattractive profile when the party is engaged in local campaigning. This may be more of a problem for the Liberal Democrats than it is for the Labour or Conservative parties, given their emphasis on community politics. Secondly, in so far as the policy priorities of a party reflect those of its members, these priorities may differ significantly from the preferences of the voters if the two groups are radically different from each other. Here, we found that the age, gender, occupational status, and income of members and voters differ considerably. If the party claims to listen to its members, it runs the risk of paying too much attention to the needs of an older, middle-class, retired electorate, and thereby risks alienating a young, working-class, employed electorate. To what extent do the preferences of Liberal Democrat voters and members differ? We examine this next.

2.5 Liberal Democrat Members and Voters: Political Attitudes

In this section we continue the comparison between members and voters by analysing the political attitudes of both groups. We have suggested that the party should be seen to be representative of its electoral supporters, and this is particularly important when we consider political attitudes. Here we shall examine the same categories of political attitudes for the voters as we used for the members, although with a more limited range of indicators available in the 1997 British Election Study.

In relation to attitudes to institutional change, our indicators show that members and voters are in agreement when it comes to two key issues. As Table 2.14 shows, Liberal Democrat voters are overwhelmingly in favour of introducing an electoral system based on proportional representation. The indicator in the election study is less specific than the indicator for the members cited in Table 2.4, but the responses to both questions show that there is support for electoral reform among both members and voters. With regards to the House of Lords, 61 per cent of Liberal Democrat voters want to see change, although they do not want the Lords abolished. A similar point can be made about members, as we observed in Table 2.4, although

Table 2.14. Liberal Democrat voters' attitudes to institutional reform (percentages)

How much do you agree or disagree that Britain should introduce proportional representation so that the number of MPs each party gets more closely matches the number of votes each party gets	
Strongly agree	31
Agree	38
Neither	24
Disagree	5
Strongly disagree	2
Do you think the House of Lords should remain as it is, or is some change needed?	
Remain as is	25
Change needed	61
Do not know	14
Do you think the House of Lords should be	
Replaced by a different body	20
Abolished and replaced by nothing	16
There should be some other kind of change	64

Source: British Election Study Survey (1997).

differences in question wording in the two surveys limit the comparisons that can be made.

Liberal Democrat voters also share the opinion of members that Britain should remain a part of the EU. In Table 2.15, nearly two-thirds (63 per cent) of the voters are in favour of continued membership. However, the interesting comparison between members and voters relates to the question

Table 2.15. Liberal Democrat voters' attitudes to Europe (percentages)

Do you think Britain should continue to be a member of the EU or should it withdraw?	
Continue	63
Withdraw	27
Do not know	10
Do you think Britain's long-term policy should be	
Leave EU	14
Reduce EU powers	41
Leave as is	16
Increase EU powers	15
Work for a single European government	6
Do not know	7
Here are three statements about the future of the pound in the European Union. Which one comes closest to your view?	
Replace the pound	20
Use both the pound and euro	27
Keep the pound as the only currency for Britain	50

Source: British Election Study Survey (1997).

of Britain's long-term policy towards Europe in Tables 2.5 and 2.15. It can be seen that 37 per cent of members and 41 per cent of voters want to see a reduction in the powers of the EU. But the members and voters differ in relation to the issue of expanding EU powers. Some 44 per cent of the members either want to increase the EU's powers or to work for a single EU government. This is true of only 21 per cent of the voters. Thus, in general, members are more enthusiastic about the EU project than are voters. A similar point can be made about Britain's membership of the European Monetary Union. While two-thirds of members think that Britain should agree to the introduction of the euro, half of the voters think that Britain should keep the pound as the only currency.

Turning next to attitudes to markets and collectivism, it can be seen from Table 2.16 that voters are in favour of the mixed economy and are generally opposed to more nationalization. In fact, their views on private education and private health care are very similar to the views of the members in Table 2.6. In both cases, members and voters do not want to see the abolition of private education, while at the same time being unenthusiastic about the growth of private medicine. In relation to nationalization, 63 per cent of members and 59 per cent of voters opt for the status quo, reflecting widespread opposition to both nationalization *and* privatization among party supporters.

The second aspect of markets and collectivism relates to public attitudes to trade unions. We saw in Table 2.6 that party members generally opposed

Table 2.16. Liberal Democrat voters' attitudes to markets and collectivism (percentages)
Do you think the government should or should not do the following things, or does it not matter either way?

	Definitely should	Probably should	Does not matter either way	Probably should not	Definitely should not
A	7	20	20	34	19
B	6	15	35	24	20
C	9	18	27	29	18
D	31	51	8	8	2

A: The government should encourage the growth of private medicine.
B: The government should get rid of private education.
C: The government should introduce stricter laws to regulate the activities of trade unions.
D: The government should give workers more say in running the places where they work.

Are you generally in favour of	
More nationalization of companies by government	31
More privatization of companies by government	9
Things should be left as they are now	59
Other	2

stricter trade union laws, and the voters take a similar view. Equally, members were supportive of workers' rights in the workplace, a position supported by the voters. Overall there is little difference between the voters and the members in relation to attitudes to the market and collect-ivism.

In relation to views on redistribution and welfare, the attitudes of members and voters to the trade-off between taxation and public spend-ing are almost identical. As Table 2.17 shows, some 81 per cent of voters favour increased taxation in order to fund more public spending. In Table 2.7, we saw that 83 per cent of party members took the same view. There are similar levels of agreement between the two in relation to government spending on poverty reduction, and on the NHS. Like party members, Liberal Democrat voters are keen on increased public spending, even if this means higher taxes. Specifically, the voters want to see increased spending targeted at health and education. Liberal Democrat voters also agree with members that income and wealth in society should be redis-tributed.

The one area of difference between members and voters with respect to redistribution is in relation to foreign aid. In Table 2.7, a majority of the

Table 2.17. Liberal Democrat voters' attitudes to redistribution and welfare (percentages)

Suppose the government had to choose between three options.
Which do you think it should choose?

Reduce taxes and spend less on health, education, and social benefits	2
Keep taxes and spending on these services at the same level as now	15
Increase taxes and spend more on health, education, and social benefits	81

Do you think the government should or should not do the following things, or does it not matter either way?	Definitely should	Probably should	Does not matter either way	Probably should not	Definitely should not
A	16	46	20	16	2
B	66	28	4	2	<1
C	6	32	26	25	10
D	82	14	2	2	<1
E	79	18	1	2	<1

A: Income and wealth should be redistributed.
B: The government should spend more money to get rid of poverty.
C: The government should give more aid to Africa and Asia.*
D: The government should spend more money on education.
E: The government should put more money into the NHS.

* Note response categories are strongly agree, agree, neither, disagree, strongly disagree.

members thought that the government should give more aid to poor countries in Africa and Asia. We can see in Table 2.17 that only just over a third of Liberal Democrat voters take this view. They are more likely to see redistribution as a domestic political issue than the members, who extend their views about redistribution to the world as a whole.

In common with the party members, voters are supportive of environmental issues, but with a reservation. We saw in Table 2.8 that members supported the idea of increasing taxation on the motorist in order to curb pollution and save the environment. As Table 2.18 shows, voters are distinctly cool on the idea that car owners should pay higher taxes, even though they do not believe that unlimited car use is a good thing. Whereas a majority of members believe that car users should pay higher taxes, only a minority of voters share this point of view.

Table 2.18 also contains indicators on moral issues, since measures of attitudes to the environment and to moral issues were rather limited in the 1997 election study. We noted in the discussion of Table 2.9 that on crime issues, members were rather illiberal, with pluralities believing that stiffer sentences should be handed out to criminals, and that life sentences should mean life. In response to both of these questions, Liberal Democrat voters are even more supportive of tough policies than the members. Seven in every ten voters believed in tougher sentencing and eight in ten believed that life sentences should be for life.

At the end of Section 2.4, which compared members' and voters' social characteristics, we raised the question of whether the differences that existed between them might cause problems for the party. We argued that they might if the two groups held very different opinions. However, having examined a wide variety of opinions of Liberal Democrat voters in this section, we conclude that social differences between the two groups are not really a cause for concern. This is because the voters and the

Table 2.18. Liberal Democrat voters' attitudes to environmental and moral issues (percentages)

	Strongly agree	Agree	Neither agree nor disagree	Disagree	Strongly agree
A	3	18	20	48	12
B	6	32	15	36	11
C	36	37	17	8	1
D	50	34	9	7	<1

A: People should be allowed to use their cars as much as they like, even if it causes damage to the environment.
B: For the sake of the environment, car users should pay higher taxes.
C: People who break the law should be given stiffer sentences.
D: Life sentences should mean life.

members have many attitudes in common, although the latter do feel more strongly on some issues than do the former. Perhaps only in relation to restrictions on car use for environmental reasons is there a danger of the two groups coming into conflict. The fact that members are more likely to be men, and also more likely to be older, wealthier, and better educated than the voters could be a problem when the party tries to recruit women, the young, and the less well off. However, this is a problem that is not unique to the Liberal Democrats; all the major parties in Britain face it.

Returning to an examination of the party members, one of the key issues from the point of view of the national party organization is how much the members are attached to the party, and how much they are prepared to work for it. Party members are a useful resource, particularly in relation to elections, but only to the extent that they are prepared to get involved. We examine this issue next.

2.6 Attachment and Activism in the Grass-roots Party

Table 2.19 shows that about one in four Liberal Democrats 'strongly' identifies with their party, and another one in two has a 'fairly strong' sense of identification. Worryingly for the party, however, there are about a quarter of the members who have no strong attachment to the party and levels of attachment have clearly declined significantly over time. In the 1993 survey, more than a third of the respondents were very strongly attached to the party, but by 1999 this had fallen to just over a quarter. Under one in five members was weakly attached to the party in 1993, but by 1999 this had increased to a quarter. Weak levels of attachment could have serious repercussions for the long-term size of the voluntary party should these members decide not to renew their subscriptions and leave.

A further disturbing implication for the party is that 70 per cent of members do not consider themselves to be at all active within the party.[1] It is also apparent that rates of activism have fallen dramatically over the six-year period between the surveys. More than a quarter were very active in 1993, but by 1999 this had fallen to 10 per cent. Low rates of activity places more responsibility upon those members who are prepared to work for the party. Altogether some 30 per cent of members regard themselves

---

[1] Among Conservative party members the level of inactivism is even higher. Eighty-three per cent of members consider themselves to be neither active nor very active within the party (Whiteley, Seyd, and Richardson 1994: 68).

Table 2.19. Activism rates of party members, 1993 and 1999 (percentages)

	1993	1999
Party identification		
Very strong	34	26
Fairly strong	49	49
Not very strong	15	22
Not at all strong	3	4
How active members consider themselves to be		
Very active	26	10
Fairly active	29	20
Not very active	32	41
Not at all active	13	29
Membership activity compared to five years ago		
More active	23	15
Less active	36	41
About the same	40	45
Amount of time devoted to party activities in the past month		
None	—	54
Up to 5 hours	—	29
5–10 hours	—	7
10–20 hours	—	4
20–30 hours	—	2
30–40 hours	—	1
More than 40 hours	—	3
Attendance at party meetings per year		
Not at all	29	53
Rarely (1–2 times)	24	17
Occasionally (3–5 times)	11	11
Frequently (5 or more times)	37	20

Source: Bennie et al. survey of Liberal Democrats (1993) and Liberal Democrat membership survey (1999)

as very active or fairly active within the party, compared with 55 per cent in 1993. This compares to the 17 per cent of Conservative members who said they were very active or fairly active in the party in 1994, and the 25 per cent of Labour party members who similarly responded in 1999 (Whiteley, Seyd, and Richardson 1994: 68; Seyd and Whiteley 2002: 88).

We also examine the levels of Liberal Democratic activism over time. Only 15 per cent of members believe that they are more active now than five years previously, while 41 per cent think that they are less active. If we subtract the former from the latter we find that some 26 per cent have become 'de-energized' over this five-year period. The comparable figure in 1993 was 13 per cent. So the rate at which activism is declining has doubled in just six years. In the case of the two other major parties in the early 1990s, the equivalent numbers who became 'de-energized' were 23 per cent for Labour (Seyd and Whiteley 1992: 89) and 17 per cent for the Conservatives (Whiteley, Seyd, and Richardson 1994: 68). This is a problem for all three parties, but for the Liberal Democrats, who stress the involvement of members in community politics, to have a grassroots party that is becoming more de-energized over time is a clear cause for concern.

Confirmation of the low levels of activism among party members is provided by a measure of the time members spend on party activities in the average month. We see that over half of the members report that they spend no time at all on party activities. When members do spend time on party business, it is normally less than 5 hours per month. Only one in ten devotes more than 10 hours a month to the party.[2] However, set against these pessimistic figures is the fact that members do attend party meetings. Nearly one-half of the members say they attend meetings and 20 per cent say they frequently attend meetings, although again meeting attendance has clearly declined over time.

2.7 Party Members' Images of the Party and the Leadership

Our data show that a majority of members renew their membership and have done so for many years. Altogether 90 per cent of members reported renewing their membership regularly since they joined the party, and the average period of membership was just over sixteen years. Therefore, we would expect members to have positive opinions of the party and the party leadership. The party is not known for internal disputes in the manner of the Conservative Party under John Major's leadership or the Labour Party during the 1970s and 1980s. On the other hand, the Liberal Democrat Party was formed as a result of the merger between the SDP and the Liberal Party, and this was not an easy process. Along the way, internal disputes amongst both partys' elites resulted in prominent members of the Liberal Democratic Alliance being unable to agree to the permanent merger of the parties. Breakaway Liberal and Social Democratic parties resulted from the exercise (Cook 1998). However, since the formation of the Liberal Democrat Party, while there have been lively debates, there has been little in the way of serious internal disputes between factions within the party. Our survey asked the members a number of questions to tap their view of the party from two angles, party organization and party image, and we

---

[2] The comparative figures for Labour and Conservative activists in the 1990s are one in ten and one in twenty respectively (Seyd and Whiteley 1992: 88; Whiteley, Seyd, and Richardson 1994: 68).

find members' views are all fairly positive. We analyse members' opinions of the party and the party leadership in Table 2.20.

Table 2.20 reveals that members believe that the party is run efficiently and is united. They do not see it as extreme. Significantly, given the middle-class status of the membership, 74 per cent of the members believe the party serves all classes. However, 40 per cent see the party as appealing only to the middle classes. Less than 6 per cent of the members see the party as right wing, while 58 per cent view the party as neither left wing nor right wing.

The members also had positive views of their party leader at the time of the survey, Paddy Ashdown. He was regarded as caring, likeable, decisive, and, like the party, centrist. After our survey had been completed, Ashdown surprised the media and political pundits alike by announcing that he was standing down as leader. This dramatic event allowed other leading figures in the party to step out of Ashdown's shadow. At the time of the survey, we had asked the hypothetical question about who would make the best alternative leader in place of Ashdown. Choosing an alternative leader when other senior figures in the party may not be very well known is difficult. The problem of finding a replacement for Ashdown was resolved when Charles Kennedy was elected as the leader, and our survey showed that prior to the leadership election, Kennedy was the most popular alternative, with nearly one in three of the membership ranking him as the alternative leader. Furthermore, his mean ranking on a 0–100 scale was higher than for any other leading Liberal Democrat (see Table 2.21). However, a little over 21 per cent of the members did not know who would be their choice of leader in place of Ashdown. This highlights the paucity of leadership material within the party and the lack of national

Table 2.20. Members' perceptions of the party and the leader (percentages)

	Very	Fairly	Neither	Fairly	Very	
Liberal Democrat party is . . .						
Extreme	<1	5	42	41	12	Moderate
United	15	60	12	11	1	Divided
Good for one class	1	4	21	38	36	Good for all classes
Middle class	4	36	52	6	1	Working class
Left wing	1	36	58	5	<1	Right wing
Efficiently run	15	59	13	11	1	Badly run
Paddy Ashdown is . . .						
Not caring	3	5	5	39	47	Caring
Likeable	43	26	5	13	12	Not likeable
Decisive	42	34	5	10	9	Not decisive
Left wing	1	28	64	7	1	Right wing

Table 2.21. Alternative party leader and ratings for the party leadership (percentages)

	Alternative leader	0–20	21–50	51–80	80+	Mean
Paddy Ashdown	—	1	8	28	63	77.3
Charles Kennedy	29	3	16	39	43	69.5
Simon Hughes	15	5	21	38	36	65.8
Malcolm Bruce	3	5	25	40	31	64.2
Menzies Campbell	12	6	21	38	31	64.9
Don Foster	1	8	37	33	23	58.4
Jim Wallace	1	9	40	31	20	56.9
Nick Harvey	1	10	45	29	16	54.4
Liz Lynne	<1	12	41	31	16	53.5
Jacki Ballard	1	12	48	25	15	52.9

figures, which has an impact on levels of support amongst the general public if not amongst the members themselves.

In this chapter, we have presented a profile of the party membership. We see that the image of Liberal Democrats that was often conveyed by the media in times past as predominantly sandal-wearing, bearded male eccentrics concerned about marginal issues is far from the truth. While we did not ask our respondents about their footware or shaving habits, we did ask them enough about their background and attitudes to know that such an image is a caricature. Liberal Democrat members are relatively mature, highly educated professionals whose attitudes reflect the core beliefs of modern Liberal Democracy.

In Chapter 3, we turn to the question of how ideological the party members are in their attitudes.

3
Ideology and the Party Members

3.1 Introduction

We have argued that the Liberal Democrat Party grew from different traditions encompassing two alternative strands of political thought—social democracy on the one hand, and liberalism on the other. The former emphasizes equality and redistribution, and the latter, individual freedom, market solutions to economic problems, and free trade. This implies that a two-strand model should capture the fundamental dimensions of Liberal Democrat ideology. However, the evidence in Chapter 2 suggests that it would be difficult to compress the range of issues that are important to party members into a simple two-strand model. It suggested that there are a number of other issues that appear relevant to members, and that do not fit into such a scheme. In addition, some members are by no means sold on the notion of social democratic redistribution, while others are far from being free-market libertarians. So there are dissenters from the two-strand model in any case.

On the other hand, the discussion in Chapter 2 was not concerned with the coherence or relative importance of beliefs amongst the party members. It might be that a number of the issues examined in that chapter are fairly peripheral to the concerns of grassroots members, and far removed from their core set of beliefs. In this chapter, we shall focus on such core beliefs and examine if the members have an underlying set of ideological principles that guide their attitudes to politics. We will attempt to discover if members' concerns about issues can be organized around a clear set of principles. This is an important task because such belief systems are important to the party in two ways. Firstly, the party is better able to develop a coherent political agenda if it is rooted in a set of clear ideological beliefs. Secondly, and closely following the first point, the party can project a coherent policy agenda to the electorate if it has clear ideological principles.

However, ideology can also produce difficulties for the effectiveness of party management. If a significant group of members are ideologues in the sense of having a coherent, ordered set of beliefs, it means that debates within the party organization could become more rancorous, since members are likely to take up entrenched positions on topics central to their ideological concerns. If attitudes to issues are linked to each other around a core set of values, challenges to these beliefs arising from changes to the party policies or programmes will be resisted. In these circumstances, policy changes are likely to give rise to cognitive dissonance among the members (Festinger 1957).

We begin this chapter by examining if there is evidence that a set of belief structures underlies the attitudes of party members. This is followed by an analysis of the sources of ideological variations in the grassroots party, paying particular attention to the social characteristics of members, as well as their political experiences and political roots. The Liberal Democrats are a comparatively young party compared with Labour and the Conservatives, and is made up of three distinct groups–ex-Liberals, ex-Social Democrats, and a third group of members who were recruited since the creation of the party in 1988. We shall explore the extent to which members from these different backgrounds exhibit ideological differences. Later on in the chapter, we extend the analysis to look for evidence of ideological thinking among Liberal Democrat voters in the 2001 general election. To start, we examine the nature of Liberal Democrat ideology at the grassroots level.

3.2 Grassroots Liberal Democrat Ideology

As mentioned earlier, we would expect at least two important strands of ideological beliefs to be present in the attitudes of grassroots party members. These have their historical roots in Liberal Party, and to a lesser extent SDP politics. The first strand comes from the Liberal tradition of 'libertarianism', and it has three aspects. The first is lifestyle libertarianism, or beliefs that stress individual rights and freedoms. These emphasize the importance of allowing people to pursue their own lifestyles without censorship or legal restrictions on their personal freedom. The second is economic libertarianism, which implies an aversion to state interference in the economy in the form of public ownership or overregulation, and which favours free-market solutions to economic problems. The third is internationalism, which links to both of the other strands of thought. Internationalism arises from the desire to remove trade and other barriers between neighbouring countries, particularly in Europe, and to spread the idea of individual freedom throughout the world. This aspect of thought would account for the long-standing support for European integration among Liberal Democrats.

The second strand of ideological thought comes from the social democratic tradition, which emphasizes the importance of equality and the need for redistribution in society to correct social inequality. This tradition stresses the importance of dealing with poverty by progressive taxation and removing gross discrepancies in income and wealth in society. It has its origins in the 'New Liberalism' of the Lloyd-George era and in the policy innovations of the last Liberal government in Britain before the First World War, but it was renewed by the arrival of former Labour party members into the party following the merger with the Social Democrats (see Crewe and King 1996).

In Table 3.1 we investigate underlying attitude structures using indicators taken from Chapter 2. The attitude indicators were chosen to reflect different aspects of these traditions of ideological thought. The principal components analysis of the indicators show that there is a modest amount of attitude structuring underlying Liberal Democrat beliefs, with four factors explaining a total of 54 per cent of the variance in fourteen attitude indicators. The indicators cluster into a fairly coherent set of factors, which capture the dimensions of Liberal Democrat beliefs discussed earlier.

The first factor, which explains 22 per cent of the variance, can be described as a *lifestyle liberalism* factor, linking attitudes to censorship, family life, the use of cannabis, homosexuality, and abortion. Thus, Liberal Democrats who oppose censorship tend also to disagree that homosexuality is wrong and are inclined to support the legalization of cannabis, but at the same time they oppose making abortions more difficult to obtain. The correlations between the indicators and the underlying factors show that this makes up a coherent strand of Liberal Democrat ideological beliefs.

The second factor explains nearly 13 per cent of the variance in the data and is clearly an *equality and redistribution* factor. It emphasizes the redistribution of income and wealth, the fight against poverty, increasing taxes in order to raise public spending and aid to the developing world. Party members who favour redistribution tend to disagree with the idea of reducing taxation and spending on health and education. They also

Table 3.1. Ideological structuring among grassroots Liberal Democrats (Varimax rotated factor matrix)

Indicator	Lifestyle liberalism	Equality and redistribution	Free market liberalism	Attitudes to the EU
Film and magazine censorship is necessary	0.67			
Government should discourage one-parent families	0.61			
Cannabis use should be legal	−0.61			
Homosexuality is always wrong	0.75			
Government should make abortion more difficult	0.69			
Income and wealth should be redistributed		0.69		
Reduce taxes and spend less on services		−0.55		
Give more aid to Asia and Africa		0.52		
Spend more money to get rid of poverty		0.73		
Production is best left to the free market			0.78	
Individuals should provide for themselves			0.58	
Private enterprise is best for the economy			0.80	
Liberal Democrat should resist EU integration				0.81
UK should agree to the EU single currency				−0.84
Eigenvalue	3.1	1.9	1.4	1.1
Percent of variance explained	22.2	13.4	9.9	8.1

favour spending more money to try to resolve the problem of poverty, both in relation to Britain and also in the developing world. Clearly, the radical liberal and social democratic egalitarian traditions are still evident in the attitudes of grassroots Liberal Democrats.

The third factor that explains about 10 per cent of the variance is an *economic liberalism* factor. Liberal Democrats who agree that 'production is best left to the free market' also tend to agree that 'individuals should provide for themselves', and they are also strong supporters of private enterprise. These themes echo the free-market liberalism of the nineteenth century, when the party was strongly identified with free trade and opposition to government interference in the market.

Finally, the fourth factor is attitudes to the *European Union*. Not surprisingly, Liberal Democrats who support Britain's membership of the single currency strongly disagree with the idea that the party members should resist further EU integration.

According to the model, these factors are uncorrelated to each other. This means that lifestyle liberalism and economic liberalism, for example, do not necessarily go together. Support for freedom of the individual in lifestyle questions does not imply support for free-market solutions to economic problems. Equally, members may strongly favour redistribution, but this does not mean that they will support or oppose lifestyle liberalism. Similarly, support for the EU does not imply egalitarian or libertarian attitudes to other issues.

It is interesting to examine the distribution of members' attitudes in relation to these four dimensions of Liberal Democrat ideology. The frequency distribution of the factor scores relating to lifestyle libertarianism appears in Figure 3.1.

It can be seen that the distribution of opinions in the grassroots party in relation to lifestyle libertarianism is close to being a bell-shaped normal distribution, but with a slight skew to the radical end of the spectrum. This indicates that there is a wide range of opinions within the grassroots party

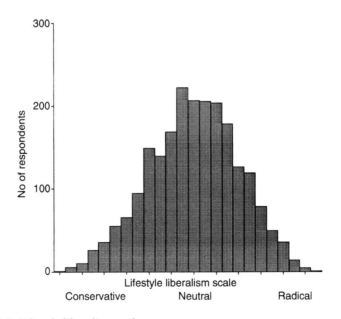

Figure 3.1 Lifestyle liberalism scale

over issues relating to homosexuality, abortion, and censorship. But there is a tendency for the members to err on the radical rather than the conservative side of this agenda.

The distribution of responses along the second dimension, which relates to equality and redistribution can be seen in Figure 3.2. The distribution is highly skewed in the direction of redistribution, and away from support for policies that increase social inequality. While there are some Liberal Democrats who oppose redistribution, a large majority come down in favour of it, and in that respect, the egalitarian tradition is very much alive and well in the grassroots party.

Figure 3.3 illustrates the distribution of opinions among members in relation to the market. Like Figure 3.1, this distribution approximates a normal distribution, except that in this case, there is a slight skew towards the free-market end of the spectrum. Thus, there is a tendency for grassroots Liberal Democrats to favour free markets in the debate over the role of markets in the modern economy. This traditional component of nineteenth-century liberal thought is very much present in the contemporary grassroots party.

Finally, Figure 3.4 shows the distribution of opinions on the issue of Britain's relationship to the EU. It shows that Liberal Democrat opinion is highly skewed in favour of closer British ties to the EU. There are Eurosceptics in the grassroots, but they are very much in a minority.

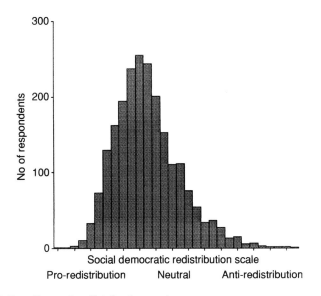

Figure 3.2 Equality and redistribution scale

53

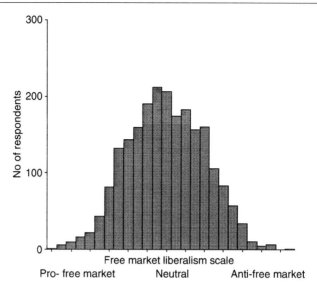

Figure 3.3 Economic liberalism scale

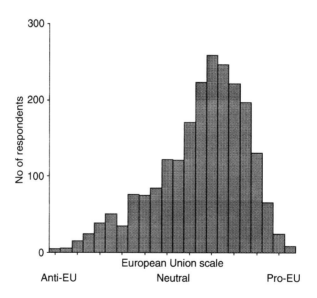

Figure 3.4 Attitudes to the European Union scale

In the light of this discussion we examine some of the sources of ideological diversity in Section 3.3.

3.3 The Sources of Ideological Diversity

Having identified four different dimensions of Liberal Democrat ideology, the question arises as to the causes of these ideological variations in the grassroots party. We will explore this question in relation to four different themes. Firstly, there is the role of socialization in helping to form the attitudes and beliefs of party members. This can be examined principally by looking at the links between the social background characteristics of the members and their ideological beliefs. Differences in age, sex, social class, and income are all associated with differences in socialization and life experiences, and therefore in attitudes and beliefs. It would be surprising if such differences did not have an influence on political ideology. Education, in particular, is associated with a greater interest in, and understanding of, politics, and so the more educated are more likely to have coherent views about different political issues than the less educated (see Pattie, Seyd, and Whiteley 2004). But other social background measures are likely to be important as well.

The political experiences of the members are also likely to affect their ideological beliefs. It is likely that long-standing party members will view the political world differently from recent recruits. This is not just an age effect, although age plays a role in this, but rather, the difference relates to the life experiences of the members at the time their political views were being formed. Research shows that the political environment of people in their late teens and early twenties has an important formative influence on their ideological beliefs that endures throughout the rest of their lives (Inglehart 1997). Since the political environment varies quite a lot over time, we should expect people of different political generations to vary in their ideological views.

A second factor likely to influence ideological viewpoints is the political roots of the party members. As Table 3.2 shows, roughly four out of ten party members joined the Liberal Democrats as their first party, with the remaining group being made up either of former Liberal party members or former Social Democrats. It seems likely that ex-Liberals will differ from

Table 3.2. The political backgrounds of the party members

Membership group	%
Ex Liberal party member	43
Ex SDP party member	14
No previous party ties	42

ex-SDP members, who in turn will differ from those who have only ever been members of the Liberal Democrats, and so we investigate this question further. We suggested earlier that the old Liberal Party had a tradition of individualism, while the Social Democrats came from a more egalitarian tradition. It seems likely that this distinction will be apparent in the responses examined in Table 3.1. Another aspect of political experience relates to the degree of involvement that individuals have with the party. As we have seen, some members are considerably more active than others and spend more of their time on party activities. This fact is likely to influence their ideological beliefs.

One rather general hypothesis about ideology in grassroots parties is that party activists are more 'extreme' than both the party leadership on the one hand and the party supporters in the electorate on the other. This is the so-called 'curvilinear disparity' thesis (May 1973), or the idea that there is a curvilinear relationship between ideological radicalism and a person's position in the party hierarchy. In this view, the people at the top and the bottom of a political party are more pragmatic and less driven by ideological considerations than the activists in the middle of the hierarchy. This produces a curvilinear relationship between ideological radicalism and status within the party organization. If this is true, activists should be more ideologically radical than passive supporters. We will investigate this question further.

A third factor that might also influence ideological beliefs is the extent to which members feel attached to, and loyalty towards, the party. The evidence in Chapter 2 showed that some members are very strongly attached to the party, while others are relatively weakly attached, even though they are members. Equally, some have very strong affective feelings towards the party, while others are relatively cool in this respect. Such different levels of attachment may be linked to ideology, with the strongly attached being more ideologically driven than the weakly attached. Another aspect of the same phenomenon relates to why the members joined the party in the first place. We examine the issue of how members came to join the party in Chapter 4. It seems likely that members who joined the party out of a sense of commitment to Liberal Democratic principles are likely to be more ideologically driven than members who joined for other reasons.

A fourth factor relates to the underlying set of attitudes that members have towards politics and the political process. This touches on the issue of political flexibility or pragmatism, discussed in Chapter 2. Some members take a very strong stand on principles, arguing that the party should put principles above everything else. Others are more pragmatic and can see the value of being flexible, particularly if this brings electoral benefits. It may be that pragmatists are much less ideologically driven than non-pragmatists.

We investigate this idea in Table 3.3, which contains the results of a principal components analysis of attitude indicators relating to political pragmatism that we first examined in Chapter 2. It can be seen that these items scale reasonably well with the highest loading being associated with: 'The Liberal Democrat party should adjust its policies to capture the middle ground of politics.' As Table 3.3 shows, individuals who agree with this tend also to agree with the proposition that party members should be willing to compromise principles for electoral reasons, and they disagree with the idea that principles should be placed before electoral consider-ations. This scale will be used in the subsequent modelling exercise to examine the influence of electoral pragmatism on ideological beliefs.

Table 3.4 contains the estimates of models of the four different com-ponents of Liberal Democrat ideology identified in Table 3.1.[1] Measures associated with each of the factors examined above are included as pre-dictors in the models. To consider the lifestyle libertarianism scale first, it can be seen that variations in this scale are influenced by several social background variables, as well as the respondents' strength of attachment to the party. The fact that political experience and electoral pragmatism have little effect on attitudes indicates that this aspect of Liberal Democrat ideology is not really driven by politics at all. Rather, it is largely driven by the individual's own socialization experiences, as well as their own life-styles. Since issues like homosexual law reform and abortion have always been handled on a non-party basis in British politics, usually by allowing free votes in the House of Commons, it is not surprising that such lifestyle issues are unrelated to political experiences or party activism.

Table 3.3. Political pragmatism and party membership

	Political pragmatism scale
Party members should be willing to compromise on their principles to achieve electoral success	0.47
The Liberal Democrat Party should always stand by its principles even if this should lose an election	−0.74
The Liberal Democrat Party should adjust its policies to capture the middle ground of politics	0.80
Eigenvalue	1.41
Percentage of variance explained	47.0

Table 3.4. The sources of ideological diversity in the Liberal Democrat grassroots

	Lifestyle liberalism	Equality and redistribution	Economic liberalism	European integration
Age	−0.21***	0.05*	0.00	0.06**
Income	0.07***	0.15***	−0.12***	0.16***
Graduate	0.08***	−0.12***	0.09***	0.12***
Sex	−0.04*	0.05**	−0.11***	0.06***
Social class	0.08***	0.01	0.03	0.08***
Religiosity	−0.30***	−0.05***	0.00	0.01
Years membership	0.05	0.01	−0.10***	0.04
Liberal Party background	0.03	−0.07*	0.07*	0.05
SDP background	0.01	−0.10***	0.09***	0.06***
Activism rates	0.01	0.11***	0.05	0.02
Time spent on party activity	0.05	−0.09**	−0.04	−0.10
Strength of partisanship	−0.12***	−0.13***	0.01	0.12***
LibDem thermometer	0.02	−0.10***	0.05*	0.09***
Joined for principles	−0.03	−0.06***	0.02	0.08***
Pragmatism scale	0.00	−0.08***	0.10***	0.02
R^2	0.23	0.10	0.06	0.14

Standardized coefficients *p < 0.10; **p < 0.05 ***p < 0.01.
The asterisks in table 3.4 denote the statistical significance of the coefficients associated with the predictor variables.

The effect of age on lifestyle issues is particularly strong, with older members being more conservative than younger ones. Religiosity also has a strong effect, with religious respondents tending to be much more conservative on lifestyle issues than respondents in general. The middle-class, educated and affluent respondents tend to be relatively radical on lifestyle issues—a finding that fits with the general idea that affluence and education tend to make people more tolerant in relation to these kinds of issues (see Pattie, Seyd, and Whiteley 2004: 48–75). In addition, there is a modest gender effect, with men being slightly less conservative than women. Finally, there is one significant measure of political attachment, the strength of partisanship of members, and it suggests that very strong Liberal Democrats are more radical in relation to lifestyle issues than weakly attached Liberal Democrats.

Turning to the second dimension, which relates to the equality and redistribution scale, the effects here are rather different from those associated with lifestyle liberalism. In this case, only some of the social background variables matter and they do so in inconsistent ways. Thus, affluent members tend to be opposed to further redistribution, but graduates tend to favour it. Clearly, education tends to offset the influence of income when it comes to views about redistribution. Again, religious members tend to be more radical than the non-religious, and are more in favour of redistribution. It is notable that several measures of political experience play a role in explaining attitudes to redistribution. Respondents with a Liberal Party background, or an SDP background, are more likely to favour redistribution than respondents who have only ever been members of the Liberal Democrats. This is particularly true of former Social Democrats whose egalitarian traditions clearly influence their views on this issue.

Activism also plays a role in influencing attitudes to redistribution. The highly active members, both those who identify themselves as such and those who devote many hours to party activity, tend to favour redistribution compared with the less active members. This evidence supports the curvilinear disparity thesis. Again, strongly attached members, and those who feel particularly warm and sympathetic towards the party, are more likely to favour redistribution than the weakly attached and the less sympathetic members. Finally, those who joined the party in order to support Liberal Democratic principles and those who feel that principles should come before electoral pragmatism tend to favour redistribution more than members as a whole. It is clear that unlike the lifestyle liberalism factor, the equality and redistribution factor is driven by more overtly political variables. The political experiences and levels of political involvement loom large in predicting variations in this scale, in a way that is not true for lifestyle concerns.

The third dimension, relating to economic liberalism, differs again from the first two. Affluent members tend to be pro-market, while graduates tend to have reservations about the role of the market in politics. Men are more enthusiastic about the role of the market than women, as are the long-established members of the party. However, those with an SDP or Liberal Party background are more sceptical about the role of the market than those who have only ever been members of the Liberal Democrats. Finally, one of the strongest effects is associated with the pragmatism scale, with relatively pragmatic members being less likely to favour the market than the less pragmatic members.

In the case of the fourth scale, attitudes to European integration, members who are affluent, middle-class, and educated are all more likely to support further integration in comparison with the poor, working-class, and uneducated members. Not surprisingly, the former members of the SDP are particularly enthusiastic about European integration. In a similar way to the redistribution scale, this aspect of Liberal Democrat ideology is influenced by the political experiences and political attachments of respondents. The latter are particularly important, with the strength of attachment to the party and the thermometer scale both having an impact on attitudes.

Looking at the findings as a whole, we see that measures of socialization and social background characteristics are important factors in explaining variations in all four scales. On the other hand, the indicators of political experience and activism have a much more mixed effect. Activism in particular is important for understanding economic and social redistribution, but it does not have an effect on any of the other scales. Attachment to the party and strength of partisanship are important for everything but lifestyle liberalism, but they operate in different ways. Finally electoral pragmatism is relevant for economic liberalism, but not for lifestyle libertarianism and internationalism.

Overall, we can say that ideological beliefs in the grassroots party are influenced by a combination of factors: early socialization, the political experiences of members, their current levels of attachment to the party, their levels of political involvement, and their attitudes to electoral strategy all play a role in influencing their ideological beliefs. What do these results tell us about the relationship of Liberal Democrat ideology to the traditional left-right dimension that underpins much of British politics? It is not clear which of these different scales, if any, relate to the left-right dimension, so we investigate this issue further in Section 3.4.

3.4 The Left-Right Dimension and Liberal Democrat Ideology

Traditionally, political ideology in Britain has been seen in terms of a left-right scale and much of the literature on party strategies is structured around this idea, as analysts speculate about the parties shifting to the left or to the right (see Downs 1957). On the face of it, all four of the scales identified earlier may be linked to traditional conceptions of the left and the right, but it is not clear how strong these links are in practice. The redistribution scale may be closer than the others to capturing the left-right dimension, since left-wing politics has always been dominated by the idea that state intervention can be used to redress the inequalities of market capitalism. However, a similar point could be made also about the economic liberalism scale, with supporters of free markets being located on the right of the political spectrum. The links between the left-right scale, lifestyle libertarianism, and attitudes to European integration are less clear, although it seems plausible that conservatives on these issues will also tend to be conservative on the left-right scale.

The survey of party members contained two nine-point scales, which measured the respondent's self-placement on the left-right dimension in politics. The first derives from the following question: 'In Liberal Democrat party politics, people often talk about the "left" and the "right". Compared with other Liberal Democrats, where would you place your views on the this scale below?' The second scale derives from a follow-up question: 'And where would you place your views in relation to British politics as a whole, not just the Liberal Democrats?' The distribution of the members along the two scales appears in Figure 3.5, where category 1 is the left-most position and category 9 the right-most position on both scales.

As Figure 3.5 indicates, the average party member is close to the median category of 5 in relation to the party left-right scale, but rather more left

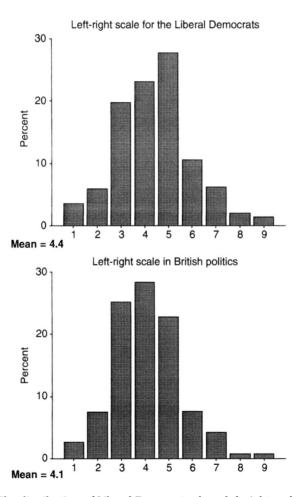

Figure 3.5 The distribution of Liberal Democrats along left-right scales

wing in relation to the British politics scale. This produces a skew to the left in the latter in comparison with the former. The correlations between the two left-right scales and the four ideology scales appear in Table 3.5. The two ideology scales are highly correlated with each other, which is not surprising because they are different indicators of the same thing. But the correlations between them and the four ideology scales are much weaker. The strongest correlation is between the equality and redistribution scale and the party left-right scale, and the weakest correlation is between the European integration scale and the party left-right scale. This evidence suggests that all four ideology scales are linked to the left-right scale in politics, but none of the relationships are strong enough for them to precisely capture left-wing and right-wing politics.

The signs of the correlations in Table 3.5 are interesting. In the case of the redistribution scale, the positive correlations imply that respondents who oppose redistribution are, not surprisingly, on the right of the political spectrum. Similarly, the negative correlation between the left-right scales and the economic liberalism factor implies that opponents of markets are on the left of the ideological spectrum. Conservatives on lifestyle libertarianism tend to be on the right of the party, and supporters of European integration tend to be on the left. Thus, the relationships make perfect sense in terms of our interpretation of left-wing and right-wing positions on these issues. But the claim that Liberal Democrat ideology does not fall easily into a simple left-right dimension is also correct. Liberal Democrat ideology certainly touches on the left-right dimension in a number of important respects, but at the same time it is more diverse than that.

We have examined ideological beliefs in the grassroots party, but are these replicated in the Liberal Democrat electorate? This important question is examined next.

Table 3.5. The correlations between the left-right scales and the ideology scales

	Left-right scale in the Liberal Democrats	Left-right scale in British politics
Left-right scale in the Liberal Democrats	1.0	0.70
Left-right scale in British politics	0.70	1.0
Lifestyle liberalism scale	−0.17	−0.21
Equality and redistribution scale	0.30	0.29
Economic liberalism scale	−0.16	−0.26
European integration scale	−0.27	−0.25

3.5 Ideology and the Liberal Democrat Electorate

Ever since Converse's seminal paper (1964) on ideological beliefs in the mass public, one prominent theme in the literature has been that the mass of the electorate lack any real ideological beliefs. The argument is that many of them have essentially no coherent attitudes, or 'nonattitudes' as it was labelled, about most political issues. This article provoked an extensive academic debate (Achen 1975; Erikson 1978; Converse and Markus 1979; Luskin 1987). In Britain, Butler and Stokes (1974: 316–37) generally supported the argument, since in their analysis of voter attitudes conducted in the 1960s, they argued that only 25 per cent of the electorate thought coherently in left-right terms. However, more recent work suggests that attitudes among voters are quite well structured into 'supra-families' of issues, one centring primarily on the economy and the other on law and order (Himmelweit et al. 1981). In addition, other researchers such as Scarborough (1984) have suggested that ideological beliefs are key to understanding voting behaviour, a view also taken by Rose and McAllister (1990).

In the present context we are less concerned with identifying very broad ideological belief structures among the electorate than with examining if the attitude structures observed among party members have their counterpart among Liberal Democrat voters. The focus is on the extent to which lifestyle issues, attitudes to redistribution, views about the free market and about European Integration form distinct dimensions in the minds of Liberal Democrat voters. To do this we use data from the 2001 British Election Study (Clarke et al. 2004). The attitude indicators in the election study are not the same as those in the Liberal Democrat membership survey, but there are enough measures linked to the four themes under consideration to be able to investigate this question further.

Table 3.6 contains the attitude indicators that are relevant to our concerns which can be found in the 2001 British Election Study. There are fewer attitude indicators than are available in the membership survey, but enough to explore attitude structures in the minds of the voters. The lifestyle indicators appear first, and it can be seen that they are linked to the themes of censorship, tolerance, and views about traditional values in the same way as those in the members' survey. The redistribution indicators are next and capture the themes of redistribution and fair shares, which also appear in the membership survey. The indicators relating to markets echo the theme of free enterprise found earlier, but they also include an indicator of attitudes to trade unions. Finally, there are two

Table 3.6. Attitude indicators among Liberal Democrat voters in 2001

	Strongly agree	Agree	Neither agree nor disagree	Disagree	Strongly disagree
A	16	41	25	11	7
B	14	48	14	19	5
C	16	45	29	8	2
D	1	11	19	56	14
E	15	54	16	14	1
F	9	27	32	27	5
G	4	24	42	26	4
H	1	7	21	52	20
I	8	31	43	16	2

Lifestyle indicators
A: Young people today do not have enough respect for traditional British values.
B: Censorship of films and magazines is necessary to uphold moral standards.
C: People in Britain should be more tolerant of those who lead unconventional lifestyles.

Redistribution indicators
D: Ordinary working people get their fair share of the nation's wealth.
E: There is one law for the rich and one for the poor.
F: In a true democracy income and wealth are redistributed to ordinary working people.

Market indicators
G: Private enterprise is the best way to solve Britain's economic problems.
H: There is no need for strong trade unions to protect employees' working conditions and wages.
I: Big international companies are a threat to democratic government in Britain.

European Union indicators

	Definitely join	Join if conditions are right	Stay out for 4–5 years	Rule out in principle
J	9	52	23	16

	Strongly approve	Approve	Neither approve nor disapprove	Disapprove	Strongly disapprove
K	12	44	17	17	9

J: Thinking of the single European currency (euro), which of the following statements would come closest to your own view?
K: Overall, do you approve or disapprove of Britain's membership of the EU?

indicators of attitudes to European integration, which are rather similar to those in the membership survey.

Looking at the distribution of opinions among Liberal Democrat voters in 2001, they were quite likely to agree with the idea that young people do not have respect for traditional British values, and also that censorship is needed to uphold moral standards. At the same time, and paradoxically, they were also likely to accept the view that British people should be more tolerant of unconventional lifestyles. With respect to redistribution, the voters were not convinced that ordinary people get their fair share of the nation's wealth, or that there is not one law for the rich and one for the poor. In contrast, they were more divided on the proposition that a true democracy should be concerned with the redistribution of income and wealth. On the indicators of attitudes to the role of the market, Liberal Democrat voters were sceptical about the effectiveness of private enterprise in solving Britain's economic problems. Similarly, they largely disagreed with the idea that trade unions were irrelevant to the task of protecting wages and workers' conditions of service. Also, a plurality, though not a majority, of them thought that international companies are a threat to British democracy. Finally, on the indicators of attitudes to the EU, voters supported the idea of joining the single currency if conditions are right, rather than the option of joining unconditionally. In addition, rather like their counterparts in the party membership, they were much more likely to approve of Britain's membership of the EU than to disapprove of it.

Table 3.7 contains the results of a principal components analysis of the attitude indicators in Table 3.6. The evidence from this table suggests that ideological structuring among Liberal Democrat voters is rather similar to that among grassroots party members. The party members' model in Tables 3.1 and the voters' model in Table 3.7 both explain around half of the variance in the data. Moreover, they have a similar structure, even though the indicators used are rather different from each other. There is one clear exception to this point, and it relates to views about lifestyles and attitudes to the EU. In the case of voters, these two items cluster together and do not form separate dimensions. In fact, this lifestyle/EU

Table 3.7. Ideological structuring among Liberal Democrat voters in 2001

	Lifestyles and attitudes to the EU	Redistribution and democracy	Markets
Youth does not respect traditional values	−0.79		
Censorship is necessary	−0.40		
Tolerate unconventional lifestyles	0.67		
Attitudes towards joining the euro	0.61		
Attitudes towards membership of the EU	0.70		
Ordinary people get their fair share of wealth		−0.50	
One law for the rich and one for the poor		0.54	
International companies threaten democracy		0.69	
A true democracy redistributes wealth		0.75	
No need for strong trade unions			0.76
Private enterprise will solve economic problems			0.73
Eigenvalue	2.4	2.0	1.3
Percent of variance explained	21.6	18.5	11.8

factor explains more variance than the other two factors, and it correlates highly with all of the indicators. The second dimension is clearly about redistribution and also about attitudes to the role of democracy in redistribution. It is noteworthy that the statement that multinational companies threaten democracy is highly correlated with this dimension, rather than the market dimension. So this factor is more concerned with democracy and redistribution than is true in the party members' survey. Finally, the market factor links two of the indicators together, and shows that members who think that private enterprise will solve economic problems are also quite likely to believe that trade unions are unnecessary to protect wages and standards of living.

Clearly, the results in Tables 3.1 and 3.7 are not exactly the same, but there is nonetheless a great deal of commonality in the attitudes of grassroots party members and Liberal Democrat voters. If members think that censorship is necessary to uphold moral standards, they are quite likely to disapprove of homosexuality and abortion. Similarly, if voters think that censorship is necessary, they are likely to disagree with the view that people should be tolerant of unconventional lifestyles. If members think that income and wealth should be redistributed, they are quite likely to think that government should spend more money to get rid of poverty. Equally, if voters think that a true democracy should redistribute wealth, they are quite likely to think that ordinary people do not get their fair share of the nation's wealth. Finally, if members think that private enterprise is best for the economy, they are quite likely to think that individuals should provide for themselves. Voters who think that private enterprise is best are quite likely to see trade unions as unnecessary, so that by implication they believe that workers can look after themselves.

3.6 Conclusions

The evidence in this chapter indicates that attitude structures or ideological beliefs exist among grassroots Liberal Democrat party members, which have their counterparts among Liberal Democrat voters. These attitude structures centre around philosophical concerns that go back to the origin of liberalism and social democracy in Britain. They concern issues of redistribution, tolerance of alternative lifestyles, the role of the market in the modern economy, and internationalism as exemplified by attitudes the EU.

The Liberal Democrat Party is unusual, in that compared to its closest rivals, it is a fairly new party. The current membership is made up of former Liberal party members, former Social Democrats, and people with no previous political ties. Over half of the membership at the time of the survey comes from outside of the Liberal tradition. Obviously this diversity of background means that we have to look beyond a simple two-factor model encompassing egalitarianism and libertarianism to explain variations in attitudes. However, it is also clear that these two themes, along with the theme of tolerance and internationalism are at the centre of the belief structures of Liberal Democrats. Moreover this is true whether they are active party members on the one hand or merely voting supporters on the other.

This concludes our discussion of Liberal Democrat ideology, and in Chapter 4 we examine the question as to why people join the party in the first place.

4

Why Join the Party?

Having examined the social background characteristics and attitudes of Liberal Democrat party members in previous chapters, we now turn to the question of why they join the party. Although the principle focus of this chapter is explaining the recruitment of party members, we will also examine the mechanics of joining and the experiences of individuals in the course of becoming members which throws light upon the effectiveness of the party organization at the local level. We begin with a discussion of the recruitment process, followed by an examination of what it means to the average respondent to be a party member. Following that, we focus on the key issue of why people join the party in the first place. In examining motives for joining, we utilize two theoretical models of political participation: the civic voluntarism and the general incentives.

4.1 Pathways to Party Membership

Since party membership in general has been declining in recent years, parties have redoubled their efforts to recruit new members. From 1994 until 1997, Labour was noticeably successful, having increased its membership by 40 per cent (Seyd and Whiteley 2002).[1] Table 4.1 provides information about how Liberal Democrat party members came to join the party in the first place. We see from the table that the party has been particularly successful in recruiting members through social contacts, which include friends, family, and workmates. It appears that existing members are keen to spread the word, so that the party has recruited 21 per cent of its membership in this way. The recruitment of

---

[1] However, as a recent analysis has shown, even the Labour Party has been losing members at an alarming rate (*The Guardian*, 27 September 2002).

Table 4.1. How members joined the party

Mechanisms for joining	%
Through telephone or door to door canvassing	13
In response to a party political broadcast	4
In response to a national party advert	7
In response to a local party newsletter/leaflet	14
I phoned/wrote to the local party	13
A member of my family persuaded me to join	7
A friend persuaded me to join	13
A colleague at work persuaded me to join	1
I joined at a local meeting/stall/rally	9
Other	19

Question: How did you join?

members through social networks highlights the importance of grassroots activists at the local level to act as a core around which the local party can be constructed and developed. At the same time, the party organization itself has been aggressively recruiting new members. Thus, the majority of members have been recruited via some form of party campaign activity, whether it is canvassing, national advertisements, or party political broadcasts. The latter frequently sign off by giving details of how the public can contact the party and join it. Table 4.1 demonstrates the different types of recruitment networks that have been deployed by the party in order to boost membership

Reaching out to the mass population and enticing more people to join the party is a constant concern. It is interesting to probe the motives that people have for joining the party. Table 4.2 lists the responses to a question about this issue. As can be seen, responses ranged across a broad spectrum, from liking the party leader and liking what the party was doing locally, to being influenced by family and friends. The most popular response, given by nearly four out of ten members, was that they joined because they believed in the principles of the party. A further 16 per cent joined because they liked the party's policies. So, one in two members joined because they were attracted by Liberal Democrat principles and policies. A generalized desire to support the party gained 9 per cent of the responses, while opposition to the Conservatives gained 10 per cent. It is noteworthy that opposition to the Conservatives was the prime reason for joining for five times as many members as opposition to Labour. The remaining members joined for a variety of other reasons, from a desire to see constitutional reform to a wish to make social contacts. Interestingly, only 3 per cent joined because they wanted to be active within the party. Once

Table 4.2. Members' reasons for joining the party

Reason for joining the party	%
Paddy Ashdown's leadership	3
Liberal Democrat policies	16
Liberal Democrat principles	38
To oppose the Conservatives	10
To oppose Labour	2
To support PR/constitutional reform	8
For social reasons	1
To support the Liberal Democrat party	9
To be politically active in the party	3
Influence of family and friends	4
Liked the work of the party locally	10
To be better informed about politics	1
To have an influence on the party	1
Other	5

Question: People join the Liberal Democrat party for a variety of different reasons. How about you; what was your most important reason for joining the Liberal Democrat Party?

members have signed up to the party it appears to be common for a majority of them not to participate further in party activities.

Another interesting aspect of the members' experience is the ease or difficulty with which they were able to join the party in the first place. Clearly, if most found it easy to join, this implies that barriers to recruitment are relatively weak. On the other hand, if joining turned out to be a difficult experience for a significant number of members, it suggests that many people could have been turned off in the face of significant barriers to recruitment. Table 4.3 shows that, for the most part, the members found it to be a relatively easy matter to join the party. We cannot infer from this, however, that barriers to recruitment do not exist in some areas of the country. This would most commonly be the absence of a local branch of the party. Clearly, if they do exist they will deter people from joining, and

Table 4.3. Ease of joining the party

Responses	%
Very easy	49
Easy	45
Difficult	5
Very difficult	1

Question: If you approached the local party when you first joined, did you find it easy or difficult to make contact with them?

Table 4.4. Expectations and experience of membership

Responses	%
Fully lived up to expectations	43
Partly lived up to expectations	49
Not really lived up to expectations	7
Not at all lived up to expectations	1

Question: How do your experiences as a member so far relate to your initial expectations?

as a consequence these potential members will not appear in the survey. However, in so far as the experience of existing members is a guide, it suggests that there are no significant barriers to recruitment.

Given that members joined for a diverse set of reasons, it is interesting to know whether they have found the experience of being a party member satisfying. Table 4.4 contains the responses to a question designed to find out if membership has lived up to expectations. For the most part, respondents were satisfied with the experience of being a party member. About half were very satisfied with the experience, and only a handful were discontented.

There is in fact a relationship between activism and satisfaction with party membership. Altogether 60 per cent of the members who described themselves as very active thought that membership had fully lived up to their expectations. In contrast, only 38 per cent of the members who were not at all active thought this to be true. While only a minority of the members are very active, those who are seem to be more satisfied with the experience of being a party member than those who are not.

In light of this discussion, it is interesting to investigate further the activities that party membership involves. This is examined in Section 4.2.

4.2 The Meaning of Liberal Democrat Party Membership

We saw in Table 2.19 that the majority of members are not involved in the day-to-day activities of the party and can be regarded as pretty inactive. Therefore, for many there is a real question about the meaning of party membership in practice. A set of questions were included in the survey to elicit information about the political activities of members. These throw considerable light on how the members see their own role in the party organization. The activities in the table were selected to give a representative picture of the full range of political activities undertaken by members. They are arranged in order of increasing cost, expressed in terms of the time and effort involved in undertaking them. They vary from a comparatively low-cost activity, such as putting up an election poster, to a very high-cost activity, like running for office at the local or national levels. Of course, perceptions of costs of the activities vary amongst respondents, but generally the early items in Table 4.5 are less costly in terms of time and effort than the later items.

Previous studies of party members (see Seyd and Whiteley 1992; Whiteley, Seyd, and Richardson 1994) found that displaying an election poster was the most popular form of low-cost activity undertaken by members. Here, we find that displaying an election poster is the second most popular activity, beaten only by the task of delivering party leaflets during an election campaign. This suggests that the Liberal Democrats are more able to recruit their members to do election campaigning than is true of other parties. The proximity of the 1997 election to the survey certainly influenced the responses to these questions. Low-cost activities dominate membership participation, but 34 per cent of members are still willing to deliver party leaflets between elections, a period when it is more difficult to sustain their motivation. We also find that 22 per cent of the members are willing to attend party meetings either occasionally or frequently. At the high-cost end of the spectrum, we find that comparatively few members are willing to canvass on behalf of the party, although more are willing to canvass door-to-door than by telephone. We will return to this question of local campaigning in a later chapter. As expected, few members are willing to stand for office, either within the party organization or

Table 4.5. Members' political activities (percentages)

	Not at all	Rarely	Occasionally/ frequently
Displayed an election poster	30	25	44
Signed a petition supported by the party	56	29	15
Donated money to Liberal Democrat funds	35	39	26
Helped with party fund-raising	63	20	17
Helped organize a party street stall	93	5	2
Delivered party leaflets during an election	38	16	46
Delivered party leaflets between elections	49	17	34
Helped at a party function	67	17	16
Attended a party meeting	59	19	22
Canvassed voters on behalf of the party door to door	72	13	15
Canvassed voters on behalf of the party by telephone	93	4	3
Stood for office within the party organization	84	8	8
Stood for elected office in a local or national election	83	8	9

Question: We would like to ask you about the political activities you may have taken part in during the last five years. How often have you done this?

in local and national elections. On the other hand, at the high-cost end of the spectrum, those members who do want to stand for office are likely to reap the largest reward in terms of achieving personal political ambitions.

One of the most important forms of political participation in Britain today is donating money to political causes of various types. Research shows that there has been a significant increase in donations of this type over time (Pattie, Seyd, and Whiteley 2004). One explanation of this growth is that individuals are increasingly willing to 'subcontract' their participation to others—in effect paying someone else to participate on their behalf (Jordan and Maloney 1997). We see in Table 4.4 that about a quarter of the party members give money occasionally or frequently to the party, so it is interesting to probe a little deeper into this form of partici-pation. Table 4.5 contains information about the level of individual con-tributions to the party. Subscriptions and donations from the members are a major source of funding for the Liberal Democrats. Unlike the Labour and Conservative parties, the Liberal Democrats are not closely associated with either the trade unions or big business, and as such cannot rely upon these sources of funding. Although at the 2002 party conference an appeal was made to trade unions disaffected by the Labour government to switch their donations to the Liberal Democrat Party, this has not really hap-pened.

From Table 4.6, we find that the level of annual subscription is not particularly high. About three-quarters of the members contribute £25 or less towards the party in subscriptions. However, the members also donate extra money to the party each year. These donations ranged from £5 to £5,000 in the year of the survey. While the higher figures are rare, the mean donation is £79.50 and the modal donation is £40. The latter is more of an indicator of the donations given by the typical party member, since it is not distorted by large payments from a few wealthy individuals.

Table 4.6. Donations by members

Donating money to the party		%
Range of contributions	Annual subscription	Total donation
Under £5	7	5
£5–15	39	8
£15–25	28	14
£25 +	26	73
		Mean = £ 79.50; Mode = £40

Question: What is your estimate of the total financial contribution that you made to the party in the last twelve months (including annual membership fee, contributions to local or national fund-raising initiatives, standing orders, etc.)?

Returning to the question of why people join the party, the reasons given in Table 4.2 are interesting but quite diverse. It is important to probe this further by examining recruitment through the lens of two alternative theoretical explanatory models of participation that are prominent in the literature. While we have evidence covering the reasons members give for joining the party, the question remains as to what prompts some party supporters to join when many others do not. In the following sections we explore this question in detail.

4.3 Rival theoretical models considered: civic voluntarism and general incentives

Joining a political party is very much a minority activity in Britain. Survey evidence from a comprehensive study of political participation conducted in the early 1980s concluded that around 7 per cent of the electorate were party members and only 2 per cent were party activists at that time (Parry, Moyser, and Day 1992). The 2001 British Election Study showed that only 5 per cent of the electorate were party members, indicating that there has been a decline in party membership over the intervening years. Of this group of party members in 2001, only 10 per cent claimed to be Liberal Democrat members (see Clarke et al. 2004). Therefore, party membership in general, and Liberal Democrat party membership in particular, is very much a minority activity.

These figures suggest something of a paradox. In the 2001 general election close to five million people voted Liberal Democrat, so why are so few of them willing to join the party? As is well known, this 'paradox of party membership' is not just confined to the Liberal Democrats. Both Labour and the Conservative parties attract many more voters than they do party members. Given this, it is reasonable to ask the question: 'Why should anyone want to join a political party?' A plausible reply might be: 'Because they want to help to promote the goals of the party—to help it to get elected so that it can implement the policies which they favour.' However, in an influential book *The Logic of Collective Action*, Olson (1965) persuasively argued that this common-sense answer is quite wrong. Olson suggested that if voters were rational individuals, in the sense of calculating the costs and benefits of their actions, it is unlikely that they would join a party, even when they strongly favoured its policies. Olson's analysis suggests that the problem of understanding party membership is not in explaining why so few join, but rather why anyone joins at all. It is possible to explain away this paradox in the general incentives theory, which is designed to provide an accurate account of why so few people join political parties.

Before examining this explanation, however, it is important to take into account a rival theoretical explanation of political participation, namely the civic voluntarism model. This is a well-known theoretical model for explaining political participation, and it focuses on the resources that individuals bring to the task of participating. We shall consider the merits of both of these models before going on to test them in Chapter 5.

4.3.1 Civic voluntarism

The civic voluntarism model (see Verba and Nie 1972; Verba, Schlozman, and Brady 1995) starts from the premise that political participation is best explained by the resources that the individual possesses. As Verba and Nie (1972: 13) put it:

According to this model, the social status of an individual—his job, education and income—determines to a large extent how much he participates. It does this through the intervening effects of a variety of 'civic attitudes' conducive to participation: attitudes such as a sense of efficacy, of psychological involvement in politics and a feeling of obligation to participate.

In this interpretation, resources give rise to civic attitudes and feelings of obligations to participate, and all of these together promote involvement. To join a political party, and in some cases to become active, individuals must possess resources in time and civic skills, and they must also have a sense of political efficacy and feelings of obligation to the party. In the most recent version of the theory, the central ideas are captured in the following quote:

We focus on three factors to account for political activity. We suggested earlier that one helpful way to understand the three factors is to invert the usual question and ask instead why people do not become political activists. Three answers come to mind: because they can't; because they don't want to; or because nobody asked. In other words people may be inactive because they lack resources, because they lack psychological engagement with politics, or because they are outside of the recruitment networks that bring people into politics (Verba, Schlozman, and Brady 1995: 269).

This implies that party members are likely to have greater resources than party supporters in general, are likely to be more interested in politics, more committed to the party, and many of them will have been mobilized by others to join the party. We have already observed in Chapter 2 that members are more likely to be middle class and university-educated than Liberal Democrat voters. We saw also in Table 4.1 that many Liberal Democrat members were mobilized to join the party either by their own networks of friends and family or by the campaigning activities of other Liberal Democrats at the local level. For some, membership of local voluntary groups and engagement in local campaigns may have stimulated them to join the party. So voluntary activity, even if it is relatively non-political in character, may be a mechanism for recruiting some people into the party. In this respect the civic voluntarism model appears to provide a plausible account of why some people become party members.

However, the civic voluntarism model has its critics. One problem with the model is that, despite the fact that high socio-economic status may correlate with party membership, most high-status individuals are not party members. This is because these people find other things to do with their time rather than participating in a political party. This means that while there is a correlation between socio-economic status and party membership, the correlation is nonetheless rather weak. An additional problem for the theory is that if high socio-economic status is the only thing that matters in predicting participation, party membership should be increasing in Britain over time, not declining. This is because Britain has changed over the last generation in that the workforce has become more white collar and less working class (Dalton 2002). There has also been a massive increase in the educational qualifications of the workforce, with many more people graduating from universities than was true a generation ago. If resources are such a good predictor of party membership, these trends should have stimulated a rise in party membership, not the decline we actually observe. A third problem with the model is that it does not address the 'paradox of party membership' referred to earlier. If Olson's analysis is correct, it is important for any theory of participation to address questions of incentives. People may have considerable personal resources and also be quite interested in politics, but if they do not have an incentive to participate, they are unlikely to get involved. Despite these critical points, the civic voluntarism model may still be useful in providing at least a partial account of why some people join a political party and become active.

4.3.2 General incentives

The general incentives model has roots in rational choice theory, which arises out of research in economics. The advantage of the general incentives model is that it addresses some of the theoretical weaknesses of the civic voluntarism model. The core idea of the model is that individuals need incentives if they are to join a political party, and to become active in that party (see Seyd and Whiteley 1992; Whiteley, Seyd, and Richardson 1994). These incentives help them to overcome the costs of participation, which are not large for inactive members, but which can become quite large for the activists. The theory hypothesizes that participation is motivated by a series of incentives. It will be recalled that Olson's thesis argues that individuals make decisions to participate solely on the basis of the costs and benefits associated with the different courses of actions open to them. Supporters of a party have an incentive to free-ride on the efforts of others, and not to contribute to the activities of the party. This free-riding comes about because parties are organizations that mainly produce public goods.

A public or collective good has two properties: jointness of supply and the impossibility of exclusion (see Samuelson 1954). Jointness of supply means that one person's consumption of the good does not reduce the amount available to anyone else. An example of this would be national defence. Everybody in a society benefits from national defence and any one individual's consumption of the good does not reduce the amount of it available to others. Impossibility of exclusion means that if one person does not contribute to the provision of the collective good, they cannot be prevented from benefiting from it. Again, if an individual avoids paying the taxes that support defence spending, they nonetheless benefit from national defence, and it is impossible to prevent them from doing so. Thus, rational individuals have an incentive to free-ride on the efforts of others and there is little reason for them to contribute.

Olson pointed out that political parties provide collective goods, in the form of policy proposals and manifesto promises, which potentially affect everyone, regardless of whether or not they are members or supporters. Consequently, rational actors who strongly support party policy proposals have nonetheless an incentive to free-ride on the efforts of others, and thereby avoid the costs of participation. In effect, they have an incentive to 'let someone else do the work'. This is how Olson explains the fact that very few of the people who support a party are willing to become members. Having said that, it is clear that some people actually do become party members, so why does this happen? Olson argues that they receive 'selective incentives' or inducements to participate, which are unrelated to the collective goals of the party. These selective incentives are private goods, in the sense that anyone who does not join will not receive them.

In his book, Olson cites the example of trade unions, which provide inducements to join such as legal advice and insurance, which are only available to members (Olson 1965: 73). In the absence of such selective incentives there would be a real problem recruiting trade union members, since the collective goods produced by the union such as pay increases and improved conditions of work are available to the entire workforce, which gives rise to the free-rider problem.

Any incentive-based theory of why people join a political party has to deal with the paradox of participation. Being an active member of a political party involves a great deal of high-intensity participation such as campaigning, organizing meetings, and running for office. Selective incentives must be important enough to overcome the problem in situations where the temptations to free-ride are great. The theory suggests that there are three types of selective incentive: process, outcome, and ideological (see Whiteley and Seyd 2002).

Process incentives refer to motives for participating that derive from the process of participation itself. Different writers have referred to a number of motives that might be counted under this heading. Tullock (1971) has written of the 'entertainment' value of being involved in revolution; Opp (1990) writes about the 'catharsis' value of involvement in political protest. For some people, the political process is interesting and stimulating in itself, regardless of outcome or goals. Party membership is a way of meeting like-minded and interesting people, and for some, this is motive enough for getting involved. Outcome incentives refer to motives concerned with achieving certain goals in the political process, but goals that are private rather than collective. Thus, a party member might harbour ambitions to become a local councillor or the local mayor, or even to be elected to the House of Commons. Others may want nomination from the Liberal Democrat Party to be a school governor or a local magistrate. There are many motives that come under this heading, but they all share the common characteristic of providing private, rather than collective, benefits from participation.

A third type of motivation is ideology, and this explains the so-called 'law' of curvilinear disparity (see May 1973; Kitschelt 1989). This is the proposition that the rank-and-file members of a political party are likely to be more radical than the voters or the party leadership. This produces a curvilinear relationship between ideological radicalism and the position of the individual within the organizational hierarchy of the party. In the case of the Liberal Democrats, it is likely to mean that the rank-and-file members are more radical than the leadership on the one hand, and the party supporters in the electorate on the other. The selective incentives to party membership deriving from ideology are related to the fact that individuals like associating with other like-minded people. The process of sharing values and beliefs with other people produces an incentive to participate in the party organization. Involvement is prompted by motives similar to those of the active churchgoer. Membership of a church allows religious people to give expression to their beliefs as well as to become part of a congregation.

It can be seen that a number of incentives exist to promote party membership that are independent of the collective incentives, which create the paradox of participation. On the other hand, these selective incentives only really apply to the active party members. People who regard their party membership as a private matter, not to be discussed or shared with other people, are unlikely to be motivated by process, outcome, or ideological incentives.

If these people do not receive selective incentives, why should they join the party? It is possible to explain why somebody would join while at the same time remaining inactive. The key to understanding this is the relationship between the costs and benefits of party membership. What matters is the individual's perceptions of both the costs and benefits. Individuals may perceive that their own contribution to the collective good is negligible, but it may still be rational for them to participate if they see the costs as being negligible as well. It is the perceived difference between costs and benefits that matters, not some 'objectively' defined measure of these benefits and costs. This has a further implication; when perceptions of both benefits and costs are small, it is not rational to calculate them precisely. The exercise of assessing costs and benefits is itself costly, and does not warrant the return when those costs are trivial. Thus, it is rational to define a threshold below which individuals do not assess the precise costs and benefits of collective action (see Barry 1970; Niemi 1976). In this situation, joining a party without having selective incentives makes sense, provided one believes that this involves making a non-zero contribution to the collective good. In addition, there are other incentives, over and above selective incentives, which might induce people to join the party.

One additional incentive is provided by 'solidaristic' motives for participation, or motives based on a group-based reasoning. Any adequate theoretical account of collective action needs to consider situations in which the individual 'thinks' collectively at the level of the group. If individuals think of the group's welfare in addition to their own personal benefits when making a decision to participate, this can make a difference. In doing this, they are asking the question 'what is best for all of us?' rather than 'what is best for me?' If this idea is applied to the task of explaining party membership, it implies that one reason why individuals join is because they believe that Liberal Democrat party members collectively make a difference to policy outcomes. Individuals will still undertake a calculus of costs and benefits, but it is focused at the level of the party as a whole, not just at their own level. If they reach the conclusion that the party as a whole can make an important difference to the lives of the people with whom they identify, they will join.

All these are ways in which individuals avoid the temptation to free-ride when collective goods are provided. The collective goods are the policy goals of the Liberal Democrat Party. Thus, individuals who think that the party will increase prosperity, promote the interests of people like themselves, and generally improve the local community or Britain as a whole will be induced to participate if they think collectively. In this case, collective action becomes an incentive to participate, rather than an incentive to free-ride. Whether or not they join the party depends on seeing it as a vehicle for achieving those goals. In a purely individualistic world of the type assumed by classical rational choice theory, in which people do not think in terms of group needs at all, most would free-ride. But in a world where people seek group benefits, it is no longer rational to do this. In that case, individuals will be motivated to participate because they feel that they are part of an effective group.

Collective incentives for joining the party can be of two kinds: positive and negative. Individuals will participate not only because they want to promote particular policy goals but also because they oppose other people's collective goals. On the one hand, they may be motivated to get involved because they support some aspect of Liberal Democrat party policy; on the other, they may participate because they oppose some aspect of Conservative or Labour policies. Positive incentives involve promoting what are seen as collective goods, whereas negative incentives involve opposing what are seen as collective bads.

The 'unity principle' introduced by Muller and his associates suggests that there is a moral dimension to all of this. A norm may exist which suggests that individuals should contribute if the collective good is to be provided (Muller and Opp 1986, 1987; Finkel et al. 1989). They describe this norm as 'calculating Kantianism'. When faced with the possibility of free-riding on the efforts of others, group members ask themselves the question: 'What if everyone did that?'; and since the answer is that the collective good would not be provided, they choose to participate.

The basic idea is that moral reasoning plays an important role in explaining participation for some individuals. They may be conscious of the paradox of participation, and they may even discount collective thinking of the type discussed earlier. But they participate anyway, out of a sense of duty or a moral imperative. This is an aspect of the 'civic culture', which is a set of norms and beliefs about how the political system should work, and what role the citizen should take within it (see Almond and Verba 1963). It provides an additional motive for joining the party in the general incentives theory. Very often, these moral motives will be expressed in terms of idealistic goals, such as the desire to 'build a better society' or because of a general belief in liberal principles. Such general motives may of course have policy implications, but a moral imperative is the driving force behind the decision to participate, not the specific policy goal.

Yet another factor, which explains participation within the general incentives framework, are incentives based on emotional or affective attachments to the Liberal Democrat Party. These motives lie outside the standard cost – benefit model of decision-making, with its emphasis on cognitive calculations. Such motives have long been discussed in the literature on party identification, since the early theorists saw partisanship as an effective orientation towards a significant social or political group in the individual's environment (Campbell et al. 1960); they have also been discussed in relation to economic voting (Conover and Feldman 1986) and in the US literature on presidential voting (Marcus 1988). A formal theory of expressive voting has been developed which postulates that voters are motivated by a desire to express support for one candidate or policy outcome over another, independently of whether or not their vote influences outcomes (Brennan and Buchanan 1984; Carter and Guerette 1992). In this interpretation, some people are motivated to join by an expressive attachment to the Liberal Democrat Party, which has little to do with the benefits obtained from membership. Such motives for joining are grounded in a sense of loyalty and affection for the party that is unrelated to cognitive calculations of costs and benefits. Frank (1988) argues that such emotional commitments provide a mechanism for overcoming collective action problems by inducing people to cooperate even in situations where significant short-term benefits accrue from free riding.

Finally, social norms constitute a fifth set of motives for joining a party. These also lie outside the scope of a narrow rational choice model of participation. A key feature of such norms is their enforcement by other people. 'Significant others' who express approval or disapproval can influence the individual's behaviour (see Elster 1989: 97–151). Thus, party members motivated by social norms are responding to the perceived opinions of individuals whose views they respect and value. We have seen in Table 4.1 that many people become party members because of their family and friends, and this illustrates how social norms can influence party membership.

Overall, then, the general incentives theory of political participation postulates that five distinct factors are at work in explaining why people join a political party or become active once they have joined. These are selective and collective incentives, altruism, affective motives, and social norms.

4.3.3 Applying civic voluntarism

Our discussion of the civic voluntarism model explains an individual's participation in terms of his or her resources, psychological engagement with politics, and sense of political efficacy, and also by the process of mobilization. There are a number of variables that are relevant for testing the civic voluntarism model in the survey. The constituent parts of the model include a measure of the individual's political efficacy and socio-economic status, and a measure of the extent to which the individual has been mobilized to be active in the party.

The first of the empirical measures relates to the individual's sense of political efficacy (Verba, Schlozman, and Brady 1995: 272). Table 4.7 contains two indicators which suggest that Liberal Democrat members' sense of political efficacy is high. Seven in every ten members believe that by getting involved they can have a political influence and eight in ten think that Liberal Democrat members can change Britain. The recruitment variable included in Table 4.7 is coded from the responses in Table 4.1. The recruitment measure focuses on recruitment by social networks, the percentage of members who were recruited by friends or family, or at the workplace. The score of 21 per cent on this variable is high in comparison with an earlier analysis of Labour and Conservative party members, which returned scores of 7 per cent for Labour and 12 per cent for the Conservatives on the same measure (Whiteley and Seyd 2002: Table 4.5, 67). The Liberal Democrat score demonstrates the importance of social networks for the recruitment of party members.

Most of the remaining predictor variables in Table 4.7 measure the individual's socio-economic status. We have already discussed the socio-economic profile of Liberal Democrat members in Chapter 2. However, it is worth repeating some of that evidence here because of its importance to

Table 4.7. The civic voluntarism model indicators

Political efficacy	%
People like me can have a real influence on politics if they are prepared to get involved (% agreeing)	70
When Liberal Democrat party members are united and work together they can really change Britain (% agreeing)	83
Recruitment	
Family, friends, and workmates	21
Resources	
Full-time employment	49
Unemployed	2
Income	
Less than £10,000	16
£10,000–20,000	27
£20,000–40,000	35
£40,000+	22
Social class	
Salariat	74
Routine non-manual	11
Petty bourgeoisie	7
Foreman and technician	4
Working class	4
Education	
Graduate	42
Non-graduate	58
Strength of party attachment	
Very strong	26
Fairly strong	49
Not very strong	22
Not at all strong	4
Membership of local groups	
None	42
One	23
Two	17
Three	10
Four or more	8

the civic voluntarism model. Based upon their socio-economic profiles, Liberal Democrat members fit the description of likely participants. We can see from Table 4.7 that the majority of them are employed full-time, enjoy a reasonable standard of living, and are middle class. Furthermore, a large proportion of them have a good educational background. In addition, the majority are fairly strongly attached to the party, which provides an important stimulus to join, are members of local groups, and are involved in community politics. In terms of the civic voluntarism model, these characteristics are all positive predictors of participation and should encourage individuals to join the party. All these characteristics suggest that resources and motivations of the type discussed in the civic voluntarism model are important in explaining why people join the party.

4.3.4 Applying general incentives

We have suggested that five factors discussed in the general incentives theory play an important role in explaining why individuals join the party, and why some of them become active once they have joined. If these factors are important, we should observe clear differences between party members and party supporters in the electorate. If we compare Liberal Democrat members and Liberal Democrat identifiers in the electorate, we would expect the former to be more highly motivated than the latter in each of the relevant variables in the general incentives model. Thus, members should be more in favour of Liberal Democrat policies, more emotionally attached to the party, and more motivated by process, outcome, and ideological incentives, although as we pointed out earlier, this depends on their rates of activism. In addition, they should feel a greater sense of duty to participate and, finally, they should be more influenced to participate by other people who are close to them. Unfortunately we do not have the data to test all these factors, since that would require a survey of Liberal Democrat voters, which contained precisely the same questions as the survey of party members. However, useful comparisons can be made between the members in the survey and Liberal Democrat identifiers identified in the 1997 British Election Study. The comparisons are limited, since that particular study was not designed to test incentive theories of participation. However, in Table 4.8 we compare the responses of party members and Liberal Democrat identifiers on a set of questions that is closely linked to the general incentives theory.

The first section of Table 4.8 relates to expressive or affective attachments to the Liberal Democrat Party. We use the same variable in this table as in Table 4.7. It is clear that members are more strongly attached to the party than are Liberal Democrat identifiers in the electorate. Twenty-six per cent of the members are very strongly attached compared to only 5 per cent of identifiers. This margin of 21 per cent compares favourably with Conservative party members where the margin is 14 per cent (Whiteley, Seyd, and Richardson 1994: 91). The evidence here is consistent with the proposition that expressive attachments motivate individuals to join the party.

Collective incentives are measured by policy goals, and in this case we compare party members with Liberal Democrat identifiers in the election study on a set of three key issue indicators in the second part of Table 4.8. The basic idea here is that if collective incentives motivate people to join the party, their policy goals should be more closely aligned with those of the party than is true of supporters in the wider electorate. Thus, policy agreement with party positions should, in part, explain why supporters become members. The items in Table 4.8 relate to public expenditure on health, welfare, and education, attitudes to nationalization versus free enterprise, and attitudes to Britain's membership of the EU.

It is necessary to get some independent measure of where the Liberal Democrat Party is located on these issues if we are to determine whether members are closer to the party than voters. This can be done using the party manifesto evidence discussed in Chapter 1 (see Budge et al. 2001).

Table 4.8. General incentives: a comparison of members and identifiers in the electorate (percentages)

Expressive incentives	Members	Identifiers in the electorate
How would you rate yourself as a Liberal Democrat?		
Very strong	26	5
Fairly strong	49	41
Not very strong	22	52
Not at all strong	4	—
Collective incentives or benefits		
The government should reduce taxes and spend less on health, education, and social benefits	1	2
The government should keep taxes and spending on these services at the present levels	16	14
The government should increase taxes and spend more on health, education, and social benefits	83	81
None of the above	3	3
In favour of more nationalization of companies by government	28	31
In favour of leaving things as they are	63	56
In favour of more privatization of companies by government	9	10
None of the above	6	4
Britain should leave the EU	6	26
Britain should continue as a member of the EU	86	65
Do not know	8	9

Perceptions of efficacy	Strongly agree +Agree	Strongly disagree +Disagree
It does not really matter which party is in power; in the end things go on much the same (members)	18	75
It does not matter which party is in power; things go on the same (identifiers)	42	38
People like me can have a real influence in politics if they are prepared to get involved (members)	70	15
People like me have no say in government actions (identifiers)	52	23

Figure 1.2 showed that the Liberal Democrat policies have taken a fairly positive view of welfare spending, so we should expect to see members being rather more supportive of welfare than identifiers in the wider electorate. Similarly, Figure 1.3 showed that the party has consistently supported European integration over time; thus, we might expect members to be more Europhile than identifiers. Party policies on nationalization were not discussed in Chapter 1, but the positive references to the subject along with positive references to free enterprise in manifestoes appear in Figure 4.1. The evidence in Figure 4.1 shows that the party has always been more favourably inclined to free enterprise than it has to nationalization, with the exception of a brief blip during 1974. As a result, we should expect party members to be the same, and be less enthusiastic about nationalization than Liberal Democrat identifiers in the electorate as a whole.

Referring to Table 4.8, we can see that party members are more positively inclined towards the EU, more sceptical about nationalization, and slightly more inclined to support welfare spending than is true of Liberal Democrat identifiers in the electorate. This supports the proposition that party members are closer to the policy positions of the party as set out in the manifesto than are identifiers in the electorate. According to the general incentives theory, this is one of the reasons why they are party members, and not just supporters.

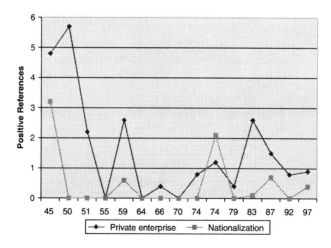

Figure 4.1 Positive references to free enterprise and nationalization in Liberal Party and Liberal Democrat manifestos 1945–97

Source: Budge et al. (2001)

A sense of personal efficacy also plays an important role in the general incentives and civic voluntarism models. Accordingly, both models predict that party members should feel a greater sense of efficacy than supporters in the electorate. We can see that the evidence in Table 4.8 is consistent with this expectation. Members are much more likely to feel that they can have a real impact upon politics in comparison with identifiers. There are differences in question wordings on these items, which make exact comparisons difficult, but it is nonetheless clear that members have a much greater sense of personal efficacy than identifiers.

Comparing the responses of members and identifiers to various issues is one way to test incentives theory. Another is to ask members why they joined the party in the first place, and then examine the answers to see if they can be classified according to the various categories of the theory. Table 4.9 clearly shows that expressive attachments play a very important role in explaining why members join the party. Expressive attachments are dominated by a liking for Liberal Democrat principles, which, as we argued in Chapter 2, were highly important for the members. At the same time, a small group of members joined because they liked the local party, which is another aspect of expressive attachments.

Table 4.9. The general incentives model indicators

What was your most important reason for joining the Liberal Democrat Party?	%
Expressive attachments	
Paddy Ashdown	3
Like work of local party	10
Liberal Democrat principles	38
	51
Collective positive	
Liberal Democrat policies	16
PR constitutional reform	8
	24
Collective negative	
Oppose Labour	2
Oppose the Conservatives	10
	12
Selective process incentives	
To be politically active	3
Social reasons	1
To be better informed about politics	1
	9
Selective outcome incentives	
To have an influence on the party	1
Social norms	
Joined because of family and friends	4

The second most popular reason for joining the party is collective incentives. Collective positive incentives include key party policy commitments framed in rather general terms. Also included in this category are the negative incentives, which are manifest in the form of a desire to oppose rival parties. Equally, selective incentives provide an insight into the private reasons for joining the party. Some members wanted to be politically active for its own sake, whereas others had social reasons. A small number wanted to have influence on the party, which is a type of outcome incentive. Finally, an important group of members were induced to join by social norms, that is, by their friends and family. More members are influenced to join by family and friends than those who join to be politically active.

It is perhaps not surprising that expressive motives for participation should predominate in the party in which most members are not active. Since inactive members are not receiving selective incentives, and collective incentives are subject to the paradox of participation, we might expect expressive motives for joining to be more important factors than other types of motives in the minds of most inactive members.

4.4 Conclusions

In this chapter we have outlined two rival theoretical explanations of why some supporters in the electorate might end up joining the Liberal Democrats. We have also looked at some evidence, which is consistent with different aspects of these theories. However, the evidence does not provide a definitive test of them, primarily because our survey did not include a sample of non-members. It is therefore impossible to model the differences between members and non-members using the same measures—something required to test the theories properly. On the other hand, if either of these theories can be used to explain why people join the party, they should also provide an explanation of why some people are active when others remain on the sidelines. Since we have data on variations in activism in the party, this can be used to test the theories applied to the task of explaining activism, and this is done in Chapter 5.

5

Explaining Party Activism

In Chapter 4, we described two rival theoretical models, which can be used to explain why some party members become politically active when others do not. The civic voluntarism model uses the idea that individual resources based upon social attributes facilitate political activity. The general incentives model suggests that political activism is driven by incentives of various kinds. In this chapter we will test the ability of these rival theories to explain party activism within the grassroots Liberal Democrat Party.

Before attempting to explain political activism in the grassroots party, it is necessary to understand precisely what activism means. At the same time, we need to get a picture of how active participation varies amongst the grassroots party members. We begin by examining the nature of party activism within the Liberal Democrat Party. Accounts of party politics, which make crude distinctions between active and inactive members, are too simplistic, since participation refers to a range of different activities. So Section 5.1 is devoted to examining this issue in detail.

This is followed by Section 5.2, which examines the relationship between party activism and the social background characteristics of the members. Examining activism rates among the members by age, social class, gender, and other related social characteristics throws further light upon the nature of political activism. One of the key features of Liberal Democrat electoral strategy over the years has been an emphasis on community politics. This is another important aspect of participation and it is examined closely in Section 5.3. Section 5.4 goes on to specify and measure the civic voluntarism and general incentives models in detail. The theoretical accounts set out in Chapter 4 are translated into models, which are then tested in order to see which gives the best account of participation. It is possible to conduct more sophisticated tests of variations in activism within the party than was true in Chapter 4, where the analysis was restricted by the lack of indicators of the attitudes and behaviour of Liberal Democrat voters. In this chapter, we are not restricted in this way, and so can develop a model, which provides the best account of activism within the grassroots party.

In Section 5.5 we examine the relationship between the incentive measures and the social characteristics of members to see how these incentives are influenced by social background. This section looks at the links between resource accounts of participation and incentive-based models, the argument being that resources might very well influence activism indirectly via their impact on incentives. We begin with a discussion of party activism.

5.1 Measuring Party Activism

Activism is not a dichotomous variable, with members either being active on the one hand or inactive on the other. Rather, it is a continuous variable, with some members being totally inactive at one end of the scale, and others being virtually full-time activists at the other. Between these two extremes lies a distribution of members who vary in their levels of activism. At the inactive end of the scale, members pay their subscription, vote for the Liberal Democrats, and possibly strongly identify with the party, but that is the limit of their commitment. At the other end of the scale, there are activists who are office holders within the organization, elected representatives on the local council, who attend important party meetings, and are prominent in local campaigns and elections.

The range of activities undertaken by the members during the previous five-year period was examined in Table 4.5. This is not an exhaustive list of all possible activities, but it does encompass most of the important types of party work. The list includes election-related activities such as delivering leaflets and canvassing, as well as more general activities such as fund raising, participating in political campaigns, and representing the party on internal and external bodies. The list covers all the most important activities undertaken by the party at the local and national levels. In Chapter 4 these activities were discussed in order of their increasing costliness. Not surprisingly, as we moved down the list and the activities became more costly in terms of time and effort, fewer party members got involved.

The evidence in Table 4.5 raises the issue of how these different types of activities are structured. Is it the case that involvement by the members in one type of activity is also associated with their involvement in other activities? It is possible that different party members undertake different kinds of political actions, or is it the same people doing every activity? Clearly, one possibility is that if members are willing to undertake high-cost types of activity like running for office, they are also likely to undertake low-cost activities like displaying an election poster and donating money to the party. On the other hand, it is clear that many members are willing to undertake low-cost activities, but not the high-cost activities. In this case, there may very well be different scales of participation, with some people doing low-cost activities but not high-cost activities, and other people being highly involved in the party organization, but doing little in the way of signing petitions or donating money to the party. We can test these alternative possibilities using a factor analysis of the activity indicators.

Table 5.1 contains the factor loadings from a factor analysis of the different indicators of party activism set out in Table 4.5. It shows clearly that there are two independent clusters of activities in the set. Firstly, there is what we have described as a high-intensity, or activist, scale, which includes items like fund-raising, attending meetings, canvassing, and running for office. For the most part, these are the high-cost types of activity discussed

Table 5.1. Factor analysis of activism indicators

Activities	Factors	
	Activist scale	Supporter scale
Displayed a poster		0.70
Signed a petition		0.45
Donated extra money		0.40
Helped with fund-raising	0.61	
Helped with street stall	0.55	
Delivered election leaflets		0.83
Delivered non-election leaflets		0.81
Helped at party function	0.61	
Attended party meeting	0.65	
Door-to-door canvassing	0.65	
Telephone canvassing	0.66	
Stood for party organization office	0.74	
Stood for elected office	0.66	
Eigenvalue	5.5	1.2
Percentage of explained variance	42.5	9.4

Note: Factor loadings less than 0.40 in value are excluded. The factor scores derive from a principle components analysis using a varimax rotation. Factors with eigenvalues <1 are excluded.

earlier. The factor loadings, or correlations between items on the scale, mean that members who do one kind of activity tend to do the others. This is the most important of the two scales in explaining variations in participation. The scale shows that the highly active members do not necessarily undertake all of the activities in the list. Individuals who run for office are not necessarily likely to display an election poster or to deliver leaflets. On the other hand, they are quite likely to attend meetings and to canvass voters.

The second scale has been labelled a low-intensity activity, or supporters, scale, and takes in activities like donating money, displaying posters, and delivering leaflets. Again, party members who do one of these activities are quite likely to do another, but they are not likely to canvass voters or run for office. Clearly, supporters undertake much less costly forms of participation than the activists, but they nonetheless undertake valuable activities, which the party depends on, particularly at election times. Their contributions, particularly in relation to donating money and leafleting, are important to the party.

The analysis indicates that participation in the high-intensity scale is independent of participation in the low-intensity scale.[1] While a member who donates money is likely to put up a poster, there is no evidence to suggest that this makes them more (or less) likely to attend meetings or to canvass voters. Altogether the two scales explain about half of the variance in these activism indicators, which demonstrates that these activities are structured to a significant extent. Thus, it would not be true to say that the members who display posters are a completely different group from the members who donate money, or that the members who attend meetings are different from members who campaign in elections. Rather there are associations between these types of activity. We began this discussion by arguing that activism was not a simple dichotomy dividing those who are active and those who are not. At the same time, the evidence suggests that it is not a single continuum either. Rather there are two activism scales required to explain the data.

In light of this analysis, each respondent can be given a score on the high-intensity and low-intensity scales, and in this way it is possible to get a visual picture of how the party members are distributed along the two scales.[2] If, for example, a particular individual regularly displays a poster at election time, gives extra money to the party, and helps to deliver leaflets,

---

[1] This does not mean that members who donate money never attend meetings or campaign in elections. Rather it means that while donating money is a reasonably good predictor of displaying a poster, it is not a good predictor of attending meetings or canvassing.
[2] The scales are the sums of scores from the analysis in Table 5.1.

but does not attend meetings or run for office, they will have a high score on the low-intensity scale and a low score on the high-intensity scale. Equally, if another individual does a lot of canvassing, attends a lot of party meetings, and runs for office, but does not give extra money to the party or deliver leaflets, they will score highly on the high-intensity scale but low on the low-intensity scale. The distribution of supporters and activists are shown in Figures 5.1 and 5.2.

It can be seen that nearly half of the members score zero on the high-intensity scale, indicating that they do none of the activities measured. The distribution of the high-intensity scale has a long tail, with a few outlier activists scoring highly on everything. But most party members who do get involved in these activities participate in a few of them but do not get involved in all. This confirms the evidence presented earlier in Chapter 4.

As Figure 5.2 shows, the distribution of members on the low-intensity scale is very different from their distribution on the high-intensity activists scale. In this case, fewer people are totally inactive, and the vast majority are involved in one or two activities. Moreover, there are quite a few

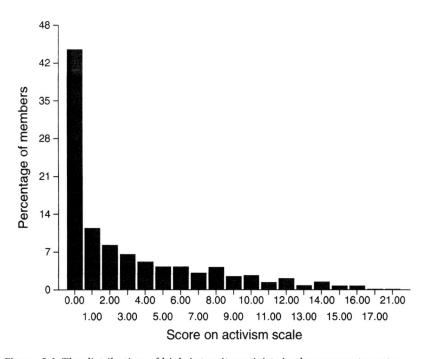

Figure 5.1 The distribution of high-intensity activists in the grassroots party

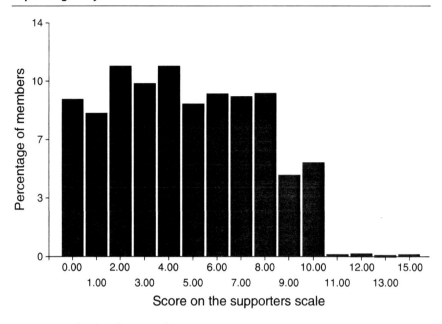

Figure 5.2 The distribution of low-intensity supporters in the grassroots party

people who are highly involved in all the activities measured by the scale. The high-intensity scale singles out the activists within our sample of party members, and separates them from supporters in the electorate in a way that the low-intensity scale does not. So from this point, we shall concentrate on explaining variations in the high-intensity scale. The starting point is an examination of the relationship between high-intensity activism and the social characteristics of party members. This subsequently leads to a discussion of the civic voluntarism and general incentives models in more detail.

5.2 Relationship between Activism and Social Background

To facilitate analysis of the relationship between activism and social backgrounds, we recoded the high-intensity activism scale into four categories and these appear in Table 5.2.[3] The categories are: not at all active, not very active, fairly active, and very active. Readers will notice that this scale is different from the one reported in Table 2.19. The earlier scale was

[3] Scores from 0 to 3 were coded 1; 4 to 7 coded 2; 8 to 11 coded 3; and 12 to the highest coded 4.

much simpler and merely asked respondents to code themselves into the four predefined categories. This scale is more sophisticated since it is constructed from a detailed analysis of activities undertaken by the members.

There are some interesting patterns in the data in Table 5.2. There is a clear tendency for the very active members to be in the 26–35 age bracket. This is particularly interesting since research into participation by the general public shows that young people are generally less likely to participate than their older counterparts (Pattie, Seyd, and Whiteley 2004; Clarke et al. 2004). Scarrow (1996: 145–6) has argued that parties are increasingly demanding more from their members in terms of participation. She points out that activists are expected to build the political visibility of the party at

Table 5.2. Social background variables categorized by levels of activism (percentages)

	Not at all active	Not very active	Fairly active	Very active
All respondents	70	16	10	4
(N)	(2006)	(459)	(287)	(115)
Age				
18–25	72	19	9	—
26–35	60	13	16	11
36–45	67	18	11	4
46–55	63	19	13	5
56–65	69	15	11	4
65+	78	13	7	2
Class				
Salariat	68	16	11	4
Routine non-manual	73	16	8	2
Petty bourgeoisie	70	17	10	3
Foreman and technician	71	17	10	2
Working class	79	13	5	3
Employment				
Employed	68	17	11	5
Unemployed	60	12	16	12
Retired	74	15	8	2
Gender				
Male	67	16	11	5
Female	73	16	9	2
Income				
Under £10,000	74	16	7	2
£10,000–30,000	69	16	10	4
£30,000+	68	15	12	5
Donations				
Under £10	88	9	2	1
£10–30	81	14	5	1
£30+	58	20	16	6
Graduate				
Yes	67	16	12	5
No	73	16	8	3

the local and national levels by campaigning and running for office. At the local level, this means the production and delivery of regular newsletters, knocking on doors, and working as 'political ambassadors' in the community. For the Liberal Democrats, this entails a high level of commitment by the members, and these findings suggest that the younger members tend to be more committed in this way. At the same time, the membership is ageing and if the older members are not very active, this inevitably signals a reduction of levels of activity in the future, unless more younger members can be recruited.

The second part of Table 5.2 describes the social-class background of activists. A lot of the research on political participation suggests that educated people are more likely to be politically active than the uneducated (Verba and Nie 1972; Parry et al. 1992). This, after all, is the basis of the civic voluntarism model. With this in mind, we find that there is a tendency for the middle-class professionals to be more active than the working class. However, amongst the fairly active, we also find that the petty bourgeoisie and the foreman/technician class categories are over-represented compared with the working class. The latter are relatively inactive compared with their higher-status colleagues. If we add the high rates of middle-class activism to greater participation amongst graduates, this provides evidence in favour of the civic voluntarism model. Resources in the form of education count when it comes to party activism.

While there are high levels of activism amongst members in full-time employment, the registered unemployed display very high levels of activism too. Rather than being demotivated, members who do not have a regular work commitment are putting their time to use by working on behalf of the party. On the other hand, retired members, who also have more spare time, are not very active as a group. In the remaining categories, we find that men are more active than women and those on high incomes are more active than those on low incomes. Finally, those who give the largest sums of money to the party in addition to their annual subscription also give more time to the party. High-intensity activists devote their lives, both in terms of time and money, to the party.

In Table 5.3 we examine the relationship between ideology and activism. In the academic literature this relationship has been formalized in the so-called 'law' of curvilinear disparity (May 1973). From the discussion of this topic in Chapter 4, it will be recalled that the theory suggests that party activists will be more radical than the party leadership and also the supporters in the electorate. In the case of Labour, this means that the activists would be to the left of the leadership and in the case of the

Conservatives, to the right. It is not absolutely clear what this would mean for the Liberal Democrats, although it is likely to mean that activists are more to the left of the leadership because they are a progressive centre party. To investigate this possibility, we use the two indicators of the members' perceptions of ideology introduced in Chapter 4. The first measures perceptions of their own ideological position on a left-right scale in relation to party members in general, and the second measures their ideological position in relation to the country as a whole. For ease of presentation, we have taken the original eleven-point left-right scales and collapsed them into five categories. We see in Table 5.3 that activism within the party on both scales is firmly rooted on the left. Respondents who score themselves to the right, both in relation to the party and in relation to Britain, tend to be significantly less active than respondents who score themselves to the left.

Up to this point we have focused on the activism scale, but another important aspect of Liberal Democrat party activity is community politics. As mentioned earlier, a common feature of Liberal Democrat election campaigns are the ubiquitous *Focus Newsletters*, which draw the voter's attention to local issues and point out how their local Liberal Democrat councillors are trying to change things for the better. How much community politics is taking place within the grassroots party? We examine this issue next.

Table 5.3. Ideological perceptions of members categorized by levels of activism (percentages)

	Not at all active	Not very active	Fairly active	Very active
All respondents	70	16	10	4
(N)	(2006)	(459)	(287)	(115)
Ideology in the party				
Left	64	16	15	5
Centre-left	66	17	12	5
Centre	75	16	8	2
Centre-right	71	17	8	3
Right	74	15	9	2
Ideology in Britain				
Left	60	18	18	4
Centre-left	69	16	11	4
Centre	75	15	8	2
Centre-right	73	18	6	2
Right	79	11	4	4

Questions: In Liberal Democrat party politics, people often talk about 'the left' and 'the right'. Compared with other Liberal Democrats, where would you place your views on the following scale?

And where would you place your views in relation to British politics as a whole (not just the Liberal Democrats)?

5.3 Community Politics and the Liberal Democrats

A starting point for understanding community politics within the Liberal Democrat Party is to examine the extent to which members are rooted in, and identify with, their local communities. If their world view is national, or even international, rather than local, it seems likely that local campaigning in the community will be less of a priority. However, if their attention is quite focused on the local community, they are more likely to emphasize community politics. The evidence in Table 5.4 shows that party members strongly identify with their local communities. For most members, this is their first priority, followed by an emphasis on their local county or their region. They appear to be quite focused on community affairs.

A second aspect of community politics is the priority given to local as opposed to national politics. Evidence on this issue appears in Table 5.5, which shows responses to a question asking members about their political priorities. It is clear from the table that they attach equal priority to local and national politics for the most part. On the other hand, this does not detract from their concern with community politics, since they see the two as going together when it comes to campaigning on behalf of the party.

Table 5.4. Levels of identification with the local community among members (percentages)

Most identify with	First	Next
The locality where you live	53	12
The county or region where you live	13	24
The country (England, Scotland, Wales)	9	15
The UK as a whole	15	21
Europe	6	21
The world as a whole	4	8

Question: Which of these geographical areas would you say you most identify with?

Table 5.5. Perceptions of the importance of local and national politics (percentages)

Most important level of politics	
Local politics is the most important	6
National politics is the most important	24
They are equally important	70

Question: In your opinion which is the most important, local politics or national politics, or are they equally important?

A third aspect of community politics is the extent to which the Liberal Democrat members are embedded in local community organizations and groups. Clearly, a strategy of community politics means working with various local groups such as tenants associations, community action groups, and local charities of various types. It is easy to see how strong local involvement in these types of groups can give members electoral advantages when it comes to running for office. This is an aspect of the role of party members as 'ambassadors in the community', serving to give the party local prominence and identity.

Table 5.6 shows that the local party members are very involved in local community groups, with a majority of them being members of at least one group. A surprising one in five of the party members are members of three or more local groups, thereby fulfilling the local ambassadorial role to the full. Such community involvement is likely to reinforce their effectiveness as local campaigners on behalf of their party. Clearly for a party which is so community-focused, some of the members are likely to be local notables, that is, individuals who serve in prominent positions as school governors, local magistrates, or members of a health trust. Holding such public offices is another way of becoming locally prominent, alongside local campaigning and participation in community groups. An effective strategy of community action will involve all these aspects of community involvement. Table 5.7 shows that some 31 per cent of the members are local notables in

Table 5.6. Local group membership (percentages)

Number of groups	
None	42
One	23
Two	17
Three	10
Four or more	8

Question: Thinking specifically about local groups (e.g. a local tenants group, community action group, women's group, or charity), how many groups do you belong to?

Table 5.7. Members' involvement with official local bodies (percentages)

Membership of official bodies	
Yes	31
No	69

Question: Are you currently on any official bodies (e.g. school governor, health authority trust, magistrate)?

this sense. Again this is likely to strengthen their effectiveness in fighting local election campaigns.

In the light of this, it is interesting to see how this extensive community involvement translates into local campaigning, both in relation to elections and of a broader community-based type. Table 5.8 charts the extent to which members have been involved in local government election campaigns, as well as other types of local campaigns, during the previous year. Perhaps not surprisingly, a majority of the members were involved in local election campaigns. Around one in five of them had fought a local election as a Liberal Democrat candidate. No doubt many of them will have been 'paper' candidates who are primarily there to show the party flag at the local level, but this is nonetheless a high level of involvement. It is also apparent that many were not paper candidates, since our survey picked up a large number of current Liberal Democrat councillors who made up nearly 10 per cent of the sample.

As a final perspective on participation, party members were asked if they had been involved in any local campaigns not directly linked to elections in the past year. Close to three out of every ten members acknowledged that they had participated in such campaigns. These covered issues like planning, education, and the environment. As a follow-up to this question, respondents were asked if they had been involved in any campaigns not associated with the Liberal Democrat Party, and almost one in five were. It appears that Liberal Democrats are engaged in a lot of community politics. This requires them to participate in local organizations, run for local office, occupy both elected and appointed positions, and get involved in local campaigns, many of which are not directly associated with the party. They are quite embedded in their local communities, and this fact, together with their localist orientation to politics, goes a long way to explaining why the party has succeeded in building a strong local electoral base in Britain (see Rallings and Thrasher 1997).

In the light of this discussion we turn next to the task of modelling the determinants of activism within the grassroots party.

Table 5.8. Members' involvement in local campaigns and local politics

	%Yes	%No
Involved in local government election campaigns	55	45
Fought a local election as a Liberal Democrat candidate, if not currently a councillor	20	80
Currently a Liberal Democrat councillor	9	91
Involved in other local campaigns in the last year	27	73
Involved in local campaigns not associated with the Liberal Democrats	19	81

5.4 Explaining party activism

5.4.1 The civic voluntarism model

In Chapter 4, we discussed how the civic voluntarism and general incentives models could be used to explain why people join the party in the first place. It will be recalled that civic voluntarism emphasizes the importance of individual resources, together with perceptions of efficacy and the extent to which individuals had been mobilized by others (Verba, Schlozman, and Brady 1995). Here we specify a model that captures each of these effects:

$$A_i = \beta_0 + \beta_1 E_i + \beta_2 M_i + \beta_3 ED_i + \beta_4 SC_i + \beta_5 INC_i + \beta_6 FT_i + \beta_7 V_i + \beta_8 P_i + \epsilon_i \quad (1)$$

where A_i is the individual's level of activism in the party; β_i are the coefficients which estimate the impact of each variable on activism; E_i is the individual's sense of political efficacy; M_i measures if the individual was asked to join the party by friends, family, and workmates; ED_i is an individual's educational attainment; SC_i is the individual's occupational status; INC_i is the individual's income; FT_i measures whether an individual works full time; V_i measures the number of local groups that the respondent belongs to; P_i measures the respondent's strength of attachment to the party; ϵ_i is the error term.

The dependent variable in the above model is the high-intensity activism scale derived from the factor analysis, which appears in Figure 5.1. The independent variables were listed in Table 4.7. To remind readers of the variables involved, the first one, E_i, measures the individual's psychological engagement with politics. The argument here is that if individuals believe that their contribution to politics can make a difference, in other words, if they feel a sense of efficacy, they are more likely to become active. On the whole, Liberal Democrats have relatively high levels of personal efficacy, in the sense of believing that they can influence the political process. Similarly, the strength of partisanship variable, P_i, measures an important aspect of motivations for involvement. Clearly, if individuals are very strongly attached to the party, they are more likely to get involved in party activity.

The variable, M_i, captures the mobilization dimension of the civic voluntarism model. Table 4.7 showed that 21 per cent of respondents were recruited into the party by family, friends, or workmates, and this variable is used to measure mobilization. Interestingly enough, recruitment by family or friends is more important for Liberal Democrats than for the other major parties. Only 7 per cent of Labour party members and 12 per cent of Conservatives were recruited in this way (see Seyd and Whiteley 1992; Whiteley, Seyd, and Richardson 1994). The expectation here is that someone drawn into politics by their family or friends is more likely to be active than someone recruited by strangers or by impersonal means such as a leaflet put through the door.

Most of the remaining predictor variables in equation (1) relate to the resources dimension of the civic voluntarism model. These are employment status, educational and occupational status, and household income. The expectation is that more highly resourced individuals, the people who are employed, educated, middle class, and affluent, will be more active than those who lack these resources. In addition, voluntary activity provides the experience of participating in a community organization. Participants in this context will acquire organizational, communication, and presentational skills, which will help them in their party activities. Moreover, community involvement can motivate individuals to participate more widely by becoming politically active. In this way, they can address issues that local community groups are unable to address in the political process.

5.4.2 The general incentives model

It will be recalled that the core assumption of the general incentives theory is that individuals need incentives if they are to participate in politics. The theory is based on a rational actor model, but it goes beyond a narrowly defined rational choice analysis to incorporate a wider set of incentives into the calculus of participation. Variables like affective attachments to the party and the influence of social norms are important, and both of these lie outside the standard rational choice analysis of decision-making.

We evaluate this model in two stages. Firstly, we derive a 'minimalist' rational actor model of activism, which contains basic measures of the costs and benefits of participation. Secondly, we go on to specify the broader general incentives model, which incorporates the minimalist model within it. The initial specification of the model includes the following variables:

$$A_i = \beta_0 + \beta_1(p_i)(B_i) - \beta_2 C_i + \epsilon \tag{2}$$

where A_i is the level of activism of individual i; p_i is a measure of political efficacy capturing the probability that i's participation will bring about the collective good or policy goals of the party; B is a measure of policy congruence with the party, that is, the collective benefits expected from the implementation of the party programme; C_i represents the costs to the individual of contributing to the collective good by participating.

To understand how these variables were measured, we can refer to Tables 4.7 and 4.8. The probability of bringing about the collective good is measured using Likert-scaled statements designed to capture the individual's sense of efficacy. As we pointed out earlier, in most cases the objective value of p_i is very small because the individual is unlikely to make any significant contribution to winning an election or changing national party policies. On the other hand, as we can see in Table 5.9, many party members have a healthy sense of their own personal efficacy, with some 69 per cent feeling that they can exert influence, and almost 90 per cent thinking that party members can collectively change Britain. In narrowly defined rational choice models, a measure like this refers to the effectiveness of an individual acting alone to influence outcomes. But party members do not act alone; rather they act collectively, and this fact gives many of them a powerful sense of their own effectiveness.

Moreover, party members have an objective basis for their feelings of efficacy, since activists have access to decision-makers within the party

Table 5.9. Indicators in the minimal rational choice model of activism (percentages)

	Strongly agree	Agree	Neither agree nor disagree	Disagree	Strongly disagree
Probability of engagement (p_i)					
People like me can have a real influence on politics if they are prepared to get involved	9	60	16	14	1
When party members work together, they can really change Britain	16	73	9	2	0
Perceptions of costs (C_i)					
Sometimes politics seems so complicated that it is difficult to know what is going on	3	34	12	40	11
Attending party meetings can be tiring after a day's work	10	66	16	7	1
Collective benefits (B)					
Liberal Democrats should resist further moves to integrate the EU	6	12	13	41	28
Britain should agree to the introduction of a common European currency	28	38	13	12	9
The English regions should have elected assemblies with taxing powers	11	36	20	28	6
Local authorities should have greater independence from central government	10	47	18	23	2
Individuals should take responsibility for providing for themselves	7	51	26	15	1

organization, and in many cases they are elected decision-makers themselves. In this situation, they have a direct influence over politics at the local level. This means that it is possible for activists to influence the provision of the collective good, in the sense of changing policies within the party organization and within local government. This type of influence is not generally available to participants in other types of collective action, such as protesting in the streets or participating in an interest group. Because political parties play such an important role in policymaking, activists are uniquely able to influence those outcomes, and thus have an objective basis for their feelings of efficacy. Our expectation is that respondents with a strong sense of efficacy are more likely to be active than respondents who lack such a sense of efficacy. The two indicators are combined into an overall efficacy scale.[4]

The indicators of costs in Table 5.9 are designed to capture the idea that politics can be difficult to understand and that activism can involve a lot of time and effort. By implication, respondents who agree with these statements are likely to be deterred from participating by perceptions of the costs involved. The two indicators are combined into an overall costs scale.[5]

The indicator of benefits in Table 5.9 further develops the ideas set out in Chapter 4, by examining members' attitudes towards the EU, to decentralization and devolution, and to welfare spending. It will be recalled from the earlier discussion that the Liberal Democrats as a party are strongly in favour of Britain's engagement with the EU and they support welfare benefits. They also have a long-standing commitment to decentralization and to regional devolution. The latter can be seen in Figure 5.3, which charts the positive references to decentralization in Liberal Democrat manifestos between 1945 and 1997.

Following the logic of the argument in Chapter 4, we would expect members who are strongly in favour of party policies on the EU, on decentralization, and on welfare spending to be more active than those who lack these attitudes. Thus, an aggregate benefits scale is constructed which reflects these perceptions.[6]

[4] Each scale was coded 5 'strongly agree'; 4 'agree'; 3 'neither agree nor disagree'; 2 'disagree'; 1 'strongly disagree'; and the respondent scores were summed up to give an overall efficacy score for each individual.

[5] In both cases respondents who strongly agree score 5 through to those who strongly disagree who score 1. The two scales are then summed up to give a 'perceptions of costs' index.

[6] Respondents who strongly disagree with resisting further EU integration or strongly agree with introducing a common currency score 5 and those who strongly agree with the first statement and strongly disagree with the second score 1, with intermediate scores assigned appropriately. Respondents who strongly agree that the English regions should have their own

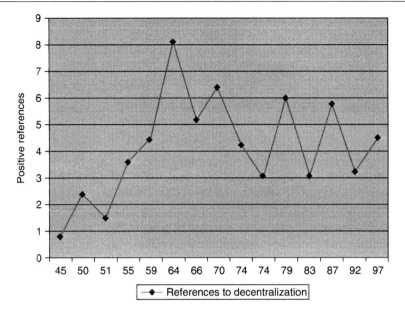

Figure 5.3 Positive references to decentralization in Liberal Democrat party manifestos, 1945–97

Source: Budge et al. (2001)

The wider, 'general incentives' model can be specified as follows:

$$A_i = \beta_0 + \beta_1(p_i)(B_i) - \beta_2 C_i + \beta_3 S(O_i) + \beta_4 S(P_i) + \beta_5 S(I_i) + \beta_6 G_i + \beta_7 E_i + \beta_8 SN_i + \epsilon_i \quad (3)$$

Where A_i, p_i, B_i, and C_i are the same as in equation (2); $S(O_i)$ are selective outcome incentives derived from the desire to develop a political career; $S(P_i)$ are selective process incentives derived from enjoying politics for its own sake; $S(I_i)$ are selective ideological incentives from participating with like-minded people; G_i are group incentives derived from being part of an effective organization; E_i are expressive attachments to the party; SN_i are social norms or the influence of other people on participation.

assemblies and that local authorities should have greater independence score 5 and those who strongly disagree with these statements score 1, with intermediate scores assigned appropriately. Those who strongly agree that individuals should look after themselves or who think that taxes and welfare spending should be reduced score 1. Individuals who strongly disagree with the first of these statements and think that taxes and spending should be increased score 5, with intermediate scores assigned appropriately. All these items are then summed up into an overall benefits scale.

Equation (3) retains the personal influence, collective benefits, and costs variables from equation (2). In addition, equation (3) includes three selective incentives measures, capturing the private benefits from participating in politics. The first, $S(O_i)$, relates to those party members who have political ambitions to become an elected representative on behalf of the party. The second, $S(P_i)$, is a measure of process incentives, or those derived from the process of participation itself. The third is $S(I_i)$ or ideological incentives, which measure the incentives derived from interacting with like-minded individuals. The latter is constructed from the data that appear in Table 5.3, and in the light of the earlier discussion we expect those on the left of the ideological spectrum to be more active than party members in general. The group incentives measure, G_i, captures the idea that individuals are more likely to participate if they feel that they are members of an effective organization. Expressive attachments, E_i, measures the individual's strength of identification with the party, the assumption being that the strongly attached are more active than the weakly attached. Finally, SN_i measures social norms, or the influence of the perception of other people's attitudes to activism. Other people's opinions can induce (or inhibit) participation within the party organization. Additional indicators of these variables appear in Table 5.10.

The indicators of selective outcome and selective process incentives in Table 5.10 are designed to capture the respondents' political ambitions and their feelings towards the process of politics itself. If individuals harbour ambitions to run for the local council or to be elected to Parliament, this is likely to give them a strong incentive to participate. Similarly, if they enjoy meeting like-minded people or learning about politics for its own sake, this will also be an incentive for involvement.[7] As the data show there are sizeable numbers of Liberal Democrats who feel like this. The group incentive indicators are designed to capture the sense of people working together in an effective organization and should motivate individuals to be active.[8]

The remaining indicators in Table 5.10 measure selective ideological incentives and expressive attachments to the party. We have already examined the ideology scale earlier, and in the case of expressive attachments respondents were asked to indicate how 'warm and sympathetic' their feelings were towards the Liberal Democrat Party—the warmer the

---

[7] Respondents who strongly agree with the statements score 5 and those who strongly disagree score 1, with intermediate scores filled in appropriately. The indicators are summed up to create the outcome and process scales.

[8] Respondents who strongly agree that the Liberal Democrats are part of a great campaign score 5, and those who strongly disagree that parties are only interested in votes also score 5. Other scores are added appropriately and the scales are summed up.

Table 5.10. Additional indicators in the general incentives model (percentages)

	Strongly agree	Agree	Neither	Disagree	Strongly disagree
Selective outcome ($S(O_i)$)					
A person like me could do a good job of being a local councillor	12	30	18	28	12
The Liberal Democrats would be more successful if more people like me were elected to Parliament	4	41	14	37	4
Selective process ($S(P_i)$)					
The only way to be educated about politics is to be a party activist	6	21	35	30	8
Being an active party member is a good way to meet interesting people	6	61	24	7	1
Group incentives (G_i)					
Liberal Democrats are part of a great campaign of like-minded people	6	51	29	13	1
Parties are only interested in people's votes, not in their opinions	6	44	15	33	2
Social norms (SN_i)					
Many people think party activists are extremists	7	50	22	21	1
The amount of work done by party members is very often unrecognized	13	57	16	14	1

The left-right ideological scale ($S(I_i)$)

%	1	2	3	4	5	6	7	8	9
Compared with other Liberal Democrats where would you place your views on the scale? (where 1 = Left and 9 = Right)	4	6	20	23	28	11	6	2	1
And where would you place your views in relation to British politics as a whole?	3	8	25	28	23	8	4	1	1

Liberal Democrat Party thermometer rating (E_i)

Score	0	10	20	30	40	50	60	70	80	90	100
%	0	0	0.1	0.1	0.3	2	6	16	32	25	18

feelings, the higher the score. As Table 5.10 indicates, respondents were skewed in the direction of a high score, the overall mean being 82.5. Despite this, there is significant variation along the scale, with the expectation being that those who feel more warmly inclined towards the party are more likely to be active.

The three models of activism are tested in Table 5.11. Controls for gender and age are included in each of the models. Model A is the civic voluntarism model and it is apparent that both resources and psychological engagement are important factors in explaining activism, though

Table 5.11. Civic voluntarism, rational choice, and general incentives models of activism (dependent variable = activism scale)

Predictor variables	A		B		C	
	β	t	β	t	β	t
Personal efficacy (p_i)	0.09	$(4.3)^{**}$				
Mobilization (M)	0.01	(0.7)				
Income (INC)	−0.02	(0.8)				
Class (SC)	0.03	(1.6)				
Full-time employment (FT)	−0.05	$(2.2)^*$				
Graduate status (ED)	0.03	(1.2)				
Voluntary activity (V)	0.14	$(7.4)^{**}$				
Strength of partisanship (P)	0.26	$(12.9)^{**}$				
Personal efficacy (x)			0.25	$(13.3)^{**}$	0.12	$(5.8)^{**}$
Collective benefits (p_i) (B)						
Perceived costs (C)			−0.09	$(4.9)^{**}$	−0.07	$(3.7)^{**}$
Outcome incentives ($S(O)$)					0.26	$(13.2)^{**}$
Process incentives ($S(P)$)					0.09	$(5.1)^{**}$
Ideological incentives (I)					−0.02	(1.3)
Group incentives (G)					0.01	(0.8)
Expressive attachments (E)					0.08	$(4.0)^{**}$
Social norms (SN)					−0.04	$(2.0)^*$
Gender	0.08	$(4.3)^{**}$	0.06	$(3.0)^{**}$	0.02	(1.1)
Age	−0.13	$(5.5)^{**}$	−0.06	$(3.3)^{**}$	−0.01	(0.5)
R^2	0.14		0.10		0.17	
F statistic		39.7^{**}		73.9^{**}		56.2^{**}

β = standardized beta coefficient.
t = t-statistics (*significant $p \le 0.05$; **significant $p \le 0.01$).
A = Civic voluntarism.
B = Rational choice.
C = General incentives.

not mobilization. Personal efficacy has a highly significant positive effect on activism, as does the strength of partisan attachments. The main effect of resources relates to full-time employment, with respondents in full-time jobs being less active than part-timers, the unemployed, or the retired. Clearly, this effect is related to the time constraints facing such individuals. In other respects, the resources measures are not significant predictors of activism, apart from voluntary activity, which as the earlier discussion indicates, provides resources in the form of organizational and communication skills. There is no evidence that social class or income has a significant impact on participation.

Turning to the model for minimal rational choice, Model B, both the measures of benefits and of costs are highly significant predictors of activism with the correct signs. Benefits weighted by efficacy have a significant positive impact on activism and perceptions of costs have a significant negative impact. Clearly, Liberal Democrats are motivated by cost–benefit considerations when they are deciding whether or not to get involved.

The general incentives model indicates that selective incentives are quite important for explaining participation, since the strongest effect in the table is associated with outcome incentives. Process incentives and expressive attachments also play a role in explaining activism. Social norms are important as well, but they appear to have the wrong sign. Thus, respondents who believe that other people recognize and value party activism are less, rather than more, likely to be involved. This is the one anomalous result in the table. This indicates that Liberal Democrats are not put off by any apparent stigma attached to being an activist. They remain activists despite the social pressures. At the same time, there is no evidence that group incentives or ideological incentives have an impact on activism, and once the additional variables in the general incentives model are taken into account, age and gender appear to be irrelevant.

The models are estimated again in Table 5.12, but this time with a different dependent variable. Instead of using the activism scale derived from Table 5.1, we use the measure of the amount of time spent on party activities, set out in Table 2.19. This provides a check on the robustness of the results, since the activism scale should produce similar results to this

Table 5.12. Civic voluntarism, rational choice, and general incentives models of activism (dependent variable = time spent on party activities)

Predictor variables	A		B		C	
	β	t	β	t	β	t
Personal efficacy (p_i)	0.10	(5.0)***				
Mobilization (M)	0.03	(1.8)*				
Income (INC)	−0.02	(0.8)				
Class (SC)	0.02	(1.0)				
Full-time employment (FT)	−0.08	(3.4)***				
Graduate status (ED)	0.04	(2.2)**				
Voluntary activity (V)	0.14	(7.5)***				
Strength of partisanship (P)	0.34	(17.4)**				
Personal efficacy (x)			0.30	(15.9)**	0.17	(8.1)***
Collective benefits ((p_i) (B))						*
Perceived costs (C)			−0.06	(3.0)***	−0.03	(1.7)*
Outcome incentives ($S(O)$)					0.21	(10.2)***
Process incentives ($S(P)$)					0.05	(2.7)***
Ideological incentives (I)					−0.04	(2.0)**
Group incentives (G)					0.01	(0.4)
Expressive attachments (E)					0.13	(6.5)***
Social norms (SN)					−0.03	(1.7)*
Gender	0.05	(2.8)***	0.04	(2.3)**	0.01	(0.6)
Age	−0.16	(7.0)***	−0.11	(5.8)***	−0.06	(3.1)***
R^2	0.21		0.13		0.18	
F statistic		60.1***		95.2***		57.9***

β = standardized beta coefficient.
t = t-statistics (*significant $p < 0.10$; **significant $p < 0.05$; *** significant $p < 0.01$).
a = Civic voluntarism.
B = Rational choice.
C = General incentives.

rather simpler indicator of participation. A comparison between Tables 5.11 and 5.12 indicates that the models are very similar. In Table 5.12, the resource measures in the civic voluntarism model appear to have more of an impact on activism than in the simpler model of Table 5.11, but the estimates are nonetheless dominated by the political engagement measures. The minimal rational choice model is the same in both tables, but there is evidence that ideological incentives play a role in the simpler model of Table 5.12 when they did not in the more complex model of Table 5.11. Apart from these minor differences, the models tell the same basic story.

In order to get a sense of which model provides the better explanation of activism, we combine them together into one large-scale model and this appears in Table 5.13. Clearly, if the civic voluntarism model was superior to the general incentives model, we would observe all of the variables in the former having a statistically significant impact on activism while none of the variables in the latter would do so.[9] However, Table 5.13 suggests

Table 5.13. Combined and best models of activism (dependent variable = activism index)

Predictor variables	A		B	
	β	t	β	t
Mobilization (M)	0.01	(0.8)*		
Income (INC)	−0.02	(0.6)		
Class (SC)	0.03	(1.5)		
Full-time employment (FT)	−0.06	(2.4)***	−0.04	(1.8)*
Graduate status (ED)	0.01	(0.3)		
Voluntary activity (V)	0.11	(5.9)***	0.10	(5.9)***
Strength of partisanship (P)	0.17	(7.6)**	0.17	(8.8)***
Personal efficacy (x)	0.07	(3.0)***	0.09	(4.3)***
Collective benefits ($(p_i)(B)$)				
Perceived costs (C)	−0.06	(2.9)***	−0.06	(3.4)***
Outcome incentives (S(O))	0.34	(11.9)***	0.24	(12.5)***
Process incentives (S(P))	0.10	(5.5)***	0.09	(5.2)***
Ideological incentives (I)	−0.01	(0.3)		
Group incentives (G)	0.02	(0.9)		
Expressive attachments (E)	0.02	(0.9)		
Social norms (SN)	−0.04	(1.9)*		
Gender	0.04	(2.1)**		
Age	−0.08	(3.4)***	−0.05	(2.2)**
R^2	0.22		0.20	
F statistic		38.5***		84.2***

β = standardized beta coefficient.
t = t-statistics (*significant $p < 0.10$; **significant $p < 0.05$; *** significant $p < 0.01$).

[9] Note that efficacy has been excluded from this combined model since it appears in the interaction term with the collective benefits measure. This is done to avoid multicollinearity.

that both models make an important contribution to explaining variations in activism. Model B is a re-estimate of Model A, with all non-significant variables eliminated. It can be seen that the psychological engagement measures from the civic voluntarism model, together with collective and selective benefits and costs from the general incentives model, all play a role in explaining activism. Resources from civic voluntarism appear to play a very modest role and mobilization plays no role at all. Overall, these results indicate that party activism can be explained by a combination of an individual's psychological engagement and the calculations of the costs and benefits of political action. Accordingly, Model B in Table 5.13 might be described as the *incentives-engagement* model of participation.

The absence of direct links between the resource measures and activism does not mean that resources are irrelevant for explaining participation, since there may be indirect links between the resource variables and the incentives-engagement model. We examine this issue in Section 5.5.

5.5 Indirect links between incentives and resources

We have seen that resources play a very modest role in explaining variations in activism within the Liberal Democrat grassroots party. But there may be links between resources and the predictor variables in the incentives-engagement model. This possibility is investigated in Table 5.14, which looks at the effects of the resource variables on the predictor variables in the incentives-engagement model. The resource measures appear in the rows and the incentive variables in the columns. It investigates the impact of the former on the latter.

The evidence in Table 5.14 confirms that there are important indirect links between resource and activism that operate via the predictor variables in the incentives-engagement model. For example, social class influences partisanship, the efficacy times benefits measure, perceptions of costs, and process incentives. For the former two variables, the effects are positive, with middle-class members being more likely to have strong partisan attachments and more likely to experience collective benefits than the working class. In the case of costs and process incentives, the effects are negative, which indicates that the middle class are less likely to perceive costs and less likely to appreciate process incentives.

Age effects are more widespread than class effects in Table 5.14, since all of the predictors in the incentives-engagement model are influenced by

Table 5.14. The influence of social background measures on the engagement-incentives model

	Voluntary activity (Vi)	Partisan strength (Pi)	Efficacy (x) Benefits (Pi) (B)	Costs (Ci)	Outcome S(Oi)	Process S(Pi)
	β	β	β	β	β	β
Class	0.02	0.05	0.05	−0.07	0.03	−0.06
t	(1.0)	(2.2)**	(2.4)**	(3.2)***	(1.2)	(2.6)***
Age	0.05	−0.09	−0.12	0.05	−0.26	0.12
t	(2.2)**	(3.6)***	(4.8)***	(2.1)**	(11.3)***	(4.8)***
Gender	−0.06	0.14	0.10	−0.14	0.19	−0.04
t	(2.8)***	(6.6)***	(4.9)***	(6.9)***	(9.6)***	(1.7)*
Income	−0.02	−0.03	0.01	−0.10	0.07	−0.12
t	(0.9)	(1.4)	(0.5)	(4.2)***	(3.0)***	(5.0)***
Graduate	0.04	0.05	0.09	−0.06	0.07	−0.03
t	(2.0)**	(2.3)**	(4.2)***	(2.5)**	(3.4)***	(1.1)
Full-time work	−0.11	0.02	0.001	0.005	−0.001	0.01
t	(4.5)***	(0.9)	(0.1)	(0.2)	(0.0)	(0.3)
R^2	0.03	0.04	0.05	0.06	0.14	0.05
F	12.8***	14.8***	18.8***	23.5***	66.0***	19.4***

B = standardized beta coefficient
t = t-Statistics (*significant $p < 0.10$; **significant $p < 0.05$; *** significant $p < 0.01$).

age. In the case of voluntary activity, perceptions of costs, and process incentives, older members are more likely to score highly on these variables than the young. In the case of partisanship, benefits weighted by efficacy, and outcome incentives, young members are more likely to score more highly than the old. Age is the one variable that has both direct effects on activism, but also indirect effects of the kind described.

Gender is also a significant predictor of all the independent variables in the engagement incentives model. In this case, men are more likely to have strong partisanship, to experience collective benefits, and to obtain outcome incentives from participation than women. In contrast, women are more likely to volunteer, to perceive costs, and to experience process incentives than men.

Income is particularly interesting, since it only appears to affect the predictor variables, which derive from the general incentives model. Not surprisingly, high income means that costs are less important to an individual, and the affluent are less likely to be motivated by process incentives. But a high income affects outcome incentives, with the affluent being more likely to respond to the incentives associated with political ambitions. Graduate status also affects all of the predictors in the engagement incentives model, except for process incentives. In this case, graduates are more partisan, and are more likely to get involved in voluntary activity, to perceive collective benefits, to feel a sense of efficacy, and to have political ambitions. At the same time, they are less likely to perceive costs as being important in the calculus of participation. The final variable in Table 5.14 is full-time work and this appears to influence only voluntary activity. Not surprisingly, those in full-time work are less likely to be involved in voluntary activities as a consequence. Overall, Table 5.14 shows that resources have an additional influence on activism via the incentive measures, apart from any direct influence they have in the civic voluntarism model. The engagement incentives model relies a lot on the fact that the party members are middle class, educated, and better off than Liberal Democrat voters to explain why they are active.

5.6 Conclusions

In this chapter we have focused on the activists within the party. From our data we have been able to describe the social profile of a typical activist. In addition, the chapter has analysed the determinants of activism and compared rival models, which explain variations in activism within the grassroots party. One of the important features of the Liberal Democrat Party is that grassroots activity appears to have laid the basis of the party's success in contesting local elections. Community activity has led to success in local government elections and eventually, this has produced success in general elections in a number of constituencies. The evidence of this chapter is certainly consistent with this interpretation, since Liberal Democrats are very involved in their local communities. However, the link between campaigning and electoral success has yet to be fully explored, an issue that is taken up in Chapter 6.

6

Local Campaigning and the Liberal Democrat Vote

6.1 Introduction

In the British general election of 1997, the Liberal Democrat's share of the vote fell by 1 per cent in comparison with the election of 1992, but at the same time, the party more than doubled its representation in the House of Commons, from twenty MPs in 1992 to forty-six in 1997. This gave the party their largest representation in the House since 1929. This, of course, was the year that the Labour Party won by a landslide, taking no less than 64 per cent of the MPs elected to the House of Commons. Labour's overall parliamentary majority of 177 was larger than the entire Conservative parliamentary party and the largest in its history.

Explanations for the defeat of the Conservative government in that year have stressed its performance from 1992 onwards. Economic mismanagement, in particular the withdrawal from the European exchange rate mechanism in September 1992, broken promises, especially on taxes and the public services, and a collapse of trust, fostered by bitter intraparty conflict and well-publicized financial irregularities by some Conservative MPs, are emphasized. In addition, Tony Blair's election as Labour party leader and his subsequent creation of New Labour is regarded as a contributory factor (Denver 1997; Butler and Kavanagh 1997; Clarke, Stewart and Whiteley 1998; King 1998).

Such explanations tend to suggest that the outcome was determined in the years prior to the election by matters of 'high politics', or national political issues, so that the local campaigns run by constituency party organizations up and down the country appeared to have little to do with it. While high-profile national politics of this type may have played an important role in explaining Labour's success, since it was the government in waiting, such an explanation is less convincing when applied to the Liberal Democrats. Indeed, if the national vote share is taken as an indicator of electoral success due to 'high politics', the Liberal Democrats lost ground in the election. There is a clear paradox in explaining a declining vote share, alongside a doubling of the party's representation in the House. This needs an explanation other than one based on the influence of national politics, and the purpose of this chapter is to provide such an explanation. The basic point is that Liberal Democrat electoral success has been largely based on local campaigning, which has taken place over many years. It was the fruit of the community politics campaigning discussed in Chapter 5. The findings of this chapter are that local campaigns are crucial to the electoral success of the party. The 1990s saw a flowering of Liberal Democrats council representation as the party took seats off its rivals, particularly the Conservatives (Rallings and Thrasher 1997). This culminated in the 1997 general election, when the party's electoral successes in local government translated into successes in winning parliamentary seats.

We begin this chapter by reviewing the debates in the literature about the importance of campaigns in elections in Section 6.2. Section 6.3 examines how Liberal Democrat grassroots campaigning was measured in the survey. Section 6.4 models the effects of local campaigning in the party's 1997 general election performance using data from the Liberal Democrat survey, together with voting and census data measured at the constituency level. Finally, we examine the implications of these findings for the future electoral prospects of the Liberal Democrats in Britain.

6.2 The Debate on Election Campaign Effects

The thesis that much of Liberal Democrat electoral success can be explained in terms of local campaigning is controversial, since a number of writers deny the relevance of such campaigns in influencing voting behaviour in a general election. Anthony King is a strong advocate of this view, and argued that in relation to the 1997 general election 'all the evidence suggests that the campaign was largely irrelevant' (King 1998: 179). He writes:

The politicians, as they always do on these occasions, puffed, panted, and rushed about the country. They stretched every sinew and strained every nerve. They gave speeches, they gave interviews, they gave their all. No camera angle was neglected, no photo opportunity was missed. At times the politicians resembled those manic characters in the jerky, speeded-up film comedies of the 1920s. But nothing happened. The audience, for whose benefit all these entertainments were laid on, remained almost completely inert. Scarcely a cough or a sneeze could be heard from the pit. (1998: 179)

In a similar vein, Crewe (1997) writes:

Had there been no campaign and no Millbank, Labour would have still won by a mile. The election was decided long before the campaign by events in the first half of the 1992 parliament.

When assessing the importance of party election campaigns, it is important to distinguish three features of their attempts to win support. Firstly, there are the national campaigns directed and run from party headquarters, which include press conferences, leaders' speeches, party election broadcasts, and advertising. Secondly, there are national attempts to direct local campaigns by targeting specific marginal constituencies. Thirdly, there are the purely local campaigns mounted by the grassroots party members in the parliamentary constituencies across the length and breadth of the United Kingdom. If the national campaign in 1997 is regarded as being irrelevant by some students of electoral politics, arguably this is even more true of local campaigns. Certainly, the 'Nuffield' election studies have consistently argued this point (see, e.g. Nicholas 1951; Butler 1952). In the 1997 general election study, Curtice and Steed's analysis of the results concluded:

The 1997 election does not appear to support claims made that local campaigning can make a difference in respect of other parties' performances too. The Labour party targeted 90, mostly marginal Conservative constituencies.... Yet... the performance in these constituencies was very similar to that in other Conservative/ Labour contests. (Butler and Kavanagh 1997: 312)

There is, however, growing evidence that contradicts these views. This work suggests that local campaigning can influence both voting behaviour and turnout in general elections. Some of this research uses campaign spending as surrogate measures of campaign activity (Johnston, Pattie, and Johnston 1989; Whiteley, Seyd, and Richardson 1994; Johnston and Pattie 1995; Pattie, Johnston, and Fieldhouse 1995); other work uses surveys of party members who do the campaigning, in order to assess effects (Seyd and Whiteley 1992; Whiteley, Seyd, and Richardson 1994; Whiteley and Seyd 1998); and a third approach uses surveys of constituency agents from the main parties who run the local campaigns (Denver and Hands 1985, 1997). All of these approaches show that local campaigns are important. The findings of this research are summarized by Denver and Hands in their study of campaigning in the 1992 general election. They concluded:

This study of constituency campaigning in the 1992 general election has shown very clearly, we would suggest, that the easy generalisation made in many academic studies—that, in modern conditions, local campaigning is merely a ritual, a small and insignificant side show to the main event—is seriously misleading. (Denver and Hands 1997: 305)

Clearly, there is a basic disagreement over this question, and in this chapter we try to resolve this debate by examining the impact of local campaigning on the vote for the Liberal Democrats in 1997. In pursuing this analysis, we have to consider the local campaigns undertaken by Labour and the Conservatives as well, since if Liberal Democrat grassroots campaigning increases their vote, it is likely that Labour and Conservative local campaigning will reduce the Liberal Democrat vote. Thus, a properly specified model of campaign effects will take into account the impact of all three major parties on the vote.

In addressing the debate about the impact of local campaigns on the vote in 1997, some arguments support and others oppose the view that local campaigns are important. To consider the opposition case first, an important point is that the general election was a landslide victory, producing an unprecedented swing from the Conservative to Labour of more than 10 per cent (Times Newspapers 1997: 280). In this context, it is possible that the local campaigns were simply swamped by the impact of national voting trends in what has been described by some researchers as a realigning election (Evans and Norris 1998). In this view, local campaigns might have an influence at the margins, but they were essentially irrelevant in the context of an election so dominated by New Labour. This kind of reasoning implies that local campaigns may only be important in 'normal' elections.

A second point is the one made by Curtice and Steed (1997) concerning the targeting of local campaigns. Clearly, to be most effective in influencing the outcome of an election, local campaigning should be targeted effectively on marginal or 'winnable' seats. The fact that the swings to Labour were no greater in the Labour target seats than in other types of seats suggests that local campaigns did not matter in 1997. In fact, this argument is less of a problem for the Conservatives and the Liberal Democrats than it is for Labour. In the case of the Conservatives, Denver and Hands (1997: 257) showed that they were very inefficient at targeting seats in the 1992 election because of the independence of their local parties from the Conservative Central Office. It seems likely that this situation continued in 1997, and if so, this would produce a weak or a non-existent relationship between Conservative campaigning and the marginality of the seat. In the case of the Liberal Democrats, Curtice and Steed conceded that the party was 'far more successful in those seats which they targeted than elsewhere' (1997: 311), which supports the argument that local campaigns matter.

Notwithstanding this last point, there is clearly a paradox, which has to be explained in the case of Labour. The paradox is that there was little difference in swings between the targeted and non-targeted constituencies, which, on the face of it, undermines the claim that targeted campaigning helps to win seats. In fact, Whiteley and Seyd (2003) explain this apparent paradox by distinguishing between the campaign objectives of the national party organization on the one hand, and the objectives of local activists on the other. Labour grassroots activists, by and large, ignored directives from the party headquarters encouraging them to campaign only in the target seats. Instead, they campaigned in a large number of seats not on the national target list, and so unsurprisingly there was not much difference between swings in the target seats and those in other types of seat. As a consequence, the national target seats list was a poor guide to the extent of local campaigning in 1997, and this explains the lack of campaign effects.

The third reason why local campaigns might well have been much less effective in 1997 derives from the fact that there is evidence from the British Election Study that campaign activities have been in decline over time. In the 1987 and 1997 British Election Study surveys, respondents were asked whether they had been canvassed by the parties during the campaign. In the 1987 survey some 47 per cent of respondents stated that a canvasser had called at their home during the campaign (British Election Study 1987). By the time of the 1997 election survey, this figure had declined to 25 per cent of respondents (British Election Study 1997). Some of the decline in canvassing might be explained by the switch to telephone canvassing from the more traditional door-to-door methods. However, since canvassing is one of the key methods of mobilizing the vote, the evidence suggests that campaigning may have weakened over time, which in turn would have reduced its impact on the vote.

A possible explanation for the evidence on the decline of canvassing is the decline of party activism in Britain, which has been established using panel surveys of Labour and Conservative party members over time

(Whiteley and Seyd 2002), and was discussed for the Liberal Democrats in Chapter 2. The decline is partly a matter of demographics, for example, the ageing of party members, which has particularly affected the Conservatives, but it is also influenced by political events and changing incentives to participate. Since parties require a core of active members to organize and run local campaigns, declining activism is likely to weaken those campaigns over time, which in turn reduces their impact on the vote.

Another factor that contributed to the decline in campaigning is the redistribution of constituency boundaries which occurred after the 1992 general election. Only 228 of the 659 constituencies in the United Kingdom were unaltered or minimally changed. This meant that local branches of the political parties had to undergo substantial reorganizations at the grassroots level, with many activists being moved from one constituency party to another. This process clearly had the potential to disrupt local party organizations and to weaken their capacity for campaigning during the general election.

If there are a number of reasons why campaigning might have been ineffective in 1997, there are also reasons for suggesting that local campaigns might have been very important in influencing the vote in that election. Firstly, there is the point that the strength of partisan attachments among voters, which has been weakening for decades, and has now reached quite low levels in Britain. In the 1997 British Election Study, only 16 per cent of the electorate very strongly identified with a political party, whereas 34 per cent had 'not very strong' attachments (British Election Study 1997). This contrasts with the 48 per cent having a strong attachment in 1964 (Heath et al. 1991: 13). In a panel study of the 1987 election campaign, Miller concluded:

[B]y the mid-eighties we have evidence that the British electorate was de-aligned and volatile. Its tendency to vote along class lines and, more directly important, its psychological attachment to parties was only half as strong as it had been twenty years earlier. (Miller et al. 1990: 11)

Since the evidence suggests that these trends have continued, with only 13 per cent of the electorate having very strong partisan attachments in 2001 (Clarke et al. 2004: 41), it is clearly much easier to influence voters by campaigning when partisan attachments have weakened in this way.

A second and related point is that when electoral swings are fairly uniform across Britain, as they were in the 1950s and 1960s, there is little scope for local campaign effects. In their pioneering research on British electoral behaviour, Butler and Stokes (1969: 121) calculated that the standard deviation of the two-party swing in the 1955 general election was 1.4 per cent, and by 1970 it was 2.1 per cent. However, by the 1990s this situation had changed, with the standard deviation of the two-party swing being 4.3 per cent in 1997 (Butler and Kavanagh 1997: 297). Clearly, there is much greater scope for local campaign effects when the changes in party support are so variable across the country.

A third factor suggesting that local campaigns might have been import-ant in 1997 relates specifically to New Labour. The party succeeded in reversing the decade-long decline in membership by an active campaign of recruiting new members after Tony Blair became the leader in 1994. This was so successful that the grassroots party increased in size by about 40 per cent between 1994 and 1997. Actually, the evidence suggests that many of these new members were not very active in their local parties (Whiteley and Seyd 1998), but nonetheless, many of them took an active part in the 1997 general election campaign. In the case of Labour at least, the successful membership recruitment strategy may well have offset the declining rates of activism referred to earlier. If so, local campaigns would have been enhanced by this influx of new members. Clearly the argu-ments that local campaigning had no influence on the vote in 1997 are not conclusive, and there are a number of arguments suggesting the opposite conclusion. In the light of this discussion, we go on to specify a model of campaign effects focusing particularly on the Liberal Democrats in 1997.

6.3 Measuring Liberal Democrat Campaign Activities in 1997

The effects of campaigning on the vote in 1997 can be assessed using data from the Liberal Democrat survey. We will also examine measures of local campaigning by Labour and the Conservatives, since these are relevant for assessing the impact of Liberal Democrat campaigning. The campaign measures for Labour come from a survey of Labour party members con-ducted in 1997 in the same constituencies as the Liberal Democrat survey (see Seyd and Whiteley 2002).[1] Both surveys had large samples, so that individual constituency samples could be identified. When this was done,

---

[1] There were no equivalent data available for the Conservatives at the time of the election although their campaigning activities had been surveyed at the time of the 1992 election (see Whiteley, Seyd, and Richardson 1994).

the average number of respondents per constituency was just under fifteen for the Liberal Democrats and just under thirty for Labour. Information about the campaign activities undertaken by the party members during the election can be obtained from these constituency samples and related to voting data and various other social and political variables at the constituency level. Both surveys asked a battery of questions designed to measure grassroots campaigning during the general election, and the responses to these appear in Table 6.1.

The activities in Table 6.1 usually take place only on one occasion during the campaign, and respondents were asked if they had done these things. As the Table shows, there were many similarities between Labour and the Liberal Democrat grassroots campaign activities during the general election. Large majorities of the members of both parties displayed election posters and donated money to election funds, while rather fewer were involved in election-day activities such as driving voters to the polls

Table 6.1 Election-related campaigning by the Liberal Democrats and Labour in the 1997 general election

Thinking about the 1997 general election, did you	Percentage of respondents saying 'Yes'	
	Liberal Democrats	Labour
Display an election poster	70	78
Donate money to party election funds	71	64
Help to run an election-day committee room	19	17
Drive voters to the polling station	19	17
Take numbers at the polling station	36	26
Remind voters to vote on polling day	27	45
Attend the count/celebration party	22	12

Table 6.2 Repeated election-related campaigning by the Liberal Democrats and Labour in the 1997 general election

Thinking about the 1997 general election, did you	Not at all		Once or more	
	Liberal Democrats	Labour	Liberal Democrats	Labour
Telephone canvass voters	94	90	6	10
Canvass voters door to door	76	76	24	24
Help with a fund-raising event	74	80	26	20
Deliver party leaflets	46	52	54	48
Attend a party rally	78	78	22	22
Help organize a street stall	96	91	4	9
Help with party mailings	75	79	25	21
Help with telephone fund-raising	98	98	2	2

or taking numbers at polling stations.[2] There were, however, some interesting differences between the parties. Labour worked harder to remind voters to vote on polling day than did the Liberal Democrats, whereas the Liberal Democrats were more involved in polling-day number taking, which focuses on getting out the vote.

The campaigning activities listed in Table 6.2 can take place many times during the election campaign. In this case, respondents were asked how many times they had done these. Again, interesting differences appeared between the parties. Labour was more involved in telephone canvassing than the Liberal Democrats, whereas the latter were more involved in delivering and mailing leaflets to the electorate. In other respects, their campaign activities were rather similar. Members of both parties were equally involved in door to door canvassing and also in attending party rallies during the campaign.

A principal components analysis of the indicators in Tables 6.1 and 6.2 was carried out for both parties to determine the extent to which the election-related activities can be combined into an overall scale. This tells us the extent to which party members who get involved in one activity also get involved in others. It can be seen from Table 6.3 that the first principal component is highly loaded or correlated with almost all the measures, for

Table 6.3 A principal components analysis of the campaign measures

Activity	Liberal Democrats	Labour
Displaying an election poster	0.43	0.34
Donating money to party election funds	0.28	0.27
Helping to run an election-day committee room	0.69	0.74
Driving voters to the polling station	0.63	0.61
Taking numbers at the polling station	0.51	0.58
Reminding voters to vote on polling day	0.65	0.57
Attending the count/celebration party	0.70	0.66
Telephone canvass voters	0.44	0.56
Canvass voters door to door	0.77	0.79
Help with a fund-raising event	0.71	0.74
Deliver party leaflets	0.71	0.72
Attend a party rally	0.67	0.70
Help organize a street stall	0.35	0.63
Help with party mailings	0.64	0.71
Help with telephone fund-raising	0.25	0.35
Eigenvalue	5.1	5.7
Percent of variance explained	34.2	37.9

[2] Taking numbers involves asking voters who emerge from the polls to provide their polling numbers. In this way the parties can record the fact that they have voted, so that subsequently they will not be contacted to vote by a party supporter.

both parties. For example, Liberal Democrats who helped to run election committee rooms were also quite likely to drive voters to the polling station and to canvass door to door during the campaign. A similar point can be made about Labour campaigners. The activities only weakly related to the first principal component among both parties were donating money to party funds and helping with telephone fund-raising. Overall, though, the evidence in Table 6.3 suggests that it is important to take into account a wide variety of activities when measuring campaign effects.

It is possible to construct an overall score on an index of campaigning for each respondent in the surveys.[3] This index was then summed up for every respondent in a given Liberal Democrat and Labour constituency party, giving an overall measure of party campaign activity in the 200 randomly selected constituencies used in both surveys. To see how this was done, we can examine the scoring for one particular constituency, Chichester, which was selected at random from the survey. There were a total of thirty-eight Liberal Democrat respondents in this constituency and their activities in relation to the 'one-off' campaign activities appear in Table 6.4, and their repeat activities appear in Table 6.5.

It can be seen in Table 6.4 that a majority of the Chichester respondents donated money to the election fund and about half put up an election poster. Only a minority of respondents were involved in election-day activities like delivering leaflets and taking numbers, but overall this sample of

Table 6.4. 'One-off' election campaigning activities by Liberal Democrat party members during the 1997 general election in Chichester (numbers of members)

	Yes	No	Total
Display an election poster	19	19	19
Donate money to party election funds	24	14	24
Help run a party election-day committee room	0	38	0
Drive voters to the polling station	5	33	5
Take numbers at the polling station	10	28	10
Remind voters on polling day to vote	9	29	9
Go to the count of votes	2	36	2
Deliver polling day leaflets	11	27	11
			Total = 80

Note: Each activity scores one point for every respondent.

[3] A respondent scored 1 for each activity in Table 6.1. Table 6.2 had four possible responses (not shown): 'not at all', 'once', 'twice', 'three or more times'. These responses were scored 0, 1, 2, and 3 respectively. Thus, the scale ran from zero (an individual did nothing at all) to 31 (an individual responded 'yes' to each of the seven items in the first sub-table and 'three or more' to the eight items in the second). An alternative approach would be to weight the activities by the factor scores, but if this is done it makes no significant difference to the findings in the subsequent analysis.

Table 6.5. 'Repeated' election campaigning activities by Liberal Democrat party members during the 1997 general election in Chichester (numbers of members)

Thinking about the 1997 general election, did you	Not at all (0)	Once (1)	Twice (2)	Three or more (3)	Total
Telephone canvass voters	34	0	0	4	12
Canvass door to door	33	0	0	5	15
Help with fund-raising	33	0	3	2	12
Deliver leaflets	22	2	5	9	39
Attend party rally	35	1	1	1	6
Help organize party street stall	37	1	0	0	1
Help with party mailings	35	2	1	0	4
Help telephone fund-raising	37	0	0	1	3
					Total = 92

Note: Each activity scores one point if a respondent does it once, two points if a respondent does it twice, and three points if a respondent does it three or more times.

respondents from a middle-England constituency got a respectable total of 80 points from their 'one-off' activities. In relation to the repeat activities of Table 6.5, the most popular one was delivering leaflets, but significant groups of respondents canvassed, both door to door and on the telephone, and a number of them helped with fund-raising. These activities gave the party a score of 92, which gives an overall total of 172 when this is combined with the one-off activities. This campaign score total for Chichester could have been improved either if the constituency had more active members or if the existing members were more active.

One complication with the campaign index relates to the size of constituencies in Britain. They are quite variable, and so variations in the campaign index may well reflect this as much as anything else, with larger constituencies getting a larger score simply because they contain a bigger pool of supporters.[4] To adjust for this, we divide the campaigning indexes for each constituency by the size of the electorate in that constituency. In effect, this means that the index measures the amount of campaigning done by Liberal Democrats per elector. This standardizes the effect of local campaigning across different-sized constituencies, although it makes all the constituency campaign scores very small.[5] This does not, however, prevent us from analysing the relationship between campaigning and voting.

The relationship between the Liberal Democrat campaign index and the percentage Liberal Democrat vote share in 1997 for the constituencies in the sample appears in Figure 6.1. It can be seen that the relationship is

[4] The largest constituency in the sample contained 101,680 electors and the smallest, 32,291 electors in 1997.
[5] The adjusted campaign score for Chichester, for example, was 0.0022135.

quite strong with a correlation of 0.82. The figure shows that there were quite a number of constituencies in the sample that did little or no campaigning. But as the Liberal Democrat vote share increased beyond about 20 per cent, the campaign index increased at almost the same rate, which produced this close relationship.

The correlation between the equivalent campaign index for Labour and the Labour vote share was a much more modest 0.32. This strong association between campaigning and the vote share indicates that Liberal Democrats use their campaign resources very effectively. This is not, however, the result of large numbers of party members migrating across the country in order to campaign in the winnable seats. The national party organizations may have precise lists of target seats, but by and large, the local grassroots activists campaigned in their own areas. Only 6.6 per cent of the respondents in the Liberal Democrat survey worked in a constituency other than their own during the election campaign, and nearly 70 per cent of these spent less than a fifth of their time in that constituency. Thus, there were really only a token number of party members who campaigned in other constituencies. It is clear that Liberal Democrat campaign success is based on activists working in their own local areas. A similar point can be made about Labour (Whiteley and Seyd 2003).

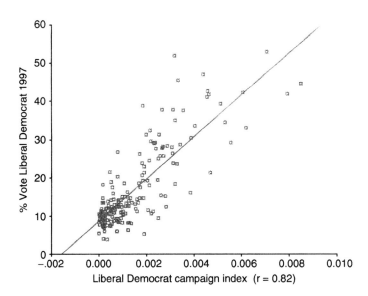

Figure 6.1 The relationship between Liberal Democrat campaigning and the party's vote share in 1997

Table 6.6. Liberal Democrat campaign scores in different types of seats in the 1997 general election ($N = 200$)

Type of seat	Mean campaign score
Liberal Democrat-held	381
Conservative-held with Liberal Democrats second	212
Labour-held with Liberal Democrats second	41
Liberal Democrats third or lower	65

After the 1997 general election the Liberal Democrats were in second place to the Conservatives in seventy-three seats, which is 44 per cent of the Tory seat total. In contrast, they were in second place to Labour in only thirty-two seats, which made up only 8 per cent of the Labour total. This meant that in the run-up to the 2001 general election, the Conservatives were much more vulnerable to Liberal Democrat campaigning than were Labour. The interesting question is whether or not this was reflected in Liberal Democrat local campaign activity.

Table 6.6 gives a breakdown of the Liberal Democrat campaign index, before it was adjusted for constituency size, in different types of constituencies following the 1997 general election. Not surprisingly, the highest campaign scores were in the seats won by the Liberal Democrats in that election. Conservative-held seats, where the Liberal Democrats came second, also had fairly high Liberal Democrat campaign scores. But the campaign scores in Labour-held seats, where the Liberal Democrats came second, were quite low. Surprisingly enough, the party did less campaigning in the seats where it came second to Labour than it did in seats where it came third or lower in the vote share rankings. This is an indication of its campaign priorities in that general election. Since these priorities were not driven by party headquarters, but rather derived from the strength of the grassroots parties themselves, this indicates that grassroots Liberal Democrat parties are much stronger in Conservative-held seats than in Labour-held seats. Given that we have a robust measure of campaign activities in the 1997 election, we can now go on to model the relationships between this and the vote.

6.4 Modelling the Effects of Liberal Democrat Campaigning on the Vote in 1997

The aggregate voting data suggest that local campaigning wins votes. Where the Liberal Democrats were in second place to the Conservatives, they increased their vote by 4.6 per cent in 1997, even though their overall vote share fell by 1.3 per cent in comparison with 1992 (Rossiter et al. 1999: 158). This can be interpreted as an example of tactical voting in which the electorate backed the party most likely to defeat the Conservatives. However, it is important to remember that local party activists play a vital role in making their electorates aware of the opportunities for tactical voting, and in that sense, it is a product of local campaigns. While the correlation between the Liberal Democrat vote share and the adjusted campaign index in Figure 6.1 is impressive, the relationship may be misleading. This is because there are a number of variables that might influence both the party vote shares and the campaigning index at the same time, and explain the correlation between them. These variables need to be controlled before any conclusions can be reached about the influence of campaigning on the vote. Without such controls, we cannot be sure if the correlation is not spurious, and is driven by factors ignored in the analysis.

One example of such a variable is social class. It is possible that the Liberal Democrats do well, both in terms of recruiting members and in winning votes, in relatively middle-class areas. It is known that the class basis of Liberal Democrat voting is rather like the class basis of Conservative voting, and is rather different from Labour, which tends to do well in working-class areas (Clarke et al. 2004: 96). If this is true, part of the explanation for the high correlation between party activism and the vote may be that both are being driven by the class characteristics of constituencies. In this case, a multivariate model containing controls for social class should demonstrate a much weaker relationship between campaigning and the vote than is apparent in Figure 6.1. Accordingly, we include a measure of social class in the model, namely the percentage of households in a constituency headed by a manual worker.[6] The argument against this is that Liberal Democrats have captured parliamentary seats in fairly working-class areas in the past, often by winning by-elections. Therefore, the class effect might be quite weak.

A second control is the percentage of public sector or council housing tenants in a constituency. Traditionally, the Labour vote has been higher among council tenants than among other working-class voters (Heath et al. 1991: 106–8). So it is possible that constituencies with a high percentage of council tenants will have both a modest Liberal Democrat vote

---

[6] This is the percentage of the working population whose occupational coding is either seg 3 (skilled manual), seg 4 (semi-skilled manual) or seg 5 (unskilled manual). The data for this exercise come from the census.

and a rather weak Liberal Democrat Party. On the other hand, sales of public sector housing initiated by the Conservatives in the 1980s have considerably reduced the size of the council housing sector, so that the political influence of housing tenure on the vote may have weakened in comparison with earlier years.

A third factor is related to the age profile of the electorate. In general, young people are less willing to participate in politics than their older counterparts (Parry, Moyser, and Day 1992: 156–61; Denver and Hands 1997). Part of the reason for this is that young people are not so strongly attached to political parties and less interested in the political process in general. However, in the context of a landslide election, it is possible that Labour had an advantage over its rivals, particularly the Conservatives, among young voters. Accordingly, a control for the percentage of the electorate under 25 years of age is included in the model. This might have the effect of reducing the size of the Liberal Democrat vote.

A fourth control is the percentage unemployed in a constituency. The unemployed are generally more likely to support Labour (Heath et al. 1991: 165–8). Moreover, some 63 per cent of Labour voters at the time of the general election thought that unemployment was the most important problem facing the country (Gallup 1997: 21). Thus, on the grounds of retrospective economic issue voting, the Labour party might expect to have an electoral advantage in constituencies with high levels of unemployment (see Miller et al. 1990: 250–5), and the Conservatives may have been blamed for this problem, given their years of incumbency. This will have an ambiguous effect on the Liberal Democrats. On the one hand, they might be expected to gain from an anti-Conservative backlash associated with unemployment, but, on the other hand, voters disgruntled by the issue may well have opted for Labour instead.

A fifth factor relates to the effects of incumbency on the vote. Cain, Ferejohn, and Fiorina (1986) have suggested that an incumbent MP can build a significant personal vote in his or her constituency, which might serve to make the local campaigns more effective. More generally, an incumbent MP's assiduous constituency work may result in electoral advantages. It is important to control this, since it might explain an important part of the relationship between campaigning and the Liberal Democrat vote. Thus, we include a dummy variable in the models that measures if a seat was held by a Liberal Democrat MP prior to the general election.

A sixth factor relates to by-elections in a constituency over the previous five-year period. Conservative by-election defeats between 1992 and 1997 steadily reduced, and finally wiped out, the government's majority, along with defections from their parliamentary party (Times Newspapers 1997: 277). Of the eighteen by-elections that took place in the period, the Liberal Democrats captured four seats from the Conservatives and Labour captured three, with the Scottish National Party taking one. Given that the local Liberal Democrat party organizations would have been mobilized to fight in most of these by-elections, it is likely that this will have given a boost to the party in fighting these seats in a subsequent general election. This potential by-election effect needs to be controlled if a true picture of the relationship between campaigning and the vote is to be drawn, and so this is included in the form of a dummy variable.

A seventh factor is linked to the earlier discussion of targeting. As Curtice and Steed pointed out, there is evidence that targeting helped the Liberal Democrats, but not Labour. However, this conclusion was drawn on the basis of a simple comparison of target seats with non-target seats. It is possible that in a multivariate model incorporating appropriate controls, targeting by the Liberal Democrats may have had no effect on the vote, even if it appeared to in the bivariate case. Equally, Labour targeting might have reduced the Liberal Democrat vote in a multivariate analysis, even if this did not appear in the bivariate analysis. These possibilities might explain part of the relationship between campaigning and the vote. Accordingly, dummy variables are incorporated into the model to control the Liberal Democrat and Labour target seats.[7]

An eighth factor, which might influence the campaign effects, is turnout. In the 1997 election the turnout of 71.5 per cent was lower than in many previous elections.[8] However, there were considerable variations in turnout and arguably a higher than average turnout would have contributed to an above-average Labour vote, given the overall swing to Labour. This could also have reduced the swing to the Liberal Democrats, given that their overall vote share declined. Of course, a high turnout might itself be explained, at least in part, by campaign activity, but it is important to see if variations in turnout are responsible for variations in the vote share, in order to identify campaign effects.

One complication with these models was mentioned earlier, namely that there is no survey-based measure of Conservative campaigning

[7] Information about target seats for Labour and the Liberal Democrats was obtained from the party headquarters. The Conservatives did not announce any target lists of constituencies in the election.

[8] The turnout in our sample of 200 constituencies was 71.4 per cent with a standard deviation of 5.6 per cent. The minimum turnout was 54.4 per cent and the maximum, 80.5 per cent.

available.[9] Clearly, an accurate estimate of the influence of Liberal Democrat campaigning on the vote can only be obtained by controlling the influence of campaigning by all of the major parties at the same time. To avoid this problem, we use a standard surrogate measure of Conservative campaigning, the percentage of the maximum campaign spending allowed by law in each constituency. By law, local party expenditure during a general election campaign must include the expenses of printing leaflets, advertising in local newspapers, telecommunications such as phone canvassing, the cost of hiring rooms and holding public meetings, fees paid to agents, and a variety of other things. It is possible that campaign spending measures aspects of the local campaign not captured by the survey-based campaign indexes. One way of thinking about this is that the campaign indexes measure the labour, or human input, into campaigning, while the spending data measure the capital, or financial, input. It is clearly desirable to measure both aspects of campaigning. Accordingly, the percentage of the maximum campaign spending by both Labour and the Liberal Democrats are included in the model, along with the Conservative spending data. This measure has been used by a number of researchers as a proxy variable, and the evidence suggests that it is a valid indicator of campaigning (see Johnston, Pattie, and Johnston 1989; Whiteley, Seyd, and Richardson 1994: 189–218; Johnston and Pattie, 1995).

The regression models of the influence of party campaigning and party spending on the Liberal Democrat vote share in 1997 appear in Table 6.7. The table contains standardized regression coefficients and t-statistics as well as the goodness of fit R^2 statistics. Model A contains all the campaign and spending variables, together with the control variables discussed earlier. A number of interesting points emerge from the table. The first is that the control variables have no significant influence on the Liberal Democrat vote, apart from the MP dummy variable. If the Liberal Democrats won the seat prior to 1997, this provided them with a significant boost to their vote in that election. But all of the other postulated effects are absent. Thus, there are no class, age, housing tenure, and by-election effects on the Liberal Democrat vote share.

---

[9] The main reason for this is that the Conservatives had no national database of members at the time of the other surveys, although they have now constructed one. This means that conducting a survey of Conservative party members comparable to that of the other parties would have meant approaching 200 different local Conservative associations to ask them for membership lists in order to provide a sampling frame. This was not a practical exercise.

Table 6.7. The influence of campaigning on the Liberal Democrat vote share in 1997 ($N = 200$)

Predictors	A	B	C	D
Incumbent Liberal Democrat MP	0.16*** (4.3)	0.21*** (6.4)	—	—
By-election in constituency, 1992–7	−0.05 (1.4)	—	—	—
Proportion of population aged 16–24	−0.06 (1.4)	—	—	—
Proportion of heads of households in working-class occupations	−0.03 (0.5)	—	—	—
Proportion of economically active people unemployed	−0.10 (1.3)	—	—	—
Liberal Democrat target seat	0.09** (2.1)	0.06* (1.7)	0.04* (1.6)	0.04* (1.8)
Labour spending as percentage of maximum	−0.22*** (4.9)	−0.23*** (6.3)	−0.13*** (5.0)	−0.14*** (5.5)
Liberal Democrat spending as percentage of maximum	0.37*** (6.3)	0.42*** (7.9)	0.12*** (2.9)	0.12** (2.8)
Labour campaign index	−0.12*** (2.7)	−0.09** (2.6)	−0.05** (2.1)	−0.05*** (2.1)
Liberal Democrat campaign index	0.35*** (5.2)	0.32*** (5.9)	0.22*** (5.8)	0.22*** (5.9)
Conservative spending as percentage of maximum	−0.00 (0.1)	—	−0.02 (0.7)	—
Proportion of households in council housing	0.07 (1.3)	—	—	—
Turnout in 1997	−0.08 (1.0)	—	—	—
Labour target seat	−0.03 (0.9)	—	—	—
Liberal Democrat vote share in 1992	—	—	0.58*** (13.8)	0.58*** (13.8)
R^2	0.86	0.86	0.92	0.92

Note: **Standardised coefficients; *t*-statistics in parenthesis;** * $p < 0.10$; ** $p < 0.05$; *** $p < 0.01$.

131

The second point to make is that the model is a very good fit to the data, with 86 per cent of the variance explained. Only a relatively modest percentage of the variation in Liberal Democrat voting across the 200 constituencies remains unexplained by the predictor variables. This is largely because the campaign measures, particularly the Liberal Democrat campaign index and the Liberal Democrat spending variable, have a very strong impact on the Liberal Democrat vote. They have a bigger impact than their equivalent measures in the Labour and Conservative models (see Whiteley and Seyd 2003). This means that much of the Liberal Democrats' voting success is explained by the campaign activities of their grassroots party members.

With regard to the other parties, both Labour campaign spending and the Labour campaign index have a significant negative impact on the Liberal Democrat vote share. However, Conservative campaign spending does not have an impact. This is partly because the measurement of Conservative campaigning is weaker in this model than for their rivals, since we are missing the Conservative campaign index. But it also reflects the fact that the Conservatives are not efficient at targeting their campaign resources—a point made earlier (see Denver and Hands 1997). Because they tend to do much of their campaigning in safe seats rather than in winnable ones, Conservative campaigns have little or no impact on the Liberal Democrat vote.

Model B in Table 6.7 re-estimates the model with all of the non-significant variables in Model A removed. When this is done, variations in the Liberal Democrat vote can be explained almost exclusively by campaign measures. The Liberal Democrat and Labour campaign indexes and spending variables remain highly significant predictors with the expected signs. If the constituency was a Liberal Democrat target seat, this had a modest though significant positive impact on the vote. In addition, incumbency by a Liberal Democrat MP continues to have a strong effect.

Model C in Table 6.7 takes a different approach to the task of controlling confounding factors. It is possible that some demographic and spatial variables exist, which have an impact on the Liberal Democrat vote, but which were omitted from the model. For example, if a community has a local political culture, which in some way favours the Liberal Democrats, this will boost their vote, and possibly their party membership. The problem is in measuring this type of effect. One way around the problem is to use the Liberal Democrat vote share in 1992 in each constituency as a control variable in the model. This acts as a generalized control variable capturing all the factors that influence the vote, but that are not measured by the campaign variables. Obviously, if a local Liberal Democrat political culture exists in a constituency, which influences the vote in 1997, it is very likely to have influenced the vote in 1992 as well. So incorporating the prior vote variable into the model controls this and other unmeasured variables.

The goodness of fit of Model C is significantly higher than that of Model B, indicating that the new control variable has picked up some effects that were unmeasured in Models A and B. An impressive 92 per cent of the variation in the Liberal Democrat votes across the set of constituencies is explained by the campaign variables, which is a very high goodness of fit indeed. Model D excludes the variables that were non-significant in Model C, and the results show that the Liberal Democrat vote share in 1997 is exclusively explained by campaign variables. The strongest predictor is the Liberal Democrat campaign index, followed by the Labour campaign index. The former has a positive effect and the latter a negative effect on the Liberal Democrat vote. The spending variables are important as well, although not for the Conservatives, and there is a modest positive effect associated with being a Liberal Democrat target seat. The MP incumbency effect disappears in these models, but this does not mean that Liberal Democrat incumbents had no effect on the vote. Rather, it implies that a Liberal Democrat MP had no additional effect on the vote over and above that measured by the campaign variables.

As an experiment, if an equivalent model is estimated for the Labour Party containing only the four campaign variables in Model D, the goodness of fit (R^2) is 0.73. If this is done for the Liberal Democrats, the goodness of fit is 0.84. Thus, the Liberal Democrat vote share in 1997 was significantly better explained by campaigning than was the Labour vote share, although campaigning variables were very important for both parties. A similar point can be made by examining the size of the campaign variable coefficients for Model D in both parties. As Table 6.7 shows, the Liberal Campaign index has a standardized coefficient of 0.22 in the vote Model D. The equivalent coefficient for a Labour vote model is 0.06 for the Labour campaign index. Thus, the Liberal Democrat campaign index is almost four times more powerful as a predictor of the vote than the Labour campaign index is of the Labour vote.

If the equivalent models of the Conservative vote share are estimated, they appear in many ways to be the mirror image of the Labour models. Thus, the demographic variables such as the percentage of working class, of young voters, and of the unemployed all have statistically significant negative effects in this model. With regard to the campaign variables in the Conservative model, only two of them appear to be important: the Labour campaign index and the Conservative spending variable, both with the expected signs. This is an interesting finding, since it indicates that the Liberal Democrat campaign variables had no measurable impact on the Conservative vote. This is not surprising, given that the Conservative spending variable had no effect on the Conservative vote. There is a ready explanation for this finding, aside from the measurement issues associated with the Conservative model discussed earlier. The Conservative vote in 1997 was only marginally influenced by campaign variables because the electorate had decided, probably as early as the 1992 Exchange Rate Mechanism (ERM) crisis, that they were going to 'throw out' the Conservative government. In this rather special sense, Antony King and Ivor Crewe are correct in arguing that campaigning had little effect on the outcome of the election. However, this point cannot be made about the Liberal Democrats and Labour. In the case of the Liberal Democrats, campaigning was crucial to determining whether or not they were going to benefit from the demise of the Conservative government. The same point can be made, but to a lesser extent about Labour, since it was the main opposition party.

The evidence to support this argument comes from a computer simulation of the 1997 general election, which evaluates the impact of the campaigning variables on the number of seats captured by the Liberal Democrats and Labour. Since the regression models in Table 6.7 are very good fits, it is possible to 'rerun' history by changing the campaign variables to see what effects that would have on the vote. These simulations suggest that if the Liberal Democrats had campaigned at twice their actual rate, the party would have won sixty-nine seats instead of the forty-six seats they actually won. Perhaps even more striking, the simulations show that if they had done no campaigning at all, they would have won a total of only three seats.

The simulation results for Labour are a bit less dramatic than those for the Liberal Democrats. If Labour had campaigned at twice the rate it actually did in the election, it would have won 142 out of the sample of 200 seats, or 76 per cent of the total. This compares with the 64 per cent of seats, which it actually won. At the other end of the scale, if Labour had done no campaigning at all, the simulations predict that the party would have won a 54 per cent seat share, or 346 seats in the House of Commons. It is interesting to note that this would have produced an overall majority for Labour of 33, instead of the 177 majority, which it actually won. Thus, campaigning was crucial, not for deciding which party won the general election, but how many seats the Liberal Democrats and Labour were going to take off the Conservatives. In the case of the Liberal Democrats, it is doubtful if they could have survived as a party in an election where they won only three seats. Thus, campaigning played an absolutely crucial role for them in the 1997 general election.

6.5 Conclusions

These results suggest that local campaigns played a very important role in influencing the vote in the 1997 general election. The campaign effects are strong and enduring in different specifications of the models, and remain highly significant in the very parsimonious best-fitting model. The evidence that campaigns mattered for Labour and the Liberal Democrats is particularly strong, but there is evidence to support this conclusion for the Conservatives as well, except in their case, the absence of any survey-based measures of Conservative campaigning makes any conclusions more tentative. The effects for the Liberal Democrats were very strong in the sense that no other variables were relevant for explaining variations in the vote across our sample of constituencies other than the campaign variables. These results reinforce conclusions from survey-based analyses of Labour party members (Seyd and Whiteley 1992; Seyd and Whiteley 2002), that local party activists play an important role in mobilizing the vote in British general elections. Arguments opposed to these conclusions are based on unreliable extrapolations of trends in opinion polls, or on an uncritical acceptance that targeting strategies by the national party organizations are a good guide to local campaign efforts, when our evidence suggests that they are not.

While it is true that Labour started the election campaign in 1997 and again in 2001 with a big lead over the Conservatives, the large changes in gross public support that can take place during the campaign indicates that opinion remains quite volatile and therefore malleable (see Miller et al. 1990). This is why campaigns, both local and national, can play a very important role in influencing the outcome. This evidence shows that the view that such campaigns are merely rituals undertaken by the parties with little or no relevance to outcomes is clearly wrong.

These results also have implications for British electoral politics. They suggest that a good deal of the credit for the gains achieved by the Liberal Democrats in recent local and national elections is due to the hard work of the grassroots activists. Estimates show that when it comes to explaining the behaviour of individual voters, national campaign effects associated with the party leadership and issues are important as well as local campaigning (Clarke et al. 2004: 167–8). So the party's electoral gains are not entirely explained by grassroots activity. But the size of the campaign effects estimated in the models suggests that parties that neglect and discourage their activists in the belief that they play only a ritualistic role in electioneering are likely to pay a significant price in terms of seats lost in a general election. Indeed, it is arguable that the decline in the Conservative grassroots party that took place while the party was in government for the best part of twenty years (see Whiteley, Seyd, and Richardson 1994) played an important role in explaining Labour's landslide win in 1997. Labour is currently repeating the Conservative pattern of neglecting and ignoring its grassroots membership, which at the time of writing is in serious decline.

These developments provide a real opportunity for the Liberal Democrats. If they continue to foster and promote grassroots activism within the party organization and to support the relatively decentralized and democratic structures that exist, they will be in a position to profit from the decline of grassroots politics which has occurred in both of their rivals. Just as the decline of the party organization had a serious effect on the electoral support for the Conservatives in the long run, the same thing will very likely happen to Labour in due course. The Liberal Democrats are the natural alternative party likely to benefit from these trends in the absence of a Conservative revival.

The evidence in this chapter, though strong, is derived from aggregate-level comparisons of campaigning by the political parties and voting behaviour at the constituency level. However, a convincing case needs to be made for the effectiveness of campaigning at the individual level. The question is: Are voters directly affected by party campaigns? This is the topic of Chapter 7.

7

Electoral Performance and Prospects

In Chapter 6, we saw that local campaigning plays a particularly important role in influencing the Liberal Democrat vote in general elections. While these campaigns are clearly significant, they are unlikely to be enough to give the party a chance of replacing Labour or the Conservatives as the second party of British electoral politics, let alone a chance of winning power. If the party is going to break out of its third-party status, it seems likely that it will take more than just local campaigning to do it. With this point in mind, in this chapter we focus on factors that explain Liberal Democrat electoral prospects in addition to campaigning. In this way, we can judge the prospects of the party replacing its main rivals to become the second, or even the first, party of British electoral politics. An additional aim is to examine the campaign effects discussed in Chapter 6 with individual-level data from the British Election Studies of 2001 and 2005. The evidence in Chapter 6 that campaigns are important is strong, but it relates to the constituency level of analysis. To make an even stronger case, we have to find out if individuals can be persuaded to change their voting intentions by campaigning.

We begin the chapter by looking at long-term support in elections and in the polls for the Liberal Democrats, to see how it has evolved over the last half-century or so. This provides a context within which to judge the party's future electoral prospects. This, in turn, leads to a discussion of the factors that influence Liberal Democrat voting support, and we model the key determinants of this over time. This dynamic analysis is limited to some extent by the availability of data, and so it is followed by a more extensive analysis of Liberal Democrat electoral support, based on the 2001 and 2005 election studies. This analysis makes it possible to determine if campaigning influences individual voters. In a final section, conclusions are then drawn about the future electoral prospects for the party.

7.1 Trends in Support for the Liberal Democrats Since 1945

To get a sense of the long-term trends in Liberal Democrat electoral performance, we can examine the record of electoral support for the party in the seventeen general elections between 1945 and 2005. Figure 7.1 plots Liberal and Liberal Democrat vote shares and seats won, and it shows that there is a strong upward trend in both over this sixty-year period. However, the increase is not uniform. The party's share of the vote hovered below 10 per cent up until about 1970, and so it appeared that the party was making little progress. However, the 1970 general election proved to be a watershed since the party began to rapidly gain support and its vote share rose to almost 20 per cent in February 1974. That election produced a tiny majority for Labour and the Liberals captured fourteen seats. Prime Minister Harold Wilson then sought a larger majority by holding a second election in October 1974, and at this election the Liberals ended up with thirteen seats.

After the two 1974 elections, support for the Liberal Democrats ebbed in 1979, but the party subsequently received a huge boost from the split in the Labour Party and the creation of the SDP in 1981. The resulting Liberal–Social Democrat electoral Alliance was created before the 1983

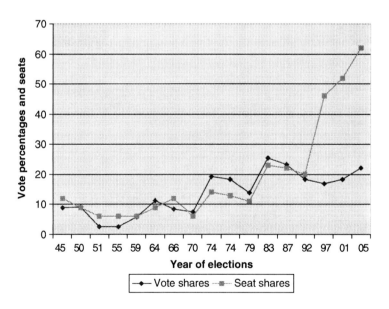

Figure 7.1 Trends in Liberal Democrat electoral support, 1945–2005

general election, and it ensured that the two parties did not challenge each other in the same constituencies in that election. As a consequence, the Alliance came very close to replacing Labour as the second party of British electoral politics.

In retrospect, the 1983 general election proved to be the high-water mark of Alliance electoral support, and in subsequent elections, the Alliance vote share dropped as Labour began the slow process of climbing back from the brink of disaster towards recovery and eventually, the creation of New Labour. This meant that the decline in the party's vote share continued even after the Alliance parties merged and the Liberal Democrats were created in 1988. A rather gentle decline in support subsequently continued until the 1997 election, at which point the party started to increase its vote share, achieving 22 per cent in 2005. It was also at that election that the number of seats it captured began to climb sharply.

As is well known, the Liberal Democrat share of seats in the House of Commons does not reflect their vote share because of the single-member plurality electoral system in Britain. In fact, the high-water mark of the party's seat share occurred in the 2005 general election, although the real breakthrough in seats occurred in 1997. In that election, the party more than doubled its representation in the House of Commons on a smaller vote share than it received in 1992. The fact that the Liberal Democrats did particularly well in 1997 was no accident. One important factor here is the nature of party competition in Britain. The party tends to pick up electoral support when the Conservatives are in power and to lose it when they are in opposition. This can be seen in Figure 7.1, where the surges in Liberal Democrat voting support occurred in 1964, February 1974, and 1983. In all three cases, there were Conservative governments in office, so the party tends to do well in picking up seats in general elections when this is the case.

The period of Labour government since 1997 has been an exception to the post-war trend of the Liberal Democrats picking up support when the Conservatives are in office. However, this is not a significant departure from the tendency of the Liberal Democrats to do well when the Conservatives are doing badly, because the latter have not really recovered from their defeat in 1997. The Conservatives obtained just under 31 per cent of the popular vote in 1997, and only just over 32 per cent in 2005. So the Liberal Democrats continued to profit in 2005 from the Conservative failure to bounce back from its defeat in 1997.

The correlation between seat shares in the House of Commons for the Liberal Democrats and Conservatives is –0.66, for the seventeen general elections between 1945 and 2005. In contrast, the same correlation for Labour and the Liberal Democrats over the same period is 0.50. The competition for seats between the Conservatives and Liberal Democrats is much greater than competition for seats between Labour and the Liberal Democrats. This is a direct measure of how both Labour and the Liberal Democrats tend to do well when the Conservatives do badly.

The latter point is underlined in Table 7.1, which examines the first- and second-placed parties in marginal seats following the 2005 general election, where marginal is defined as a seat with a majority of up to 10 per cent of the vote. It can be seen that the Liberal Democrats came second in a third of the marginals held by the Conservatives, and second in only 12 per cent of those held by Labour. Futhermore, the Conservatives came second in 59 per cent of the marginals held by the Liberal Democrats, whereas Labour was second in 41 per cent of these seats. Clearly, following the 2005 general election, the electoral competition between the Liberal Democrats and Conservatives is significantly greater than between the Liberal Democrats and Labour.

It should be noted, however, that electoral competition between the Liberal Democrats and Labour is growing over time. In the 2001 election, the Liberal Democrats came second in only 7 per cent of Labour marginals, and Labour challenged the Liberal Democrats in only 11 per cent of their own marginals. So Labour has become more of a challenge to the Liberal Democrats following the 2005 election. Having said that, however, there is still some way to go before Liberal Democrat competition with Labour is as strong as it is with the Conservatives. This makes the party much more vulnerable to a resurgence of the Conservative vote than it does to an increase in the Labour vote.

The main reason why the Liberal Democrats did well in winning parliamentary seats at the 2005 election is that their vote is now much less

Table 7.1. The seat battlegrounds in marginal seats after the 2005 general election

Marginal seats won in 2001	Conservatives 2nd	Labour 2nd	Liberal Democrats 2nd	Total
Conservatives	—	30 (67%)	15 (33%)	45 (100%)
Labour	75 (88%)	—	10 (12%)	85 (100%)
Liberal Democrats	17 (59%)	12 (41%)	—	29 (100%)

Note: Marginal is defined as seats having majorities of up to, and including, 10 per cent of the vote.

evenly spread across the country than it was in the past. In the 1983 general election, the relatively even spread of their vote ensured that despite the high vote share they won few seats; they came second or third in a lot of constituencies, piling up the votes while failing to win seats. By 2005, the Liberal Democrat vote had become much less evenly spread, allowing them to win more than three times as many seats as in 1983 with a reduced share of the vote compared with that year. Russell and Fieldhouse (2005: 199) suggest that this development is largely the result of locally targeted campaigns, in particular the 'Key Seats Initiative', which concentrated campaigning resources into selected constituencies. Thus, the analysis of Chapter 6 is very relevant for understanding the long-term trends in Liberal Democrat support. More generally, regional variations in voting behaviour have become more pronounced over time, and this has given the Liberal Democrats an opportunity to win seats, particularly in places like the west country (see Denver 2003: 152–4).

Trends in Liberal Democrat support over time can be tracked in monthly opinion polls, which provide many more cases to analyse than is true of general elections. Differences in party competition are also apparent in the polls. Figure 7.2 examines trends in voting intentions for the Conservatives and the Liberals/Alliance/Liberal Democrats in monthly opinion polls between 1947 and 2004.[1] There are two striking features in this figure. Firstly, for most of the period between 1947 and 2004, when the Conservatives experienced an upswing in their support, the Liberals, and subsequently the Liberal Democrats, experienced a loss of support. Thus, peaks in the Conservative series coincide roughly with troughs in the Liberal and Liberal Democrat series, and vice versa. This is most dramatically demonstrated in the middle of Figure 7.2, when for a short period the Liberal–Social Democrat Alliance was more popular than the Conservative government in the vote intentions measure. This was a by-product of the split in the Labour Party and the creation of the SDP in 1981. The exception to this general trend comes at the end of the series, during the New Labour period, when the Conservative vote trends upwards at the same time as the Liberal Democrat vote.

The second trend apparent in Figure 7.2 is the narrowing of the gap between the Liberals/Liberal Democrats and the Conservatives over time. At the start of the series in the 1950s, the gap between the parties was wide. But later on, particularly after the creation of the Liberal Democrats in

---

[1] We are grateful to Professor David Sanders for supplying these data.

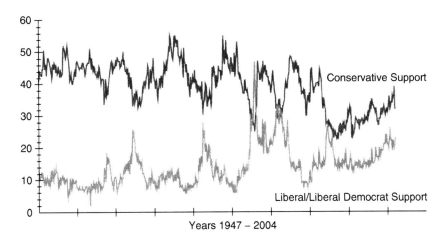

Figure 7.2 Voting intentions for the Conservatives and Liberals/Liberal Democrats in Britain, 1947–2004

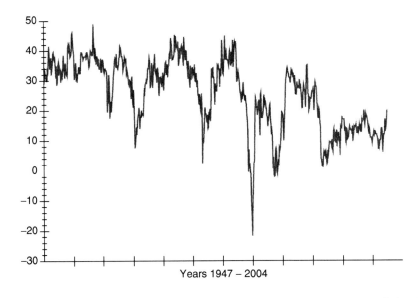

Figure 7.3 Voting intentions for the Conservatives minus the Liberals/Liberal Democrats in Britain, 1947–2004

1988, the gap became much narrower. This suggests a long-term trend in British electoral politics involving the Liberal Democrats gradually catching up with the Conservatives in the opinion polls. This trend can be seen most clearly in Figure 7.3, which measures the difference between the

Conservative and the Liberal/Liberal Democrat voting intentions series. This trends more or less continuously downwards over time, although there are wide fluctuations in the series.

The relationship between Liberal/Liberal Democrat voting intentions and Labour support shows a different pattern from that of Figure 7.3. Figure 7.4 contains the equivalent series to Figure 7.3, showing the difference between Labour and Liberal/Liberal Democrat vote intentions. The striking thing about this figure is that with the exception of a big 'valley' in the middle of the series, the gap between Labour and the Liberal/Liberal Democrats remains fairly constant over time. The 'valley' has been referred to already, and occurred when the SDP–Liberal Alliance was created in the early 1980s. After the arrival of New Labour in the 1990s, the gap between the two parties more or less reverted to its pre-Alliance size. This underlines the point that, in the long run, the Liberal Democrats represent more of an electoral challenge to the Conservatives than they do to Labour.

In light of this discussion, we examine the factors that are likely to influence the Liberal Democrat vote intentions over time, before going on to develop and test a model of these trends in Section 7.2.

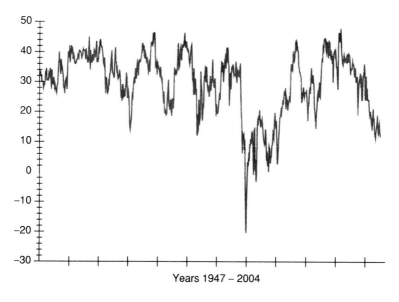

Figure 7.4 Voting intentions for Labour minus the Liberals/Liberal Democrats in Britain, 1947–2004

7.2 The Determinants of the Liberal Democrat Vote

The analysis of voting behaviour can be approached with two alternative methodological strategies. One involves modelling the behaviour of individual voters using cross-sectional data from national surveys of the electorate. This has been a common approach since the first electoral surveys were conducted in Britain in the 1960s (see Butler and Stokes 1969). A refinement of this approach, which makes it possible to capture some of the important dynamics, is to use panel data in which the same respondents are interviewed on two or more occasions (see Clarke et al. 2004). This is obviously preferable to conducting a single set of interviews at one point of time, not least because it can identify those who change their minds and examine why this happened. The group of 'switchers' are particularly interesting, since the causal mechanisms that drive the vote must also change for this group, otherwise they would not be 'switchers'. An alternative methodological approach is to model relationships over time at the aggregate level, using monthly or quarterly observations from opinion poll data of the type observed in Figures 7.2–7.4.[2] In this case, we are looking at the behaviour of averages of voters rather than individual voters. This type of analysis has been used to examine the links between the state of the economy and political support over time (see Whiteley 1986).

In this chapter, we will use both approaches to model the factors that influence the Liberal Democrat vote. We start with an examination of the dynamics of support using monthly time series observations over a period of roughly twenty-five years. Data availability limits the extent of the analysis, but it greatly facilitates the identification of the dynamic factors at work over a long period, which explains the trends we observe in Figures 7.1–7.4. Subsequently, we will examine a more complex model of the Liberal Democrat vote using individual-level data derived from the British Election Studies of 2001 and 2005. The latter analyses take place over a much shorter period of time. By combining these approaches, it is possible to identify the key variables that influence Liberal Democrat support and that are likely to be important in the future. The time series analysis throws light on support over the period of a generation, and the panel analysis brings the analysis up to date with a more detailed analysis of two recent elections. We begin with an examination of trends over time.

---

[2] It is not generally possible to model relationships using the data from Figure 7.1, since there are too few observations to estimate effects.

7.3 The Dynamics of Liberal Democrat Support, 1974–2005

Originally, time series models of party support were used to investigate the effects of changes in the economy, such as in unemployment and inflation, on political support for the incumbent government or main opposition party. This modelling strategy was introduced by Goodhart, Charles, and Bhansali (1970) in a seminal article, which used a simple reward–punishment model of the effects. According to this, if the economy does well and unemployment and inflation are at low levels, the governing party will be rewarded for its success in the polls. If, on the other hand, the economy does badly, the governing party will be punished and the opposition parties will do well. Later models incorporated voters' subjective judgements about the state of the economy, which were found to be better predictors of support than the objective measures such as unemployment data (Whiteley 1986; Sanders 1991, 2005). Generally, these models showed that voters' economic expectations really matter in predicting their voting behaviour. If they were optimistic about their own economic futures or the economic future of the country, they tended to support the incumbent party. If, on the other hand, they became pessimistic about the future economy, they would be willing to switch to the opposition parties.

During the 1970s, inflation and unemployment became an increasing problem for UK governments. This was the era of 'stagflation' or a combination of rising unemployment and inflation, which proved to be a toxic mix for incumbent parties. Incumbents lost general elections in 1970, in 1974, and again in 1979, and the economy played a key role in explaining why this happened. During the Thatcher era of the 1980s, interest rates were increasingly used to try to manage the macroeconomy with the principle goal of reducing inflation. This was the era of 'monetarism' and it achieved its objectives, but at a huge cost in terms of unemployment (Maynard 1988). However, towards the end of the eighteen years of Conservative government, unemployment started to decline both in Britain and across the EU, and the country entered a period of relatively low inflation.

When New Labour was elected in 1997, the task of determining interest rates was given to a group of experts, the Monetary Policy Committee of the Bank of England. This meant that the government no longer directly controlled interest rates. Handing over interest rate policy to the Bank of England appears to have taken the issue out of politics to some extent, since it is apparent that the objective economy is now no longer a good predictor of party support (Sanders et al. 2001). This development has reduced the government's electoral vulnerability to a poor economic performance to a degree. In addition, interest rates, unemployment, and inflation have all stopped fluctuating widely like they did in the 1970s and 1980s, and have been held at relatively low levels. As a result, they have become much less salient to the electorate.

To examine the influence of both the objective and subjective economy on Liberal Democrat party support, we need a more sophisticated model than a simple reward–punishment model. This is true for two reasons. One is that electors are well aware of the fact that the Liberal Democrats are unlikely to win a general election outright and form a government, so the party is not seen as a main contender in the economic management stakes in the same way as its rivals. The Liberal Democrats are in a different position from Labour and the Conservatives in this regard. When control of government is confined to a duopoly of parties, the third party is unlikely to be judged in the same way as its rivals. To take this into account, we need to modify the reward–punishment model to apply it to the Liberal Democrats. Normally, if the governing party is doing well in managing the economy, then, other things being equal, voters are likely to continue supporting it. If, on the other hand, the governing party is doing badly, voters will turn to the main opposition party, *providing that it presents a credible alternative*. If the main opposition party, whether Labour or the Conservatives, does not present a credible alternative, disaffected voters may well turn to the Liberal Democrats.

There have been periods over the last quarter century when the main opposition parties were not credible alternatives. For Labour, this was true in the 1980s following its split and the creation of the SDP. We observed in Figure 7.1 that the Alliance parties received a huge boost in their support during this period. Similarly, after New Labour's landslide victory in 1997, Liberal Democrat support started to increase. This may, in part, be explained by the fact that voters who were pessimistic about their economic prospects switched from Labour to the Liberal Democrats instead of to the Conservatives, because of a widespread perception that the latter did not provide a credible alternative to Labour. From the point of view of modelling these trends, it means that we need to take into account support for both the governing and main opposition parties when investigating the impact of the economy on Liberal Democrat support. It can be described as a modified reward–punishment model.

In addition to the economy, there are other issues that might encourage voters to switch to the Liberal Democrats, rather than to the main opposition party when the latter lacks credibility. For example, the Liberal

Democrats were the only major party to oppose Britain's involvement in the Iraq war of 2003. Many Labour voters who opposed the war would not switch to the Conservatives on this issue, since that party supported the Labour government's policies. Consequently, in 2005 many of them switched to the Liberal Democrats. However, it is difficult to model all these issues over time, since data are not available to do so. Accordingly, we simply examine the effects of Conservative and Labour voting intentions on Liberal Democrat voting intentions. The earlier discussion suggests that the Conservatives have a bigger influence on Liberal Democrat support than Labour, and this possibility can be investigated empirically in the analysis.

Apart from the other parties, there is another factor that is clearly important in explaining support for the Liberal Democrats in the polls. This is the popularity of their leader. If the leader receives relatively favourable publicity and is thought to be doing a good job, this might persuade wavering voters to turn to the Liberal Democrats. This process operates by means of a 'leadership heuristic' (Sniderman et al. 1991; Clarke et al. 2004). This is the idea that when voters are faced with a complicated choice about which party to support, they can use their feelings about the party leader to make a choice, rather than conducting a complex evaluation of the policies and credibility of the party. The latter would require an extensive exercise in gathering, processing, and analysing information. In addition to knowing what the parties are promising, voters would need to know the likelihood that parties will deliver on those promises if elected. Since it is not rational for voters to undertake such a calculation, given that their vote is unlikely to make any difference to the outcome, they are likely to use information short cuts, or rules of thumb, which enable them to judge the parties more easily. This has been described as a process of 'low information rationality' (Popkin 1991). One such short cut is to evaluate the rival party leaders and to decide who is the most attractive, and then to use this information to make a vote choice.

However, if voters do use a leadership heuristic to make a decision about which party to support, this is not a straightforward matter in a three-party setting. In a two-party system like that of the United States, if they do not like the Republican candidate, they can choose the Democrat. In Britain, it is not enough for voters just to dislike the current prime minister. Rather they need to dislike both the current prime minister and the leader of the opposition to consider switching to the Liberal Democrats. Again, from a modelling point of view, it means that we must take into account support for the prime minister and the leader of the opposition when estimating the influence of the party leader on support for the Liberal Democrats.

Monthly observations of the popularity of Liberal and Liberal Democrat leaders over the period from 1974 to 2004 appear in Figure 7.5. It can be seen that there have been wide fluctuations in the popularity of the leaders over time. When David Steel took over from Jeremy Thorpe as leader in the summer of 1976, this coincided with a slump in the Liberal leader's popularity. But after the 1979 election, Steel became significantly more popular and maintained this level of popularity until after the 1987 general election. At this point, the wrangling between the Liberals and the Social Democrats over their post-election merger had a damaging effect on his popularity. When Paddy Ashdown was subsequently elected leader of the newly established Liberal Democrats in October 1988, he started from a fairly low base of popularity, as Figure 7.5 makes clear. Again, the run-up to the 1992 general election and the election campaign itself gave him a significant boost, and his popularity reached a high point in 1997. When Charles Kennedy took over as leader in 1998, he also started from a low base of popularity, but fairly rapidly improved his position to reach a high point by the time of the 2001 general election.

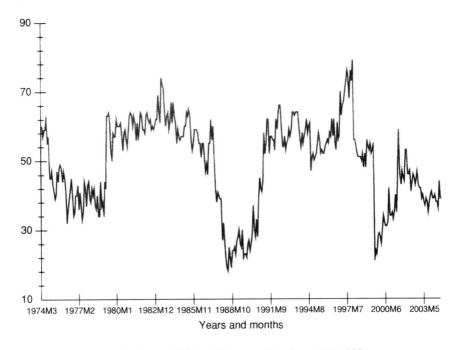

Figure 7.5 Approval ratings of Liberal Democrat leaders, 1974–2004

The common pattern in Figure 7.5 is that Liberal Democrat leaders tend to start their terms of office with relatively low levels of popularity, in part because the voters do not know who they are. Subsequently, their popularity ratings tend to increase, particularly at election times, as they get more public recognition and media exposure. If the popularity of the leader has a significant impact on the Liberal Democrat vote, it is clear that the impact is likely to be greater at election times, so this needs to be taken into account in any model of Liberal Democrat support.

In the light of this discussion, we go on to specify and test a model of Liberal Democrat voting intentions over time in Section 7.4.

7.4 A Model of the Dynamics of the Liberal Democrat Vote

In Section 7.3, we suggested that Liberal Democrat voting intentions might be influenced by the state of the objective and subjective economies, providing that we take into account levels of support for the other two parties. A similar point can be made about support for the party leaders. Accordingly, the estimating model contains four types of variables: (a) measures of voting support for both Labour and the Conservatives; (b) measures of the popularity ratings of all three party leaders; (c) subjective and objective economic variables; and (d) measure of the proximity of a general election. In this section, we examine each of these measures in detail.

The dependent variable in a multiple regression model of Liberal Democrat voting support is the time series data in Figure 7.2. The starting point of the model is to try to determine how this changes over successive months, so the first predictor variable in the model is that the Liberal Democrat voting support lagged one month.[3] This specification means that we are modelling the changes in Liberal Democrat support over time. The second type of predictor variable is support for Labour and the Conservatives. However, if we incorporate these measures into the equation at the same time point, it leaves the causal status of the relationships ambiguous. That is, if we use current Labour and Conservative vote intentions to predict current Liberal Democrat support, we cannot be sure if the

---

[3] As Figure 7.2 shows, there is a Liberal Democrat vote intention percentage for each month. If we shift last month's scores into the present month throughout the entire series, this is referred to as lagging the series, so that every month's score moves up, so to speak, one period. This makes it possible to estimate the influence of the vote in the previous month on its current value and hence determine the change in support over successive months.

declining popularity of the two major parties is responsible for an increase in support for the Liberal Democrats, or if the process is actually working the other way round. If, in fact, changes in Liberal Democrat support drive changes in the popularity of Labour and the Conservatives, the model will face technical problems and the estimates will be unreliable.[4] To avoid this problem, we include Conservative and Labour support lagged one period as predictors in the model. Thus, the model estimates the effect of last month's support for the two major parties on this month's support for the Liberal Democrats. Since observations made this month cannot causally influence observations made last month, this estimation strategy deals with the potential problem of two-way causation.

The third type of predictor variable is measures of the popularity of the party leaders. As well as the approval rating of the Liberal Democrat leader, we also include approval ratings for the prime minister and the leader of the opposition in the equation. Again, the causal status of the relationships is ambiguous if we incorporate current leadership approval ratings into the equation, so in order to avoid that problem we use lagged versions of all three measures as predictors of Liberal Democrat voting. In this way, support for rival leaders influences the Liberal Democrat vote, rather than the other way round. In addition to measuring the effects of leader popularity on voting support, we include dummy variables for David Steel, Paddy Ashdown, and Charles Kennedy.[5] The estimates from these variables will indicate if one of these leaders was more or less popular than their predecessors or successors.

In addition to party and leadership variables, we include issue measures in relation to the state of the economy. These measures are of two types. Firstly, there are indicators of the objective state of the economy such as unemployment, inflation, and interest rates. These may or may not be perceived as being important by the electorate. Secondly, we include a measure of the subjective economy, personal economic expectations, which captures the extent to which electors feel optimistic or pessimistic about their own economic prospects for the future. Finally, we include a dummy variable, which measures 1 in the month of a general election and zero otherwise. This captures the idea that the Liberal Democrats get a boost to their support during an election campaign because of all the extra

---

[4] If the causal sequence is the reverse of that specified in the model, or alternatively there is two-way causation between the variables, the model is subject to bias and the estimates are unreliable. This is referred to as the endogeneity problem in econometric textbooks (see Greene 2003, ch. 15 for a full discussion).

[5] A dummy variable scores 1 when each of these leaders was in office and 0 otherwise.

publicity they receive. This works directly, in the sense that their policy proposals are discussed in the media, but it also works indirectly, in the sense that their leaders are given more prominence during the election campaign.

The estimates of the Liberal Democrat voting model appears in Table 7.2, which contains unstandardized regression coefficients, together with *t*-statistics and some diagnostic tests. The full model appears in the left-hand column and the best model in the right. The latter has the non-significant variables omitted in order to provide more efficient estimates of the effects. In the case of the full model, it can be seen that current Liberal Democrat voting intentions are, not surprisingly, strongly influenced by lagged Liberal Democrat voting intentions, with the coefficient of 0.60 measuring the speed of adjustment of the series to an exogenous or unexpected shock.[6] The goodness of fit of the model (R^2) is very high and it passes two diagnostic tests reported in the table. There is no significant serial correlation in the model residuals as the chi-squared test indicates, and secondly, the test for functional form suggests that the model is well

Table 7.2. Time series models of Liberal Democrat voting intentions, 1974–2001

Dependent variable: Liberal Democrat voting intentions Predictors				
Liberal Democrat vote intention (lagged)	0.60***	(6.6)	0.60***	(7.0)
Conservative vote intention (lagged)	−0.26***	(2.8)	−0.29***	(3.7)
Labour vote intention (lagged)	−0.18**	(1.9)	−0.24***	(3.0)
Liberal Democrat leader approval (lagged)	0.03*	(1.8)	0.02*	(1.9)
Prime ministerial approval (lagged)	0.01	(0.7)	—	—
Opposition leader approval (lagged)	−0.01	(0.5)	—	—
Prospective economic evaluations	−0.01	(0.5)	—	—
Unemployment rate	0.39***	(2.9)	0.28***	(3.8)
Inflation rate	−0.02	(0.3)	—	—
Base interest rate	0.13*	(1.8)	—	—
David Steel incumbency	−0.76	(1.1)	—	—
Paddy Ashdown incumbency	−1.86*	(1.9)	−1.22***	(3.3)
Charles Kennedy incumbency	0.03	(1.2)	—	
Month of election	1.52*	(1.7)	1.40*	(1.6)
Incumbent Conservative government	−0.04	(0.1)	—	—
R^2	0.90		0.90	
Serial correlation chi-squared test	10.8		9.97	
Reset functional form test	1.43		0.78	

Note: t-statistics in parentheses; *$p < 0.10$; **$p < 0.05$; ***$p < 0.01$.

---

[6] Since $LD(t) = 0.60\ LD(t - 1)$, then $LD(t) = (0.60)(0.6)LD(t - 2)$, and so on, where $LD(t)$ is Liberal Democrat Voting Intentions at time t. After about four or five months the influence of past voting intentions on the current is negligible, so anything that affects current voting intentions will be 'forgotten' by then.

specified.[7] This means that the model is well-behaved and does not appear to have any statistical problems, which might distort the results.

If we examine the predictor variables in the model, we can see that Conservative and Labour vote intentions both have a significant impact on Liberal Democrat voting intentions. If the Conservative vote intentions series were to increase by about 5 per cent in a single month, this would reduce Liberal Democrat voting intentions by just under 1.5 per cent in the following month. A 5 per cent increase in Labour's voting intentions would produce a reduction in Liberal Democrat vote intentions by just under 1 per cent in the same period. This reinforces the earlier conclusion that competition between the Conservatives and Liberal Democrats is greater than competition between Labour and the Liberal Democrats. It is important to note, though, that the Liberal Democrats benefit from a reduction in both Labour and Conservative support. Both the major parties are rivals of the Liberal Democrats.

In addition to the party effects, an increase in the approval ratings of the Liberal Democrat leader by 5 per cent would increase Liberal Democrat voting intentions by about 0.15 per cent in the subsequent month. Thus, the leader has a clear impact on support for the party, but it is weaker than the impact of the Liberal Democrat's main rivals. It should be noted that while these leadership effects exist, the Liberal Democrat vote is not influenced by the popularity of the prime minister or leader of the opposition. Once support for Labour and the Conservatives is taken into account, their respective leaders have no additional influence on the Liberal Democrat vote. In addition, the estimates show that Paddy Ashdown experienced significantly lower levels of popularity when he was leader than did David Steel and Charles Kennedy.

Alongside the leadership effect, there is a surprising relationship between unemployment and Liberal Democrat voting intentions. If unemployment rose during the period, that increased support for the Liberal Democrats. This means that they benefited to some extent from the reward–punishment process discussed earlier. Intriguingly, there is no evidence of a similar effect associated with interest rates or inflation, and no evidence that economic optimism or pessimism had any influence on the vote. It appears that, historically, the objective economy has influenced Liberal Democrat support rather than the subjective economy. A good deal of this may have resulted from the politics of the Thatcher era, when unemployment mushroomed after 1980 at a time

---

[7] These issues are more fully discussed in Greene (2003).

when Labour was split and did not provide a credible alternative to the Conservatives.

The Liberal Democrats clearly receive a surge in support at election times. The estimates show that, on average, the party obtain about 1.5 per cent more support in the election month than at other times. This is consistent with the argument that media exposure associated with an election campaign benefits the party in the polls. A final point is that there is no evidence of the Liberal Democrats gaining or losing more ground during a Conservative administration than a Labour administration. Once the other factors are taken into account, Conservative incumbency has no impact on Liberal Democrat support. This finding does not contradict the earlier point that electoral competition between the Liberal Democrats and Conservatives is greater than competition between the party and Labour. What it does show is that, once we have taken into account the other variables in the model, particularly voting support for the Liberal Democrats' main rivals, the party receives no additional boost to its support from a Conservative government as opposed to a Labour government.

Figure 7.6 shows the relationship between actual Liberal Democrat voting intentions and voting intentions predicted by the best model in Table 7.2. It can be seen that the two series track each other very closely, suggesting that the model is very successful in accounting for variations in Liberal Democrat support over this period of twenty-five years. The results of Table 7.2 indicate how reliant the party is on the electoral fortunes of both Labour and the Conservatives. Changes in support for these parties will feed through to the Liberal Democrats fairly quickly and in predictable ways. But trade-offs exist in this process. If Labour were to lose 5 per cent of its support and the Conservatives gain 5 per cent in a given month, the Liberal Democrats would lose votes as a consequence. If, on the other hand, the Conservatives were to lose 5 per cent and Labour gain 5 per cent, the Liberal Democrats would gain votes. This is because changes in Conservative support have a bigger impact on the Liberal Democrat vote than changes in Labour support. But this is not the whole story, since it is clear that the Liberal Democrat leader can make a difference to their voting support as well. At the same time, it is also true that different Liberal Democrat party leaders have had a different impact on the party's fortunes over time.

Given that the predictor variables in the Liberal Democrat voting models are lagged, we know that the causal sequence runs from Conservative and Labour voting to Liberal Democrat voting. But it is interesting

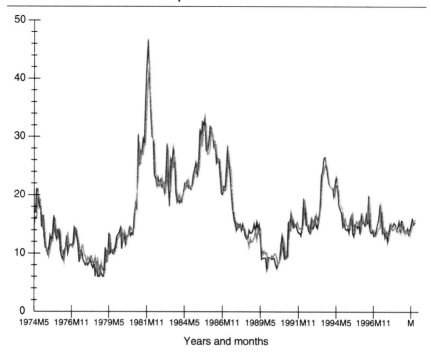

Figure 7.6 Actual Liberal Democrat support and predicted support from the best model

to explore this issue further in order to establish if changes in the Liberal Democrat vote intentions have any subsequent impact on Conservative and Labour vote intentions. If they do, the causal relationships between voting support for the three major parties would be interactive, with three-way links operating between all of them. We will pursue this issue in Section 7.5.

7.5 Causality and the Liberal Democrat Vote

In the best model of Table 7.2, we avoided the distortions of two-way causation by means of lags, but it is still possible that the current Liberal Democrat support has an impact on future Conservative and Labour vote intentions, not to mention the Liberal Democrat leadership approval ratings. We can address this issue with the help of a Granger causality test, a method for untangling causality in time series analysis developed by economists (see Granger 1990). Granger causality is defined as follows:

A variable x is said to Granger-cause y if prediction of the current values of y is enhanced by using past values of x. (Kennedy 2003: 74)

This idea can be tested in the following way. Firstly, we determine if past values of x have an influence on y, while at the same time taking into account the past values of y. This was done in Table 7.2, where one of the x variables, for example, was voting intentions for Labour. At the same time, the past values of Liberal Democrat vote intentions were included in the model to control for the past history of y. So Table 7.2 confirms that Liberal Democrat leadership evaluations and support for the other major parties have an impact on Liberal Democrat support. But does this work in reverse? Do past Liberal Democrat voting intentions influence contemporary leadership evaluations or contemporary support for Labour and the Conservatives? This is tested in Table 7.3.

It is clear from Table 7.3 that support for Labour, the Conservatives, and Liberal Democrat leadership evaluations are not influenced by past Liberal Democrat voting intentions. This means that Conservative and Labour voting support, together with Liberal Democrat leaders' approval ratings, Granger-cause Liberal Democrat voting support. The causal process runs one way only and there is no evidence of feedback at work. This is an important finding, since it suggests that Liberal Democrat support feeds off, but does not directly influence, support for Labour and the Conservatives. Similarly, the Liberal Democrat leader influences voting support for the party, but again the process does not work the other way round. The clear conclusion is that if the party is to build its electoral base in the future, it will have to rely on a loss of support for its rivals. Put another way, a necessary condition for the Liberal Democrats to build their electoral support is for the electorate to become disillusioned with one or both

Table 7.3. Tests of two-way causation in the Liberal Democrat voting models

Predictors	Conservative vote intentions	Labour vote intentions	Liberal Democrat leadership approval
Conservative vote intentions (lagged)	0.95*** (58.4)		
Labour vote intentions (lagged)		0.92*** (48.5)	
Liberal Democrat leadership approval (lagged)			0.92*** (37.8)
Liberal Democrat vote intentions (lagged)	0.01 (0.4)	−0.01 (0.6)	0.01 (0.2)
R^2	0.90	0.87	0.86
Serial correlation chi-squared test	17.7	21.8*	14.1
Reset functional form test	3.78*	0.17	3.47*

Note: t-statistics in parentheses; * $p < 0.10$; ** $p < 0.05$; *** $p < 0.01$.

of the other parties. The party cannot climb out of its third-party status by its own actions or policies.

We suggested earlier that the gap between the Conservatives and Liberal Democrats in Figure 7.3 had narrowed, and that this implies a more competitive situation between these parties than exists between Labour and the Liberal Democrats. The evidence in Tables 7.2 and 7.3 shows how this process works. The Conservatives lose support, which the Liberal Democrats then gain along with Labour, something which occurred particularly during the 1990s. It does not work by the Liberal Democrats gaining popularity for some outside reason, which subsequently attracts Conservative voters. A similar point can be made about Labour. In the early 1980s, the Liberal Democrats had to wait for a split in the party to occur in order to reap electoral rewards. They did not promote some new policy initiative or leadership change, which subsequently had the effect of attracting large numbers of Labour voters.

These are important findings, since they imply that the party is to a significant extent waiting for the other parties to make mistakes before it can profit by winning over the voters. This is a political version of 'waiting for Godot', and it means that to an important extent, the Liberal Democrats are not the masters of their own fate. In the following sections, we examine a more detailed model of Liberal Democrat support using data from the 2001 and 2005 British Election Studies. We shall see if these findings and those of Chapter 6 are confirmed at the individual level. We begin by looking at the 2001 election, and then we replicate the model in 2005 to investigate what changes occurred between these two elections.

7.6 Liberal Democrat Voting Support in 2001

The models in Table 7.2 are interesting, but they are limited. There are a number of additional factors that might influence the Liberal Democrat vote, which need to be taken into account. The lack of key measures made this impossible, so the models had to be simple. In addition, aggregate trends do not throw light on the question of why some individuals choose to vote for the Liberal Democrats when others do not. The well-known ecological fallacy (Robinson 1950) suggests that aggregate-level findings may not mirror individual-level relationships. This means, for example, that although prime ministerial approval did not appear to influence the Liberal Democrat vote at the aggregate level, we cannot infer from this finding that Tony Blair had no influence over individual Liberal Democrat voters in 2001 or 2005. The aggregate-level analysis highlights the average outcome of individual-level processes, and we can find many voters who do not behave in the same way as the average.

The British Election Study of 2001 carried out an analysis of the determinants of voting behaviour for all the major parties in that election (see Clarke et al. 2004). The study was able to evaluate the impact of a number of measures, such as partisan attachments, on the Liberal Democrat vote. These could not be assessed in the time series models because of a lack of data. As a consequence, a detailed analysis of individual voting behaviour throws light on a number of questions, which are neglected in the time series analysis. One such question is whether or not the party obtains electoral benefits for the specific issue positions it adopts. In the election study survey, respondents were asked to indicate the issue that was most important to them, and at the same time to say which party best handled this issue. These questions make it possible to determine the extent to which Liberal Democrat voting support was issue-based. If we select the respondents who said that the Liberal Democrats were best at handling the issue that these respondents said was most important to them, the range of issues they were most concerned about in 2001 appears in Table 7.4. The responses are quite varied, with education topping the list, closely followed by the NHS. Relationships with the EU were also prominent, as were the economy and taxation. Clearly, issues matter to Liberal Democrat supporters.

Another neglected question relates to the role of ideology in influencing the vote. The party has always sought to place itself in the centre ground of British politics, and one influential line of academic research associated with the work of Downs (1957) suggests that voters will support parties at

Table 7.4. The range of issues that respondents thought the Liberal Democrats handled best in 2001

Issue	Percentages
UK membership of EMU or relationships with the EU	13
Law and order	4
Education	25
The economy	7
The National Health Service	22
Taxation	5
The environment	2
Other	22

Note: The table contains percentages of those respondents who thought that the Liberal Democrats handled their most important issue best. The data come from the 2001 pre/post-election panel survey. $N = 2,303$.

157

the centre of the left-right ideological spectrum. Actually, in Downs' interpretation, voters support the party they think is closest to their own position on some contested issue dimension. But since most voters are to be found in the centre, this means that centre parties have an advantage in a two-party system. In a three-party system, things are more complex, since in this case, a centre party can be squeezed between its rivals. To assess the impact of this type of spatial voting, we need to determine if distances between the Liberal Democrats and voters on a salient issue do indeed influence the Liberal Democrat vote. A third issue, which can be probed more fully at the individual level, is the impact of partisan attachments on the vote. Partisans are electors who think of themselves as regular supporters of one or other of the major parties. They are different from independents, who are often referred to as 'floating' voters, and who are more likely to switch between parties in successive elections. It is important to assess the electoral impact of such partisan attachments, both in relation to the Liberal Democrats and also in relation to their main rivals.

A fourth issue concerns the party leader, who, as we have already seen, has an important causal influence on electoral support for the party. The interesting questions are to know how big this influence was in 2001 and how it affected individual voters. Again, though it appears that rival leaders had no influence on the Liberal Democrat vote at the aggregate level over a twenty-five year period, it is important to determine if this is true at the individual level in 2001. Finally, we observed in Chapter 6 that Liberal Democrat campaigning had a significant influence on their vote in 1997. Clearly, it is interesting to assess the effect of campaigning in another election and at the individual level, while taking into account the other factors referred to above. The 2001 election study makes it possible to measure campaign effects using a different methodological approach to that of Chapter 6. The study contained questions about voters' perceptions of local party campaigns. Thus, it is possible to assess the extent to which campaigns were directly perceived by the voters, and to estimate if they had an influence on Liberal Democrat electoral support.

7.7 Estimating the Liberal Democrat Voting Model in 2001

The Liberal Democrats won just over 18 per cent of the popular vote in the 2001 general election. The British Election Study post-election survey found that just over 19 per cent of its respondents claimed to be Liberal Democrat voters, which is well within any margin of error due to sampling. Thus, the Election Study survey is a reliable guide to Liberal Democrat voting. We can use it to develop a predictive model for explaining why some voters were Liberal Democrats. The study was a panel survey, in which electors were interviewed prior to the campaign and then again after polling day. To avoid the problems of two-way causation discussed earlier, we use the pre-election measures to predict the post-election voting behaviour. The single exception to this is in relation to the campaign measures, which for obvious reasons need to be evaluated after the election is over. Thus, the data come from the British Election Study 2001 pre-post election panel survey, which contained just over 2,300 respondents.

As the earlier discussion indicated, partisan attachments are quite likely to be important influences on the vote. Respondents were asked: 'Generally speaking, do you think of yourself as Labour, Conservative, Liberal Democrat, or what?' This identifies partisans for each party, and in the pre-election survey, some 36 per cent of respondents identified with Labour, 19 per cent with the Conservatives, and 7 per cent with the Liberal Democrats. Clearly, the party has many fewer partisan supporters than its main rivals. The impact of the party leaders can be assessed by means of a set of thermometer scales. These are questions that asked respondents to indicate the extent to which they liked or disliked the leaders using an 11-point scale varying from 0 to 10. These measure were designed to capture the leadership heuristic referred to earlier. Respondents who strongly disliked a leader would give him a score of 0, and those who strongly liked him a score of 10. Needless to say, most people gave the leaders intermediate scores. The average scores were 5.0 for Charles Kennedy, 5.3 for Tony Blair, and 3.9 for William Hague. So the Liberal Democrat leader was considerably more popular than the Conservative leader, and slightly less popular than the prime minister.

The importance of issues was assessed in a variety of ways. One has already been referred to, namely the most important issue perceived by respondents. Another is the economy, and to assess this respondents were asked: 'How do you think the financial situation of your household will change over the next twelve months?' Replies varied from 'get a lot worse' to 'get a lot better' on a 5-point scale, which incorporated the neutral category 'stay the same'. The expectation is that economic optimism on the part of respondents will tend to reduce support for the Liberal Democrats and increase support for Labour, and economic pessimism will have the reverse effect. A third issue, also mentioned earlier, which is particularly identified with the Liberal Democrats, is Britain's relationship to the EU, particularly the question of entry into the European single currency.

Respondents were invited to opt for various alternatives, from a list that included 'join as soon as possible' to 'rule out in principle'. A dummy variable was created in which respondents who chose the first of these options were coded one, and all others were coded zero. This was then used as a predictor variable in the model. The expectation is that an individual's support for UK membership of the single currency will tend to boost their support for the Liberal Democrats. Finally, in relation to issues, the survey contained a series of questions about the government's performance in handling the public services as well as various other policy concerns. A preliminary analysis of these questions showed that respondents tended to group evaluations of public service performance together. These services included education, the NHS, and transport. This analysis produced a 'public services evaluations' scale, which was used as a predictor in the Liberal Democrat Voting model.[8] The expectation is that discontent with the government's handling of these issues should help the Liberal Democrats to win votes.

As regards the important issue of taxation, respondents were asked to locate themselves on an 11-point 'taxation versus spending' scale, while at the same time locating all of the political parties on the same scale. If individuals placed themselves at the 0 point, it would mean that they strongly supported cuts in both spending and taxation. If, on the other hand, they placed themselves at 10 it would mean that they strongly supported increases in both taxation and spending. The average position for voters was 6.5 and the average position for the Liberal Democrats was 6.1. In fact, the Liberal Democrats were closer to the average respondent than either of the other two parties, since Labour was placed at 5.9 and the Conservatives at 4.8. The absolute distance between the voter's position and the position he or she assigned to the Liberal Democrats is used as a predictor in the model. The expectation is that respondents who place themselves close to the Liberal Democrats are more likely to vote for the party than respondents who place themselves a long distance away.

In relation to campaigning, in the post-election survey respondents were asked to indicate if they had seen a party political broadcast, been canvassed, or had been reminded to vote on polling day by a party. These measures of campaigning were evaluated separately for all three parties, and were aggregated into party campaign scales. These scales were then

---

[8] This was a factor analysis and the dominant factor that explained most variance related to evaluations of the public services. The factor scores from this analysis are used in the Liberal Democrat vote model.

used to predict Liberal Democrat voting.[9] Given the analysis in Chapter 6, an additional indicator was incorporated into the model, namely, whether or not the respondent lived in a Liberal Democrat target constituency. These were defined as constituencies in which the Liberal Democrats either came first or second in the 1997 general election, and so they were assumed to be areas where the party might be expected to put in extra effort to campaign.

Finally, voters were asked if they 'really preferred' another party to the one they voted for in the election. This was an indicator of tactical voting, and the best estimate was that about 14 per cent of respondents voted tactically in the 2001 general election (see Clarke et al. 2004: 83). The analysis in the British Election Study volume *Political Choice in Britain* indicates that tactical voting greatly helped the Liberal Democrats (Clarke et al. 2004: 116), so this is included in the model.

The logistic regression estimates of the Liberal Democrat voting models appear in Table 7.5.[10] There are three versions of the model, and the first one includes all of the indicators described above. Thus, the model takes into account the respondents' partisanship, their evaluations of the party leaders, their issue perceptions, their social characteristics, and their perceptions of the campaigns. In this model, the Conservative, Labour, and Liberal Democrat partisanship variables are all statistically significant predictors of Liberal Democrat voting with the correct signs. Similarly, evaluations of Charles Kennedy, Tony Blair, and William Hague are also significant predictors. The coefficients suggest that, not surprisingly, the strongest effects were associated with Liberal Democrat partisanship and evaluations of Charles Kennedy. However, Conservative partisanship had a stronger negative effect on Liberal Democrat voting than Labour partisanship, and evaluations of William Hague had a slightly stronger effect than evaluations of Tony Blair. Thus, the strong competition for votes between the Liberal Democrats and Conservatives is partly explained by partisanship and leader evaluations. A rather surprising finding in the model is that none of the issue measures are significant predictors of Liberal Democrat support, with the sole exception of the most important issue indicator. The respondents' views about the economy, about the government's handling of public services, and about UK membership of

---

[9] The summary scale is simply the number of times respondents were exposed to these activities calculated for each party.

[10] This model uses a dummy dependent variable and therefore is estimated by means of a logistic regression. A full discussion of this type of model can be found in Pampel (2000).

Table 7.5. Logistic regression models of Liberal Democrat voting in 2001
Dependent variable: Liberal Democrat voter in the 2001 ($N = 2,303$)

Predictors						
Liberal Democrat prior vote	—		—		2.49***	(10.0)
Liberal Democrat partisanship	2.24***	(8.1)	2.26***	(8.2)	1.29***	(4.2)
Conservative partisanship	−0.65**	(2.5)	−0.61**	(2.4)	−0.55**	(2.2)
Labour partisanship	−0.45**	(2.0)	−0.45**	(2.0)	−0.50**	(2.3)
Evaluations of Charles Kennedy	0.23***	(4.4)	0.24***	(4.6)	0.17***	(3.2)
Evaluations of Tony Blair	−0.07*	(1.8)	−0.08**	(2.2)	—	—
Evaluations of William Hague	−0.08***	(2.2)	−0.09**	(2.4)	—	—
Liberal Democrats can best handle respondent's most important issue	1.05***	(2.9)	1.13***	(3.2)	0.99***	(2.7)
Personal economic expectations	0.01	(0.2)	—	—	—	—
Britain should definitely join EMU	0.15	(0.5)	—	—	—	—
Closeness to LibDems on the taxation versus spending scale	0.06	(1.3)	—	—	—	—
Evaluations of government handling of public services	−0.05	(0.5)	—	—	—	—
Liberal Democrat local campaigning	0.59***	(3.5)	0.57***	(3.4)	0.49***	(3.1)
Labour local campaigning	−0.33**	(2.0)	−0.32**	(1.9)	—	—
Conservative local campaigning	−0.44***	(2.7)	−0.42***	(2.6)	−0.67***	(4.1)
Respondent tactical voter	1.10***	(5.4)	1.08***	(5.4)	1.17***	(5.7)
Liberal Democrat target seat	1.05***	(4.5)	1.07***	(4.6)	1.17***	(4.8)
Social class	−0.01	(0.2)	—	—	—	—
Ethnicity	0.15	(0.4)	—	—	—	—
Gender	0.01	(0.0)	—	—	—	—
Age	−0.01**	(2.1)	−0.01**	(2.1)	−0.01**	(2.1)
Education	0.46**	(2.5)	0.50***	(3.0)	0.41**	(2.3)
Pseudo R^2	0.31		0.31		0.37	
Percentage classified correctly	87		87		88	

Note: t-statistics in parentheses; *$p < 0.10$; **$p < 0.05$; ***$p < 0.01$.

the European Monetary Union played no role in influencing their decision to vote Liberal Democrat, once their most important issue was taken into account. Clearly, for some people the economy is the most important issue, but as Table 7.4 shows, this is far from being true for everyone.

The campaigning variables are very important predictors in the model, which confirms the analysis of Chapter 6. Exposure to Liberal Democrat campaigning increases, and exposure to Labour and Conservative campaigning decreases, the probability that a respondent will vote Liberal Democrat. Again, the effect associated with the Conservative campaign is a little stronger than the effect associated with the Labour campaign. Not surprisingly, the effect associated with Liberal Democrat campaign is strongest of all. In addition, if the individual is a tactical voter or lives in a Liberal Democrat target constituency, the probability of voting Liberal Democrat is considerably higher than elsewhere. Again, these variables measure campaign effects. Finally, there are two demographic variables that influence the Liberal Democrat vote. These are age and education, with older voters being rather less likely to vote Liberal Democrat, and the educated being rather more likely to vote for the party, other things being equal. It is also apparent that social class, gender, and ethnicity played no role at all in influencing the Liberal Democrat vote, once all the other variables are taken into account.

The second model in Table 7.5 excludes all the non-significant variables from the first model and provides more efficient estimates of the effects. When this is done, it is clear that Liberal Democrat voting behaviour is largely explained by three factors. The first is partisanship, the second is leadership evaluations, and the third is local campaigning. In addition, the most important issue indicator has a very small effect in the model, and the controls for age and education remain significant. The third model adds a lagged Liberal Democrat voting intentions measure to the equation of the best model. This takes advantage of the panel design to assess the effects of the variables in the best model on the changes in support for the Liberal Democrats between the start of the campaign and polling day. In effect, it allows us to determine which variables influenced the Liberal Democrat vote during the election campaign itself. The results are very interesting, and show that evaluations of the Labour and Conservative party leaders had no influence on voting intentions, which is consistent with the finding in the time series models in Table 7.2. It is important, however, to emphasize what this model means. It does not mean that Tony Blair or William Hague had no influence on the Liberal Democrat vote. Rather, it implies that they had no influence beyond the start of the election campaign. Thus, any influence they might have had on Liberal Democrat voters was already in place at the start of the campaign.

The estimates in the third model also show that Labour's local campaigning had no influence on the Liberal Democrat vote, although the vote was influenced significantly by the Conservative campaign, The latter had about the same impact as the Liberal Democrat campaign, but in the opposite direction. It is also clear that targeting paid off for the Liberal Democrats during the campaign, as did tactical voting. All the other important effects in the second model in Table 7.5 also appear in this model, but generally they are weaker in their impact. In the light of these findings, we examine the evidence for the 2005 general election in Section 7.8, to see if the same basic model applied then.

7.8 Estimating the Liberal Democrat Voting Model in 2005

The 2005 election provides an opportunity to replicate the 2001 model to see what changed between the two elections. If the basic model is sound, the 2005 estimation should produce very similar results, when it was replicated using the British Election Study Rolling Campaign Panel Survey.[11] Altogether 24.9 per cent of the survey respondents who voted in 2005 claimed to have supported Liberal Democrats, which is quite close to the 22.7 per cent vote share that the party took in Britain as a whole. So the survey is a good guide to Liberal Democrat voting behaviour. Compared with the 2001 model, the 2005 model was revised in one key respect. Russell and Fieldhouse (2005) make the plausible claim that the Liberal Democrat vote is boosted significantly by the perception that the party can win in a given constituency. They write:

Perhaps the main strategic problem for a third party in a simple plurality system is the wasted vote syndrome. Only by establishing electoral credibility (demonstrating the ability to win locally and preferably nationally) can a third party hope to increase its representation. (Russell and Fieldhouse 2005: 201)

By means of an analysis of aggregate voting data in 2001, they infer that the probability of the Liberal Democrat winning is a key variable in influencing the vote for the party. However, a decisive test of this hypothesis requires individual level data. The 2005 British Election Internet panel study contained a question that asked people to indicate the probabilities that each of the three parties could win in their constituency. The responses to this question for the Liberal Democrats appear in Figure 7.7, which shows the percentages of voters who assign a particular value out of ten that the Liberal Democrats will win in their constituency.

The average score on the 11-point scale in Figure 7.7 was 3.1, which compares with mean scores of 5.5 and 4.4 on the Labour and Conservatives scales respectively. Altogether about 21 per cent of respondents gave the Liberal Democrats a probability of winning score larger than the midpoint value of 5. Clearly, if the probability that the party can win influences the vote, we should expect to see this measure having a significant positive impact on the Liberal Democrat vote.

Table 7.6 contains the logistic regression estimates of the Liberal Democrat vote model updated to the 2005 general election. The variables in this model were designed to replicate the 2001 model as closely as possible.

---

[11] The details of this survey, together with the data that can be downloaded, can be found on http://www.essex.ac.uk/bes.

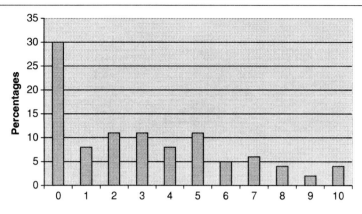

Figure 7.7 Perceptions of the probability that the Liberal Democrats can win in the respondent's constituency in 2005
Question: On a scale that runs from 0 to 10, where 0 means very unlikely and 10 means very likely, how likely is it that the Liberal Democrats will win the election in your constituency?
Source: BES Rolling Campaign Panel Survey (2005); $N = 6,117$

The first model replicates the 2001 election model exactly, and it can be seen that the estimates are very similar to those in Table 7.5. Partisanship and leadership are all significant predictors of Liberal Democrat voting support with the correct signs. The test statistics are larger in this table than they were in the earlier one, mainly because the sample size was roughly three times larger than in 2001.

In one important respect, the 2005 model does differ from the earlier one, in that the issue variables had a statistically significant impact on the probability of voting Liberal Democrat. If respondents were optimistic about their own economic prospects, they were less likely to vote Liberal Democrat (and more likely to vote Labour) as a consequence. If they felt that Britain should definitely join the European Monetary Union, they were more likely to vote Liberal Democrat. Finally, if they were close to the party on the taxation versus spending scale, then, again, they were more likely to vote for it. The only issue measures that had no effect on Liberal Democrat voting were evaluations of the government's handling of public services. In relation to the campaigning variables, Liberal Democrat campaigning continued to have a positive impact of support, except that in 2005 voting was not influenced by Conservative or Labour campaigning. On the other hand, tactical voting and the target seat effect observed in Table 7.5 continued to be important.

Table 7.6. Logistic regression models of Liberal Democrat voting in 2005
Dependent variable: Liberal Democrat voter in 2005. ($N = 6{,}117$)

Predictors						
Liberal Democrat prior vote	—		—		1.53^{***}	(13.7)
Liberal Democrat partisanship	1.03^{***}	(8.6)	1.01^{***}	(8.1)	0.38^{**}	(2.8)
Conservative partisanship	-1.25^{***}	(7.3)	-1.15^{***}	(6.6)	-1.06^{***}	(5.9)
Labour partisanship	-0.44^{***}	(3.7)	-0.44^{***}	(3.5)	-0.46^{***}	(3.7)
Evaluations of Charles Kennedy	0.21^{***}	(9.8)	0.20^{***}	(8.9)	0.15^{***}	(6.7)
Evaluations of Tony Blair	-0.12^{***}	(6.2)	-0.12^{***}	(6.1)	-0.11^{***}	(6.3)
Evaluations of Michael Howard	-0.11^{***}	(5.8)	-0.12^{***}	(6.1)	-0.09^{***}	(4.6)
Liberal Democrats can best handle respondent's most important issue	0.75^{***}	(6.2)	0.70^{***}	(5.6)	0.39^{***}	(3.0)
Personal economic expectations	-0.11^{**}	(2.3)	-0.11^{**}	(2.2)	-0.12^{**}	(2.4)
Britain should definitely join EMU	0.29^{**}	(2.4)	0.32^{***}	(2.6)	0.26^{**}	(2.0)
Closeness to LibDems on the taxation versus spending scale	-0.16^{***}	(5.9)	-0.16^{***}	(5.7)	-0.11^{***}	(4.0)
Evaluations of government handling of public services	0.10	(1.6)	0.10	(1.6)	—	—
Liberal Democrat local campaigning	0.75^{***}	(7.0)	0.73^{***}	(6.6)	0.88^{***}	(10.9)
Labour local campaigning	0.03	(0.3)	0.05	(0.5)	—	—
Conservative local campaigning	0.09	(0.9)	0.08	(0.8)	—	—
Respondent tactical voter	0.42^{***}	(3.9)	0.38^{**}	(2.5)	0.36^{***}	(3.2)
Liberal Democrat target seat	0.71^{***}	(6.5)	0.31^{**}	(2.5)	0.32^{***}	(2.5)
Probability of Liberal Democrats winning the seat	—	—	0.11^{***}	(6.6)	0.09^{***}	(5.3)
Social class	0.02	(1.3)	0.02	(1.3)	—	—
Ethnicity	0.40^{*}	(1.7)	0.31	(1.3)	—	—
Gender	0.03	(0.4)	0.07	(0.8)	—	—
Age	-0.00	(0.5)	0.00	(0.0)	—	—
Education	0.13^{**}	(4.0)	0.13^{***}	(3.9)	0.13^{**}	(4.3)
Pseudo R^2	0.30		0.31		0.34	
Percentage classified correctly	86		85		86	

Note: t-statistics in parentheses; $^{*}p < 0.10$; $^{**}p < 0.05$; $^{***}p < 0.01$.

The second model in Table 7.6 contains the probability of winning scale from Figure 7.7, and it has a highly positive effect on Liberal Democrat voting. This supports the argument of Russell and Fieldhouse (2005) that individuals can be persuaded to vote for the party if they think that it has a chance of winning in their constituency. This effect works independently of all the other factors that influence the Liberal Democrat vote. As Table 7.1 showed, the party came second in fifteen Conservative marginals and ten Labour marginals in 2005, so this perception should boost its chances of winning these seats in any future general election. The third model contains the lagged Liberal Democrat vote variable, which again allows us to measure the impact of the predictors during the election campaign. It can be seen that all of the variables that are significant predictors of voting in the second model continue to be significant in the third model. So all the predictors were relevant in explaining changes in the Liberal Democrat vote during the general election campaign itself.

The coefficients in Tables 7.5 and 7.6 are rather hard to read since they are based on the log odds ratio of voting Liberal Democrat. Figure 7.8 contains estimates of the impact of each of the predictors in the second model of Table 7.6 on the probability of voting Liberal Democrat.[12] We can

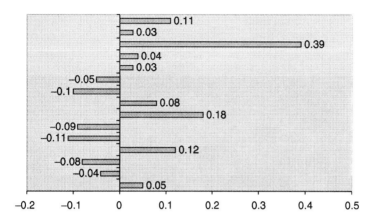

From top to bottom, the variables are:

Perception that the Liberal Democrats can win in the respondent's constituency (0.11)
The constituency is a Liberal Democrat target seat (0.03)
The impact of Liberal Democrat local campaigning (0.39)
If the respondent is a tactical voter (0.04)
If the respondent definitely wants Britain to join the euro (0.03)
Perceptions of personal prosperity (–0.05)
Distance from the Liberal Democrats on the taxation versus spending scale (–0.10)
Perceptions that the party is best at handling the respondent's most important issue (0.08)
Evaluations of Charles Kennedy (0.18)
Evaluations of Michael Howard (–0.09)
Evaluations of Tony Blair (–0.11)
Liberal Democrat partisanship (0.12)
Conservative partisanship (–0.08)
Labour partisanship (–0.04)
Education (0.05)

Figure 7.8 The effects of variables in the best model on the probability of voting Liberal Democrat, 2005

[12] The probabilities were estimated using the Clarify programme obtained from Gary King's website at Harvard University. They are calculated by holding all of the predictor variables at their mean values while changing the variable of interest from its minimum to its maximum, and observing the impact of this on the probability of voting Liberal Democrat. See Tomz, Wittenberg, and King (2001).

see that Liberal Democrat local campaigning was easily the most important variable in influencing the vote in 2005. Following this, evaluations of
Charles Kennedy and Liberal Democrat partisanship were the second and
third most important variables respectively. Other variables in the model
all had modest, but significant, impacts on the Liberal Democrat vote.

7.9 Conclusions

This analysis of the Liberal Democrats' electoral support has several implications for the party's future electoral strategy. A first implication is that
the party needs to build a stronger base of party identifiers. It has suffered
in the past from having a relatively weakly attached set of voters, who,
because they lack strong identification with the party, are willing to desert
it in a subsequent election. Party identification provides an electoral bal-
last, and the party needs to consider ways in which it can create and foster
such loyalties among voters in the future. The evidence suggests that
partisan attachments are weakening generally throughout the electorate,
so all of the parties have a problem in this respect. It may be in the future
that the Liberal Democrats will have less of a disadvantage in relation to
this issue in comparison with their main rivals.

A second implication follows from the finding that the party generally
does well when its policies and leaders are more prominently displayed in
the public's mind. This naturally occurs at election times, but if the party
were able to attract more publicity and attention in the period between
elections, it could win more support. In other words, the party may not be
presenting itself very effectively in between election campaigns. This is a
difficult task because it relies on the media. But media strategy may be
something the party needs to review to try to make it more effective than
at present.

A third implication is that the party cannot afford to have an unpopular
leader. We saw earlier that William Hague was much less liked than Tony
Blair or Charles Kennedy at the time of the 2001 general election. After
they lost office in 1997, the Conservatives went on to appoint two unpopular leaders in a row. William Hague resigned immediately after the
1997 election, and was followed as leader by Iain Duncan Smith and
subsequently Michael Howard, both of whom were relatively unpopular.
These Conservative leaders helped the Liberal Democrats to win votes,
and if in the future, the party were to make the same mistake as the
Conservatives, it would suffer badly as a consequence. This means that

Liberal Democrat members, when they are selecting a new leader, have to pay close attention to the electoral attractiveness of rival candidates. They cannot afford the luxury of selecting a leader who might be popular with the rank-and-file members, but unpopular with the voters.

A fourth implication is that the party needs to do everything possible to foster an active grassroots campaigning organization, since targeted local campaigns are much more important to the Liberal Democrats than they are to the Conservatives and to Labour. As we have seen, the party pioneered a community politics form of electioneering, and this strategy was successful in building active local organizations and also in winning local elections. Ultimately, this community politics strategy really paid off in 1997, when the party won a number of Westminster seats in areas where it already had established strong roots in local government. The importance of local campaigning is highlighted in Figure 7.8, and so in the future, the grassroots activists are going to be crucial to the task of building electoral support. For this reason, the party needs a strategy for developing the grassroots membership.

The Liberal Democrats may have an advantage in being out of power for so long, since it is clear that incumbency tends to damage the grassroots of its major rivals. During the long period of Conservative ascendancy in British politics in the 1980s and 1990s, the grassroots Conservative Party suffered badly from declining activism and from an ageing membership (Whiteley, Seyd, and Richardson 1994). A similar point can be made about the Labour Party after 1997 (Seyd and Whiteley 2002; Whiteley and Seyd 2002). This comes about because governing parties tend to neglect their grassroots organizations and take them for granted. We will consider this issue more fully in Chapter 8.

Having examined the sources of electoral support in this chapter and in Chapter 6, we look to the future in the next and final chapter. The major question to be addressed here is: Can the Liberal Democrats break through the present barriers they face to become the second, or even the first, party of electoral politics in Britain?

8
Conclusions

8.1 Introduction

By many accounts, the Liberal Party should have been dead and buried decades ago. It suffered major internal party splits during and after the First World War, it was ill-equipped to deal with the depression years of the 1920s, and it was undermined by class conflicts that emerged in the inter-war years. By the 1950s, the Liberal Party was a mere parliamentary rump, and the British electoral system deals harshly with minor parties. Yet it refused to die, and along with its social democratic allies, it has emerged phoenix-like from the ashes to become a major force in contemporary British politics. We have argued in this book that the party's survival and rebirth is primarily the result of the commitments of very dedicated people over several generations. It is the Liberal grassroots that has nourished the party back to life again.

One hundred and five years after the last Liberal government was elected, is it possible that a Liberal Democrat government could be elected to office? How does it become the second, or even the first, party of electoral politics? What are the circumstances under which this might happen? This is the principle concern of this concluding chapter. We begin with an analysis of the necessary conditions for the Liberal Democrats to replace one of the other parties as the second party of British politics. This leads into an examination of the likelihood that these conditions will be met in the foreseeable future. In fact, the evidence suggests that the party has a real opportunity to break the existing two-party hegemony at a general election in 2009 or 2010, and we discuss this fully. Finally, we think about some broad conclusions that emerge from this analysis.

We have shown that grassroots campaigning plays a particularly important role in explaining the electoral performance of the Liberal Democrats, and that the party activists are a key factor in accounting for the party's growing success at the polls. However, it is important to remember that the party is still a long way from power. Figure 7.1 showed that the party's vote shares and seat shares have been increasing at each successive election since 1992, but with sixty-two seats won in the 2005 election, the party still has a long way to go to replace the Conservatives as the second party of British politics. For reasons discussed earlier, the party faces an even bigger task in replacing Labour. Moreover, it is possible that the task of improving the party's electoral performance may become more difficult in the future.

Figure 6.1 showed how the Liberal Democrats were able to concentrate campaign resources in order to maximize the impact of their campaigning in general elections. Similarly, Figure 7.8 showed how important local campaigning is in influencing the Liberal Democrat vote in general elections. But as the party begins to defend more seats, while at the same time seeking to win new ones, campaign resources will become more thinly spread on the ground. The earlier analysis suggested that the party is largely unable to move people around the country in order to target particular constituencies, except in the case of by-elections. Instead, active local parties have been created by the hard work of a few party members who have gradually and painstakingly built up the local organization. In the past, this has been done by raising local issues, working on campaigns in the community, and winning seats in local government elections. In the right circumstances, such as in the 1997 general election, these resources can then be used as a springboard to winning parliamentary seats. If the campaigning effort becomes diluted, this will get harder to do in the future. Of course, this development can be prevented if the party recruits many new members, but the evidence in Table 2.19 suggests that activism in the grassroots party is declining, rather than increasing. Similarly, the 2005 British Election Study survey suggests that Liberal Democrat membership fell by about 6 per cent between then and 2001.[1] In this respect, the party has the same problem as its major rivals in recruiting and retaining members. The implication of Table 2.19 is that Liberal Democrat electoral progress may very well be stalled if the party has to rely on new activists to win additional seats. While building the activist base must be part of any electoral strategy, it is unlikely to be enough to bring the breakthrough to make the party a real contender for power.

---

[1] The number of Liberal Democrat party members is small in the election study surveys, and so this figure should be interpreted with care.

8.2 Moving Up from Third Place

In the three successive elections between 1997 and 2005, the Liberal Democrats won an average of fourteen extra seats per election. At that rate of increase, it would take the party nineteen general elections or approximately seventy-five years to win a majority in the House of Commons. This, of course, assumes that the progress in winning seats does not stall, when there is a real possibility that it might do so for the reasons mentioned earlier. Clearly, the party is not going to break through the present barriers and become the second party of electoral politics by merely continuing its present rate of progress.

Insight into to the size of the task awaiting the Liberal Democrats can be gained from the history of the early twentieth century, when Labour became the second party. We mentioned in Chapter 1 that the some writers viewed the 'strange death of Liberal England' as something occurring mainly prior to the First World War, as a consequence of the rise of class politics, but the evidence to support this thesis is weak. In the last general election before the war in December 1910, the Liberals captured 44 per cent of the vote and 272 seats in the House of Commons (Butler and Butler 1994: 214). In the so-called 'coupon' election of 1918, the Asquith Liberals took 28 seats, and the coalition Liberals led by Lloyd-George took a further 133 seats. The two factions had a combined share of 26 per cent of the vote. In contrast, Labour captured forty-two seats with a 7 per cent share of the vote in 1910, and sixty-three seats with a 22 per cent share in 1918.[2] By a curious historical accident, Labour was in the same electoral position after the First World War as the Liberal Democrats were after the 2005 general election. With a combined total of 161 seats in 1918, the Liberal Party, though split, was far from being dead. More to the point, it was still in second place with near to three times as many seats as Labour.

The crucial problem for the party was that the coalition Liberals, like Addison, Shortt, Fisher, and of course, Lloyd-George, attached more importance to remaining in the coalition government dominated by the Conservatives than they did to preserving their party. After such a devastating war, the country faced immense problems of reconstruction. The Liberal Party had been in power during the war years, and just as Churchill reaped the consequences of being in power during an equally

---

[2] There were a further ten coalition Labour party members in 1918 who took 1.5 per cent of the vote (see Butler and Butler 1994: 214).

traumatic war in the 1945 election, the Liberal Party experienced great losses in the 1918 election. However, unlike the Conservative Party, which went into opposition in 1945 and was able to rethink its policies and reform the organization before winning again in 1951, the coalition Liberals clung on to power. The new cabinet contained eight Liberals, including Lloyd-George, who continued as prime minister, although the most senior posts in the cabinet were in Conservative hands (Cook 1998: 77–90).

This was a pre-Keynesian era, and in response to the recommendations of the ultra-orthodox Geddes report, the government rapidly started to dismantle the social policies put in place by the pre-war Liberal government, in pursuit of a balanced budget. As soon became apparent, these policies helped to reinforce a post-war slump and by 1921 unemployment exceeded 1 million and remained above that level until 1939 (Butler and Butler 1994: 377). The new government also embarked on a policy of repression in Ireland, carried out with great brutality by the 'Black and Tans', despite the protests of coalition Liberal ministers like Addison and Shortt. These ministers fought hard in cabinet for more moderate policies but were overruled. In retrospect, it is easy to see that what happened was a failure of valence politics. A government that had already been damaged by the 1918 election and that faced huge post-war problems failed to deliver on the key issues which mattered to the electorate. These were a prosperous economy, effective public services, supportive welfare policies, and internal peace and security.

The electoral consequences of the failure rapidly became apparent as the coalition Liberals began to lose by-elections to Labour. As Cook (1998: 79) writes: 'With each by-election disaster, dreary reports came in of the lack of any Coalition Liberal organisation.' Lloyd-George's faction was a top-down affair, which had emerged from the crises of the First World War with more MPs than its rival, but it had attracted few grassroots Liberal party activists. The need for an effective local party organization was particularly pressing at the time, because large numbers of newly enfranchised voters had been added to the electoral rolls. The electorate of 1910 was just short of 8 million people, whereas the electorate of 1918 was more than 21 million people (Butler and Butler 1994). Winning these first-time voters required effective local party organizations, which the coalition Liberals lacked. The upshot of all this was that the coalition Liberals lost more than half their seats in the 1922 election, compared with only nine losses by the Asquith Liberals, who had retained their local party organizations. In that election, Labour eclipsed the combined Liberal factions in terms of its vote shares and in the number of seats in the House of Commons. The split in the Liberal Party was not healed until much later and it never again regained its position as the second party of electoral politics.

It was not the rise of class politics that explained Labour's success; rather, it was the split in the Liberal Party and the coalition Liberals' decision to cling on to power in a failing government. They were in the invidious position of having responsibility without much power, and since Lloyd-George was prime minister throughout this whole period, they reaped the electoral consequences for the failures of that government. Admittedly, the momentous events of the First World War provided the background to the split in the first place, since war on that scale puts a tremendous strain on any political system. But the way in which the leaders responded to these strains was crucial in explaining why the party went into decline.

There is no such thing as alternative history, but it is reasonable to conclude that the party could have avoided this fate if these events had been handled differently. Firstly, if the Asquith–Lloyd-George split had been healed quickly after the end of the war, this would have greatly helped the party's recovery. A reunited party would have been much more effective in campaigning than a divided party. Secondly, if the coalition Liberals had withdrawn from the government and gone into opposition after the 1918 election, or once it became apparent that the government was failing to handle the emerging crisis, this would have helped too. Churchill's defeat in 1945 gave the Conservatives time to recover and rethink their policies, whereas the Liberal administration continued to cling on to power despite the losses in 1918. A mass resignation by Liberal ministers would have very likely precipitated a general election in which the party could have opposed budget cuts and repressive policies in Ireland. In that event, it is likely that the party would have retained its second place, and eventually recovered to win again after a suitable period in opposition. Certainly, a later election in which the party campaigned on the policies advocated by the two great liberal thinkers of the twentieth century, Keynes and Beveridge, could have put it in power for years, as the Democratic Party's New Deal in the United States demonstrated.

The relevance of all this for contemporary politics is clear. The Liberal Democrats can achieve an electoral breakthrough if two conditions are met. Firstly, either the Labour or Conservative Party should split, ideally the latter, given the competitive situation in constituency electoral politics.

Secondly, the single-member plurality electoral system for Westminster elections should be replaced by a more proportional system. The importance of a split in a rival party can be seen in relation to the earlier discussion of the coalition government in the First World War. But it is also apparent from the evidence of Chapter 6, which showed how the Alliance came very close to replacing Labour as the second party of electoral politics in 1983.

It is possible that a large enough split in a rival party will deliver the prize of second-place status to the Liberal Democrats without electoral reform, but it is unlikely. Such a split would have to be on the scale of 1916, and it would have to last for years for it to deliver this result. It is worth remembering that when Labour split in 1981, and the Alliance parties took 25 per cent of the vote in the1983 election, they nonetheless won only twenty-three seats. On a pure proportional system, in which the vote shares are translated exactly into seat shares, Labour would have obtained 228 seats, the Conservatives 209 seats, and the Liberal Democrats 143 seats in the 2005 general election. The latter would still have ended up in third place, but in a much better position to take advantage of a split in a rival party than from the base of the sixty-two seats they actually won. Thus, the combination of electoral reform and a split in a rival party would deliver the breakthrough to put the Liberal Democrats in second place.

There is, of course, another possibility, which is that electoral reform takes place and neither of the rival parties split. In that event, the Liberal Democrats are quite likely to end up in a coalition government, so it may not matter if they become the second or first party of British politics if their goal is merely to share power. In the general election of 2005, for example, a pure proportional system would have very likely produced a Lib-Lab coalition government similar to the one in Scotland after devolution. So if one reduces the party's ambitions to that of sharing power in a coalition, electoral reform is the only change that really matters. In fact, such a reform is likely to transform the party system in any case. Supporters of minor parties such as the Greens and the UK Independence Party, who are currently deterred from voting for them by the wasted vote argument, are very likely to vote for them under a proportional representation system. It is even possible that electoral reform could trigger a split in the Conservative or Labour party, as factions within these parties see better prospects for themselves outside the big tent of the present party system. This suggests that electoral reform may be a more important condition than a split in a rival party, if the Liberal Democrats are to achieve second-party status. If electoral reform appears to be the key, what are the conditions under which it might occur? And more specifically, what is the likelihood of this occurring as a result of a general election in 2009/10? We consider these questions next.

8.3   The Prospects for Electoral Reform

It may be recalled that Labour included a pledge to hold a referendum on electoral reform in its 1997 manifesto. The party had been opposed to reform for many years, but during the long years of opposition, it began to change its mind. In 1990, Neil Kinnock established a working party to consider the issue, under the chairmanship of Raymond Plant, Professor of Politics at the University of Southampton. After the 1992 election, and in response to the report of the Plant commission, the new leader, John Smith, adopted the policy of holding a national referendum on the issue (Stuart 2005: 295). After winning power in 1997, the party then set up the Jenkins Commission to investigate alternative electoral systems, and this recommended a specific system for Westminster elections (TSO 1998). The report described its preferred alternative in the following terms:

The Commission's central recommendation is that the best alternative for Britain to the existing First Past The Post system is a two-vote mixed system which can be described as either limited AMS or AV Top-up. The majority of MPs (80 to 85%) would continue to be elected on an individual constituency basis, with the remainder elected on a corrective Top-up basis which would significantly reduce the disproportionality and the geographical divisiveness which are inherent in FPTP. (http://www.archive.official-documents.co.uk/document/cm40/4090/chap-9.htm)

As is well known, the recommendations of the Jenkins Commission were never implemented and Labour lost interest in the issue, notably after winning a second landslide victory in 2001.

There is what might be described as the 'paradox of electoral reform' to be overcome before the electoral system can be changed. This is the fact that the majority party in the House of Commons has to back electoral reform in order to get it through, but since that party has won an election on the existing system, it has a strong incentive not to do so. This means that electoral reform is unlikely to be implemented by a majority government in Britain, because it involves asking MPs in the majority party to vote for a system that jeopardizes their own seats. There is, however, one scenario in which electoral reform could become a real possibility. This is a general election, which produces a 'hung Parliament', or no party with an overall majority. In this situation, the largest party may have to negotiate with one of its rivals, most likely the Liberal Democrats, in order to achieve a coalition government. In this case, the Liberal Democrats can insist on electoral reform as the price of participating in the coalition.

Alternatively, the largest party might try to govern with only a minority of seats, while challenging its opponents to vote it out of office. The relevance of either scenario depends on the likelihood of a hung Parliament occurring as a result of a general election in 2009 or 2010. In either case, the Liberal Democrats could be the arbiter of electoral reform. In the first scenario, they would have to insist on electoral reform as the non-negotiable price of cooperation. This means that a commitment to reform would have to be in the Queen's speech of the new Parliament. If they wavered on this condition, or accepted some type of vague commitment, they would lose a historic opportunity to bring about reform. In the second scenario, where the largest party tried to govern on its own, the Liberal Democrats would need to be able to threaten it with a rival coalition. As a result, the largest party would either have to concede electoral reform or go into opposition. To make this credible, the Liberal Democrats would have to pursue a policy of 'equidistance' between Labour and the Conservatives. This was their traditional stance until Paddy Ashdown changed it to a policy of favouring Labour in the run-up to the 1997 general election.

It may, of course, be argued that these scenarios are unrealistic, since neither of the two major parties are currently committed to electoral reform. Labour is committed to holding a referendum, but in practice will do nothing about it as long as it has a majority, and the Conservatives are opposed in principle. But the prospect of power, most obviously for the Conservatives who, by 2010, will have been out of office for thirteen years, provides a powerful incentive to agree to reform. But all of this is irrelevant if the prospects for a hung Parliament at the next general election are remote. So the crucial issue is how likely is it that a hung Parliament will occur after the next general election in 2009/10? We consider this issue next.

8.4 What are the Chances of a Hung Parliament after the next Election?

In the 2005 general election, Labour captured 356 seats, the Conservatives 197, the Liberal Democrats 62, and other parties 30, giving Labour an overall majority of 66. Between 2001 and 2005, the Labour share of the vote fell by 5.4 per cent, the Conservatives rose by 0.6 per cent, and the Liberal Democrats increased by 3.8 per cent. It is possible to simulate the outcome of the next general election in 2009 or 2010 in terms of the number of seats captured by different parties, by making various assumptions about how the party vote shares change over time.[3] If this is done it turns out that a hung Parliament is quite likely to happen at the next election. This makes the earlier discussion about Liberal Democrat tactics in the case of a hung Parliament highly relevant.

To see why this is the case, recall that a party must capture at least 324 seats in the House of Commons if it is to win an overall majority. We begin the simulations by assuming that the minor parties such as the Nationalists and the Ulster parties win a total of thirty seats in such an election, the same number that they won in 2005. Figure 8.1 shows how the number of seats captured by Labour, the Conservatives, and the Liberal Democrats change in response to various uniform swings across the country from Labour to the Conservatives. Figure 8.1 assumes that there is no swing from Labour to the Liberal Democrats, which is not realistic, but it facilitates seeing the electoral consequences of a straight fight between Labour and the Conservatives.[4] If either Labour or the Conservatives fall below the horizontal line of 324 seats in the Figure, they do not have an overall majority in the House of Commons. Figure 8.1 shows that if the swings from Labour to the Conservatives range from about 2 per cent to just under 8 per cent, neither of these parties will have a majority. Considering that the average swing between the two parties was 3.8 per cent in the seventeen general elections between 1945 and 2005, this is quite likely to happen. Thus, a hung Parliament will result from a wide range of plausible swings from Labour to the Conservatives.

It is interesting to see the consequences of a straight fight between Labour and the Liberal Democrats. This is done in Figure 8.2, which repeats the earlier analysis, but this time looks at uniform swings from Labour to the Liberal Democrats, assuming no overall swing from Labour to the Conservatives. In this scenario, Labour loses its overall majority

---

[3] The simulations were done using the British Parliamentary Constituency Database, 1992–2005, compiled by Pippa Norris. The data can be downloaded from Pippa_Norris@Harvard.edu.

[4] The uniform swing or 'Butler swing' is calculated from the following formula:

$$[|Con\ 09 - Con\ 05| + |Lab\ 09 - Lab\ 05|]/2$$

where Con 09 and Lab 09 are the percentages of the vote obtained by the Conservatives and Labour in a hypothetical election in 2009. Con 05 and Lab 05 are the percentages of the vote obtained by the parties in the 2005 election.

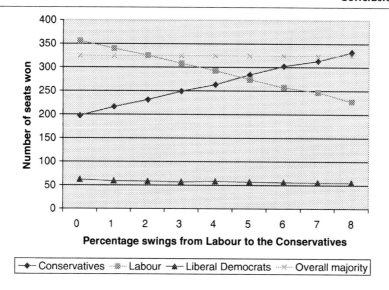

Figure 8.1 Simulated outcomes of elections with uniform swings from Labour to the Conservatives

if the swing to the Liberal Democrats is about 3.5 per cent. The average swing between the two parties was 3.9 per cent in the seventeen elections from 1945 to 2005, and to repeat an earlier point, the swing from Labour to the Liberal Democrats in 2005 was actually 4.6 per cent. So, once again, a hung Parliament will result from a wide range of plausible swings from Labour to the Liberal Democrats.

The assumption of a swing between only two of the three major parties is unrealistic. It is much more likely that swings from Labour to the other two parties will be shared between them in varying proportions. It is interesting to see what would happen if any swings from Labour are shared equally between both parties; for example, if Labour lost 2 per cent of its vote, and the Conservatives and Liberal Democrats picked up 1 per cent each. The results of this simulation appear in Figure 8.3, and they show that when this happens Labour loses its overall majority with a swing of just over 3 per cent to the other two parties. One interesting feature of Figure 8.3 is that the Conservatives do not obtain an overall majority in the range of swings depicted. This is because the Liberal Democrats share Labour's misfortune, and this prevents the Conservatives from winning enough seats to form a majority. Again, the lesson of this simulation is that a hung Parliament is quite likely to occur.

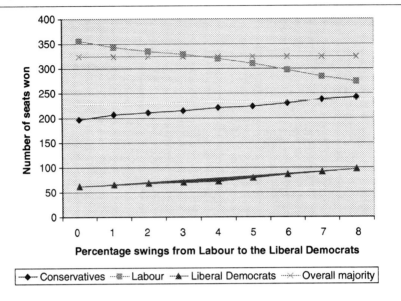

Figure 8.2 Simulated outcomes of elections with uniform swings from Labour to the Liberal Democrats

It is well known that electors who defect from Labour generally find it easier to switch to the Liberal Democrats than they do to the Conservatives (see Clarke et al. 2004). This means that the assumption that a swing from Labour will be shared equally between the Conservatives and the Liberal Democrats is unrealistic. The swing from Labour to the Liberal Democrats in 2005 (4.6 per cent) was larger than the swing from Labour to the Conservatives (3.0 per cent). So, in a final simulation, we assume that the two parties share the swing from Labour in the same proportions as they did in 2005. Roughly speaking, the Liberal Democrats took about two-thirds of the combined swing in that election, leaving the Conservatives to pick up the remaining third. This simulation appears in Figure 8.4, and it looks rather like that in Figure 8.3. Again, Labour loses its majority with a swing to the other two parties of about 3 per cent, and the Conservatives do not gain an overall majority in the range of values considered. In fact, the shared swing from Labour to the other two parties has to be around 12.5 per cent before the Conservatives get an overall majority. This makes the chances of a hung Parliament rather greater than in the earlier simulations.

There is one important qualification to make to this analysis. The 2009/10 general election will be fought on new constituency boundaries. The

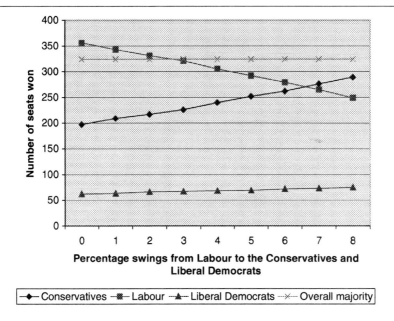

Figure 8.3 Simulated outcomes of elections with equal swings from Labour to the Conservatives and Liberal Democrats

revisions in the boundaries will almost certainly work to the disadvantage of Labour, since the latter had a big advantage in 2005. Labour-held constituencies had significantly fewer electors than Conservative- or Liberal Democrat-held constituencies, making it easier to elect a Labour MP.[5] The boundary revisions are designed to reduce this advantage, making it more difficult for Labour to retain its majority as a consequence. From the point of view of the simulations, this has the effect of making Labour lose its overall majority with smaller swings than those depicted in the Figures. This makes a hung Parliament more likely with a small swing against Labour, although at the same time, it will help the Conservatives to win an overall majority with a smaller swing. In effect, the points at which both parties cross the overall majority line shift to the left. However, and this is the important point, the boundary revisions are unlikely to change the fact that a wide range of plausible swings will give rise to a hung Parliament at the next election.

[5] The average electorate in Labour-retained seats in 2005 was 66,857, and the average electorates for Conservative seats was 72,956 and for Liberal Democrat seats 69,431.

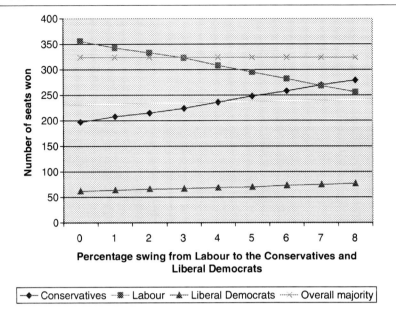

Figure 8.4 Simulated outcomes of elections with the same swing shares from Labour to the Conservatives and Liberal Democrats as in 2005

The implications of this analysis are clear. The Liberal Democrats should prepare themselves to be the pivotal party after the next general election. If a hung Parliament does happen, it is likely that both Labour and the Conservatives will try to entice them into a coalition without conceding cast-iron guarantees of electoral reform. If the party were to go along with this, it would be throwing away an opportunity to push through electoral reform, which might not recur for a generation. Once the Liberal Democrats have unlocked the present electoral system, they can start to exert significant influence over government, in a way they have not been able to do since the First World War.

Electoral reform will not necessarily make the Liberal Democrats the second party of British politics, but it will shake up the whole British party system. If a small party can win representation in the House of Commons without having to overcome the formidable barrier of the First-Past-The-Post electoral system, it gives incentives to factions inside the major parties to consider breaking away. In these circumstances, one can imagine many possibilities, for example, the emergence of a socialist party along the lines of the Scottish Socialist Party. This might involve a breakaway group of Labour MPs. Another possibility is that a right-wing populist party emerges, along the lines of the National Front in France, which could take MPs from the Conservatives. There are numerous possibilities that would allow the Liberal Democrats to really boost their electoral prospects.

8.5 Conclusions

The evidence in this book suggests that the Liberal Democrats can gain a strategic advantage over their rivals by fostering and promoting grassroots activism. The decline in the voters' attachments to the major parties in Britain is one of the best established trends in British politics (Sarlvik and Crewe 1983; Clarke et al. 2004). It means that the voters can be persuaded to desert their traditional allegiances more easily, and this is likely to work to the advantage of the Liberal Democrats for a number of reasons.

Firstly, when party loyalties weaken, it gives more scope for a more localist and candidate-centred electoral politics that fits well with the tradition of community politics, now long established in the grassroots party. Secondly, as the earlier analysis shows, grassroots campaigning plays a particularly important role in explaining Liberal Democrat electoral success. Local campaigning is likely to have a bigger impact on voting behaviour in a world of weak partisanship than one in which most people are strongly attached to the major parties. So current developments in British party politics favour the campaign style of the Liberal Democrats.

In addition, the party will obtain an advantage because its rivals have gone much further down the road towards the 'electoral professional' model of party organization than the Liberal Democrats (Panebianco 1988). The electoral professional model sees political parties as being hierarchical organizations dominated by leaders in which full-time professional communicators control the agenda. In this situation, leaders dominate followers, and the party members are there basically to obey orders from the top, much as in an army. Such a structure has evolved in response to the needs of the continuous election campaign, which is now such a feature of modern politics. The continuous election campaign is based on the principles of advertising, and it reduces policies to sound bites, which are repeated endlessly in order to have maximum effect. Policies themselves are the product of market research and focus groups, and do not generally emerge from a democratic debate within the party organization. The task assigned to the party members in this model is to act as cheerleaders, and to sell policies decided by the leadership to the wider electorate. Since this model is highly inimical, both to deliberation and to democracy, and the members lack any sense of ownership of the policies, not surprisingly, it undermines grassroots activism. Essentially it shuts down 'voice' or deliberation, and as a consequence produces 'exit' as members leave the party (see Hirschman 1970).

The Liberal Democrats have escaped the worst aspects of this model for a number of reasons. The fact that they have been out of power for a long time means that the leadership has less of a need to try to control the media agenda by staying 'on message'. Parties in power tend to neglect their grassroots, in part because their leaders are very preoccupied with the task of governing. But this also happens because such leaders are the focus of relentless lobbying by special interests, many of who have louder voices and deeper pockets than the grassroots members of their own parties. The members are increasingly seen by leaders as just another special interest that has to be managed, rather than an asset that has to be nurtured. The Liberal Democrats have the advantage of not being in power and therefore of not falling into this 'winner's curse' of electoral politics. Equally, so much of modern government is about presentation, and the demands of governing often conflict with those of democracy. Non-governmental parties in general are freer to debate their differences in public, without the media interpreting these as splits and faction fighting. In contrast, debate in governing parties is often interpreted as division and weakness and therefore an indicator of a lack of ability to govern.

Secondly, the Liberal Democrats have a decentralized structure reflecting the party's long-standing federalist organization. This structure inhibits the growth of top-down control of the type common in New Labour and in the Conservative Party. The latter has always had a strong top-down culture and New Labour acquired it during the modernization process starting in the 1980s and culminating in Tony Blair's leadership of a reinvented party. As the pathologies of such a culture become apparent over time, producing falling party membership and declining support, the two major parties may try to reinvent themselves again. The Liberal Democrats start with the advantage of having a strong ethos of community politics, which inhibits these developments in the first place.

Thirdly, the Liberal Democrats rely more on their grassroots members than do the other parties. The members play more of a role in funding the party, and as the evidence in this book demonstrates, they are crucial in explaining the party's electoral successes. This makes the party leadership more aware of the value of the members as a key asset, which needs sustaining rather than ignoring.

If the analysis in this book is correct, the Liberal Democrats may be poised to take a major leap forward towards achieving political power in their own right, something which has eluded them since the early part of the twentieth century. They have an opportunity to unlock the British party system, and to place themselves in the driving seat in a way that has not been seen for nearly a century. It will, however, require astute leadership, which has both a sense of long-term strategy and also the ability to manoeuvre tactically in order to take advantage of new opportunities. Time will tell if this comes about.

THE METHODOLOGY OF THE LIBERAL DEMOCRAT MEMBERSHIP SURVEY

The Questionnaire

A draft questionnaire was initially produced in September 1998. The questionnaire repeated questions from previous surveys of Labour and Conservative party members (see Seyd and Whiteley 1992, 2004; Whiteley, Seyd, and Richardson 1994); and added questions from other surveys, including an earlier survey of Liberal Democrat members (Bennie, Curtice, and Rudig 1996), the 1997 British Election Study survey (Heath, Jowell, and Curtice 2001) and the 'World Values Study' survey (Inglehart 1997). In addition, some entirely new questions were added covering key issues relevant specifically to the Liberal Democrats, such as community politics and relationships with the Labour party. In October 1998, the questionnaire was piloted with the help of local Liberal Democrat party members from Sheffield Hillsborough and Hallam constituencies. As a result of the piloting process, minor adjustments were made to the wording and layout of the questionnaire.

Sampling

In order to provide a comparison with data derived from the survey of Labour party members conducted in 1997 (Seyd and Whiteley, 2002), the same 200 constituencies in Great Britain were again used in the Liberal Democrat survey. These were a random sample of constituencies in England, Wales, and Scotland, stratified by region. In addition, 34 extra constituencies were added in order to cover all the Liberal Democrat held seats at that time. The sampling frame was the list of party members held in Liberal Democrat party headquarters in Cowley Street in London. In order to achieve a target number of cases of 5,000, a 1-in-5 sample was randomly selected from this list of members in these 234 seats. This sampling exercise provided a total list of 7,640 members, the larger number of cases being selected to allow for non-response.

Mailing Details

The survey was conducted by mail in the following stages:

1. From November 1998, 7,640 introductory letters were sent to the complete sample informing them of the survey and asking them for their cooperation. An accompanying letter from Chris Rennard, the campaigns director of the party, was enclosed asking members for their cooperation with the survey. This initial mailing revealed a total of 50 members who were no longer reachable, since they had moved away from their previous addresses, left the party or had died.
2. In December 1998, 7,590 questionnaires were sent out, along with a covering explanatory letter and a pre-paid reply envelope.
3. In February 1999, 4,010 reminder letters were sent to non-respondents.
4. In April 1999, 3,564 second reminder letters were sent out to non-respondents with second copy of the questionnaire and a pre-paid reply envelope.
5. In May 1999, 2,454 third reminder letters were sent out to non-respondents.

Response Rates

At the final count, 4,442 completed questionnaires were received, constituting a response rate of 58 per cent. In order to ascertain whether the completed questionnaires represented a biased sample of the membership, a non-respondent telephone survey was undertaken. 300 members were randomly selected from all those who had failed to respond to any of the original survey mailings. This sub-sample of individuals were then asked to respond to a short set of questions covering the date they had joined party, their strength of party identification, and their employment status, together with their age and gender. No significant differences emerged between respondents and non-respondents from this exercise, suggesting that the sample was not biased by non-response.

Analysis

All statistical analysis was carried out in SPSS, except for the logistic regression models in Chapter 7, which were analysed using STATA. All the analysis in this book was done using data from 200 constituencies to ensure that this was a representative sample of Liberal Democrat constituency parties.

THE QUESTIONNAIRE

DEPARTMENT OF POLITICS
UNIVERSITY OF SHEFFIELD
NORTHUMBERLAND ROAD
SHEFFIELD
S10 2TU

SURVEY OF LIBERAL DEMOCRAT MEMBERS
1998/99

The aim of this survey is to understand more about the backgrounds, beliefs and activities of ordinary party members. The views of people like yourself may be ignored in political debate and our research will help to put this right. We are therefore sending this set of questions which we would ask you to answer. Please return the completed questionnaire to us in the enclosed postage paid envelope as soon as possible.

We obtained your details at random from a list of party members held by Liberal Democrat headquarters. Your individual anonymity is guaranteed by law and we can assure you that we will not pass on your individual replies to anyone else. The Liberal Democrat Party will receive our general conclusions based on an overall analysis of the replies. If you would like to receive feedback from this survey please mark the box on the last page.

The numbers below include an identification number for mailing purposes only. This is so that we can cross your name off the mailing list when your questionnaire is returned to us. Your name and address will never be placed on the questionnaire.

If you have any questions at all about the project, please feel free to ring Ms Janet Allaker on 0114 2221677 or email J.Allaker@Sheffield.ac.uk. The questionnaire should take roughly 45 minutes to complete.

Thank you in advance for your help

Professor Patrick Seyd Professor Paul Whiteley Ms Janet Allaker

OFFICE USE ONLY

JOINING THE PARTY

1. Would you call yourself a very strong, a fairly strong, a not very strong, or a not at all strong Liberal Democrat?

PLEASE FILL IN ONE BOX ONLY

Very strong

Fairly strong

Not very strong

Not at all strong

2a. Were you a member of the Liberal Party or the Social Democratic Party (SDP) before the 1988 merger?

Yes, I was a member of the Liberal Party

Yes, I was a member of the SDP

No

2b. In which year did you first join the Liberal Democrat/SDP/Liberal party?

PLEASE WRITE IN   1 9

3. Have you continuously been a member since that time?   Yes   No

4. People join the Liberal Democrat party for a variety of different reasons. How about you, what was your **MOST IMPORTANT REASON** for joining the Liberal Democrat party? was it:

PLEASE FILL IN ONE BOX ONLY

Paddy Ashdown's leadership

Liberal Democrat policies

Liberal Democrat principles

To oppose the Conservatives

To oppose Labour

To support moves towards PR/constitutional reform

For social reasons

To support the Liberal Democrat party

To be politically active in the party

The influence of your family and friends

You liked what the party was doing locally

To be better informed about politics

To have an influence on the party

Other (please specify)

OFFICE USE ONLY

OFFICE USE ONLY

5. How did you join?
PLEASE FILL IN ONE BOX ONLY

Through telephone or door to door canvassing ☐
In response to a party political broadcast ☐
In response to a national party advert ☐
In response to a local party newsletter/leaflet ☐
I phoned/wrote to the local party ☐
A member of my family persuaded me to join ☐
A friend persuaded me to join ☐
A colleague at work persuaded me to join ☐
I joined at a local meeting/stall/rally ☐
None of these ☐
Other (please specify) ☐

6. If you approached the local party when you first joined, did you find it easy or difficult to make contact with them?
PLEASE FILL IN ONE BOX ONLY

Very easy ☐
Easy ☐
Difficult ☐
Very difficult ☐

7. How do your experiences as a member so far relate to your initial expectations?
PLEASE FILL IN ONE BOX ONLY
Membership has:

Fully lived up to my expectations ☐
Partly lived up to my expectations ☐
Not really lived up to my expectations ☐
Not at all lived up to my expectations ☐

CONTACT WITH PARTY

8. What annual membership subscription do you pay to the party?
PLEASE FILL IN ONE BOX ONLY

Under £5 ☐
£5 up to £15 ☐
£15 up to £25 ☐
£25 plus ☐

9. What is your estimate of the TOTAL financial contribution which you made to the party in the last 12 months (including annual membership fee, contributions to local or national fund-raising initiatives, standing orders, etc)?

PLEASE WRITE IN THE AMOUNT   £

10. Thinking back over the LAST YEAR, how often have you had contact with people active in your local branch or constituency Liberal Democrat party?

PLEASE FILL IN ONE BOX ONLY

Not at all

Rarely

Occasionally

Frequently

11. Are you satisfied or dissatisfied with the level of contact from your local Liberal Democrat party?

PLEASE FILL IN ONE BOX ONLY

Very satisfied

Satisfied

Neither satisfied or dissatisfied

Dissatisfied

Very dissatisfied

12. Thinking back over the LAST YEAR, how often have you attended a LOCAL Liberal Democrat meeting (e.g. ward business meeting, constituency open meeting)?

PLEASE FILL IN ONE BOX ONLY

Not at all

Rarely (once or twice)

Occasionally (three to five times)

Frequently (more than five times)

13. If you attended AT LEAST ONE party meeting within the LAST YEAR, please indicate your reactions to it using the following scales. If, for example, you found the meeting very interesting, you would fill in the box on the left-hand side. If you found it very boring, you would fill in the box on the right-hand side. If you found it neither boring nor interesting, you would fill in the middle box.

If you attended more than one meeting, think about the LAST meeting you attended.

If you did not attend within the LAST YEAR, please go on to question 14.

PLEASE FILL IN ONE BOX FOR EACH DESCRIPTION

	very	fairly	neither	fairly	very	
Interesting						Boring
Unfriendly						Friendly
Efficiently						Badly run
United						Divided
Hard to understand						Easy to understand
Left wing						Right wing
Old fashioned						Modern

14. Have you received or seen any of the following in the last twelve months?

PLEASE FILL IN AS MANY AS APPLY

informed

Liberal Democrat News

A request for money from the Federal party

Telephone calls from the local or national party

Any other communication from a Federal, state or regional party

15. Would you say that the party (local or national) does enough to keep you informed about what is going on?

PLEASE FILL IN ONE BOX

The party does enough

The party does not do enough

ACTIVITIES IN THE PARTY

16. Do you at present hold any office(s) within the Liberal Democrat party?   Yes   No

17. If YES, at which level do you presently hold office within the party?

PLEASE FILL IN ALL BOXES THAT APPLY

Ward/Branch Level

Constituency Level

Regional Level

State Level

Federal Level

European Level

18. How active do you consider yourself to be in the Liberal Democrat party?

PLEASE FILL IN ONE BOX ONLY

Very active

Fairly active

Not very active

Not at all active

19. How much time do you devote to party activities in the average MONTH?

PLEASE FILL IN ONE BOX ONLY

None

Up to 5 hours

From 5 to 10 hours

From 10 to 20 hours

From 20 to 30 hours

From 30 to 40 hours

More than 40 hours

20. Next we would like to ask you about political activities you may have taken part in during the LAST FIVE YEARS. How often have you done the following?

PLEASE FILL IN ONE BOX FOR EACH ACTIVITY

	Not at all	Rarely	Occasionally	Frequently
Displayed an election poster in a window				
Signed a petition supported by the party				
Donated money to Liberal Democrat funds (other than paying a membership subscription)				
Helped with party fund-raising				
Helped organise a party street stall				
Delivered party leaflets *during* an election				
Delivered party leaflets *between* elections				
Helped at a party function (eg social event, jumble sale)				
Attended a party meeting				
Canvassed voters on behalf of the party door to door				
Canvassed voters on behalf of the party by telephone				
Stood for office within the party organisation				
Stood for elected office in a local or national election				

21. Are you more active or less active within the party than you were five years ago (or when you joined if less than 5 years ago), or about the same?

PLEASE FILL IN ONE BOX

More active

Less active

About the same

22. If you are MORE ACTIVE than five years ago (or when you joined if less than 5 years ago) please highlight the most important reason for this change. Was it:

PLEASE FILL IN ONE BOX ONLY

Because I am now an elected representative/officer of the party

Because of my increased opposition to the Tories

Because of my increased opposition to Labour

Because of having more time to spare

Because of a change in family circumstances

Because I have retired from work

Because of changes within the Party

Because of my increased awareness of political issues

In order to support my political career

Because of another reason, please specify

OFFICE USE
ONLY

23. If you are LESS ACTIVE than five years ago (or when you joined if less than 5 years ago) please highlight the most important reason for this change: was it?

PLEASE FILL IN ONE BOX ONLY

Because of a lack of spare time/pressure of other commitments

Because of a deterioration in my health

Because of a move of home

Because of a change in work circumstances

Because of my current disillusionment with politics

Due to my no longer being a party official

Due to my frustration at being unable to influence the party

Because of a change in family circumstances

Because of a lack of contact from the local party

Because of another reason, please specify

COMMUNITY POLITICS

24. Which of these geographical areas would you say you most identify with?

PLEASE FILL IN ONE BOX FOR EACH COLUMN   a) first of all?   b) and the next?

The locality or town where you live

The county or region where you live

The country (England, Scotland, Wales)

The U.K. as a whole

Europe

The world as a whole

25a. Some party members have been involved in local government election campaigns over the years. How about you?   Yes   No

25b. If YES, have you campaigned in a local authority other than where you live?   Yes   No

26a. Are you currently a local Liberal Democrat councillor?   Yes   No

26b. If not currently a councillor, have you ever fought a local election as Liberal Democrat candidate?   Yes   No

26c. In the last year have you been involved in other local campaigns? (eg planning issues, the environment, education etc).   Yes   No

26d. If YES, were any of these campaigns not associated with The Liberal Democrats?   Yes   No

27a. Have you been involved in parliamentary By-election campaigning?   Yes   No

27b. If YES, have you worked in a parliamentary By-election outside the constituency in which you live?   Yes   No

27c. In your opinion which is the most important, local politics or national politics, or are they equally important?

PLEASE FILL IN ONE BOX ONLY

Local politics is the most important

National politics is the most important

They are equally important

28. Please look carefully at the following list of voluntary organisations and highlight which you support, belong to, or currently do unpaid work for.

PLEASE FILL IN ALL THAT APPLY

	Support (but not a member)	Belong to	Do unpaid work for
Trade Unions			
Groups that help the elderly, disabled or disadvantaged people			
Religious or church organisations			
Education, arts, music or cultural groups			
Local community action groups on issues like poverty, employment, housing, racial equality			
Third world development or human rights groups			
Conservation, environmental, ecology groups			
Professional associations			
Youth work (e.g. scouts, guides, youth club, etc)			
Sports or recreation groups			
Women's groups			
Peace movement groups			
Animal rights groups			
Health related voluntary group			
Other groups			
None			

29. Thinking specifically about local groups (e.g. a local tenants group, community action group, women's group or charity) how many groups do you belong to?

PLEASE FILL IN ONE BOX ONLY

None   One   Two   Three   Four or more

OFFICE USE ONLY

30. Are you currently on any official bodies?
(e.g. school governor, health authority trust, magistrate)

Yes   No

If YES, please write in which one(s)

196

THE 1997 GENERAL ELECTION

31. Did you vote in 1997's General Election?   Yes ⸱⸱⸱ No ⸱⸱⸱

32a. During the election campaign some party members were involved in campaigning work for a constituency party other than their own. How about you? Did you work for another constituency party?   Yes ⸱⸱⸱ No ⸱⸱⸱

32b. If YES, were you asked or did you volunteer?   Asked ⸱⸱⸱ Volunteered ⸱⸱⸱

32c. If you did, which other constituency did you work for? (If more than one, write the constituency in which you did most work)

32d. Would you estimate the percentage of your time spent campaigning in another constituency other than your own.

PLEASE FILL IN ONE BOX ONLY

0% 10% 20% 30% 40% 50% 60% 70% 80% 90% 100%

33. Thinking about the 1997 General Election, we would like to ask you about your activities during the campaign. Did you:

PLEASE FILL IN ONE BOX FOR EACH ACTIVITY

	Yes	No
Display an election poster		
Donate money to party election funds		
Help run a party-election-day committee room		
Drive voters to the polling station		
Take numbers at the polling station		
Remind voters on polling day to vote		
Go to the counting of votes/party celebration		
Deliver polling day leaflets		

34. Again, thinking about the 1997 General Election, did you:

PLEASE FILL IN ONE BOX ONLY

	Not at all	Once	Twice	Three or more occasions
Telephone canvass voters on behalf of the party				
Canvass voters on behalf of the party door to door				
Help with party fund-raising events				
Deliver party leaflets				
Attend a party rally				
Help organise a party street stall				
Help with party mailings				
Help with telephone fund-raising for the party				

35. We would like to ask you how effective you think various election activities are in helping the Liberal Democrat party.

PLEASE FILL IN ONE BOX FOR EACH ACTIVITY

	Very effective	Effective	Not very effective	Not at all effective
Displaying an election poster in a window				
Delivering party leaflets				
Attending a party rally				
Canvassing voters door to door				
Canvassing voters by telephone				
Helping run a party election-day committee room				
Driving voters to the polling station				
Reminding voters on polling day to vote				
Helping with party mailings				

36. Thinking about the last year's General Election, please give your general impressions of the LIBERAL DEMOCRAT CAMPAIGN at national level, describing them using the following scales.

If, for example you think the campaign was very effective, you would fill in the box on the left-hand side. If you think it was very ineffective, you would fill in the box on the right-hand side. If you think it was neither effective nor ineffective you would fill in the middle box.

PLEASE FILL IN ONE BOX FOR EACH DESCRIPTION

	very	fairly	neither	fairly	very	
Effective						Ineffective
Efficiently run						Badly run
United						Divided
Uncaring						Caring
Principled						Unprincipled
Negative						Positive
Left wing						Right wing
Modern						Old fashioned

37. In your opinion, what was the single most important reason behind the success of the Liberal Democrat general election campaign?

OFFICE USE ONLY

---◇———◇———◇———◇———◇———◇———◇———

POLITICAL ATTITUDES

38. In Liberal Democrat party politics, people often talk about 'the left' and 'the right'. Compared with other Liberal Democrats, where would you place your views on this scale below?

PLEASE FILL IN ONE BOX ONLY

	1	2	3	4	5	6	7	8	9	
LEFT										RIGHT

39. And where would you place your views in relation to British politics as a whole (not just the Liberal Democrats)?

PLEASE FILL IN ONE BOX ONLY

	1	2	3	4	5	6	7	8	9	
LEFT										RIGHT

40. Next there is a set of statements about important political issues. We would like to know if you agree or disagree with them.

PLEASE FILL IN ONE BOX ONLY FOR EACH QUESTION

	Strongly agree	Agree	Neither	Disagree	Strongly disagree
It is better for Britain when trade unions have little power					
The Labour government should fine the parents of juvenile delinquents as a way of curbing youth crime					
The Liberal Democrat party should adjust its policies to capture the middle ground of politics					
Liberal Democrats should place less priority on achieving equal rights for women					
The government should give more aid to poor countries in Africa and Asia					
The Liberal Democrat party places more emphasis on its media image than it does on its principles					
Modern methods of farming have caused great damage to the countryside					
The production of goods and services is best left to the free market					
Individuals should take responsibility for providing for themselves					
Restrictions on immigration into Britain are too tight and should be eased					
Liberal Democrats should resist further moves to integrate the European Union					
Britain should agree to the introduction of a common European currency					
High income tax makes people less willing to work hard					
Income and wealth should be redistributed to ordinary working people					
Ordinary people should do more to protect the environment even if it means paying higher prices					

199

	Strongly agree	Agree	Neither	Disagree	Strongly disagree
Parliamentary constituencies should be clustered into groups of three with at least one female Liberal Democrat candidate in each group					
The reformed House of Lords should be a wholly elected chamber with no appointed members					
Child Benefit should not be taxed					
Compulsory second pensions are an infringement of Liberal Democrat principles					
Regional variations in the minimum wage are unfair and should be opposed					

41. Are you generally in favour of:

PLEASE FILL IN ONE BOX ONLY

More nationalisation of companies by government

More privatisation of companies by government

Or should things be left as they are now

42. Suppose the government had to choose between the following three options. Which do you think it should choose?

PLEASE FILL IN ONE BOX ONLY

Reduce taxes and spend less on health, education and social benefits

Keep taxes and spending on these services at the same level as now

Increase taxes and spend more on health, education and social benefits

43. Generally speaking, would you say that most people can be trusted or that you can't be too careful in dealing with people?

PLEASE FILL IN ONE BOX ONLY

Most people can be trusted

You can't be too careful with people

Don't know

44. Generally speaking, would you say that most politicians can be trusted or that you can't be too careful in dealing with politicians?

PLEASE FILL IN ONE BOX ONLY

Most politicians can be trusted

You can't be too careful with politicians

Don't know

45. Next there is a set of statements about important political issues. We would like to know if you agree or disagree with them.

PLEASE FILL IN ONE BOX ONLY FOR EACH STATEMENT

	Strongly agree	Agree	Neither	Disagree	Strongly disagree
Liberal Democrats should have maintained the policy of equidistance between Labour and the Conservatives					
Community politics should be much more important than national politics for Liberal Democrats					
The only time Liberal Democrat members hear from the party is when they want some money					
There is one law for the rich and one for the poor					
Young people today don't have enough respect for traditional British values					
Censorship of films and magazines is necessary to uphold moral standards					
There is no need for strong trade unions to protect employees' working conditions and wages					
Private enterprise is the best way to solve Britain's economic problems					
It is the government's responsibility to provide a job for everyone who wants one					
It is a good thing for schools to be made to compete against each other for pupils					
Liberal Democrats spend too much time discussing the distribution of wealth instead of wealth creation					

ATTITUDES TO THE LIBERAL DEMOCRAT PARTY

46. Please think about your general impressions of the LIBERAL DEMOCRAT PARTY, and describe them using the following scales.

If, for example, you think the party is very extreme, you would fill the box on the left-hand side. If you think it is very moderate, you would fill the box on the right-hand side. If you think it is neither moderate nor extreme, you would fill the middle box.

PLEASE FILL IN ONE BOX FOR EACH SCALE

	very	fairly	neither	fairly	very	
Extreme						Moderate
Efficiently run						Badly run
United						Divided
Good for one class						Good for all classes
Middle class						Working class
Left wing						Right wing

47. Please think about your general impressions of PADDY ASHDOWN, and describe them using the same type of scale

PLEASE FILL IN ONE BOX ONLY FOR EACH SCALE

	very	fairly	neither	fairly	very	
Not caring						Caring
Likeable as a person						Not likeable as a person
Decisive						Not decisive
Left wing						Right wing

48. For each of the following indicate which option best describes the LIBERAL DEMOCRAT party nowadays. A party that:

PLEASE FILL IN ONE BOX FOR EACH STATEMENT

Keeps its promises	OR,	breaks its promises
Is capable of being a strong government	OR,	is not capable of being a strong government
Stands up for Britain abroad	OR,	does not stand up for Britain abroad

49. And for each of the following which option best describes PADDY ASHDOWN

PLEASE FILL IN ONE BOX FOR EACH SCALE

Someone who sticks to his principles	OR,	someone who does not stick to his principles
Someone who keeps his promises	OR,	someone who breaks his promises
Someone who listens to reason	OR,	someone who does not listen to reason
Capable of being a strong leader	OR,	not capable of being a strong leader

50. If PADDY ASHDOWN was to step down as party leader who would you like to see elected as leader?   PLEASE WRITE IN

OFFICE USE ONLY

51. Next there are some statements about Liberal Democrat party politics. We would like to know if you agree or disagree with them.

PLEASE FILL IN ONE BOX FOR EACH STATEMENT

	Strongly agree	Agree	Neither	Disagree	Strongly disagree
The role of the party member is to support decisions made by the leadership					
Party members lack the knowledge necessary to make policy					
A problem with the Liberal Democrat party today is that the leader is too powerful					
The party conference should be the ultimate source of authority in the Liberal Democrat party					

ATTITUDES TO POLITICS

52. Next there are some more statements about politics in Britain. We would like to know if you agree or disagree with them.

PLEASE FILL IN ONE BOX FOR EACH STATEMENT

	Strongly agree	Agree	Neither	Disagree	Strongly disagree
It doesn't really matter which party is in power in the end things go much the same					
People like me can have a real influence in politics if they are prepared to get involved.					
Sometimes politics seems so complicated it is difficult for a person like me to understand what is going on.					
The party leadership doesn't pay a lot of attention to ordinary party members					
Parties in general are only interested in peoples' votes, not in their opinions					
Liberal Democrat party members are part of a great campaign of like-minded people who work together in solidarity.					
Many people find party meetings rather boring					
A person like me could do a good job of being a local Liberal Democrat Councillor					

	Strongly agree	Agree	Neither	Disagree	Strongly disagree
The people who are most active in the Liberal Democrat party are the ones who have most say in deciding party policy					
The only way to be really educated about politics is to be a party activist.					
The Liberal Democrats would be more successful if more people like me were elected to parliament.					
Attending party meetings can be tiring after a day's work					
Being an active party member is a good way to meet interesting people					
Party activity often takes time away from one's family					
Many people think party activists are extremists					
The amount of work done by ordinary party members is very often unrecognised					
When Liberal Democrat party members are united and work together they can really change Britain.					
By and large, Liberal Democrat MPs try to represent the views of ordinary party members.					
For the Liberal Democrats to have a reasonable chance of success every member must contribute as much as they can					

PERSONAL DETAILS

53. Which of these descriptions applies to what you were doing last week, that is, in the seven days ending last Sunday?

IF MORE THAN ONE APPLIES PLEASE FILL IN THE BOX FOR THE ACTIVITY WHICH IS MOST IMPORTANT TO YOU

In full-time education

On a government training/employment scheme (e.g. Employment Training, New Deal)

In full-time paid work

In part-time paid work

Waiting to take up paid work already accepted

Unemployed and registered at a benefit office

Unemployed and NOT registered

Permanently sick or disabled

Wholly retired from work

Looking after the home full-time

In full/part-time voluntary (unpaid) work

Doing something else, please write in

54. Which type of organisation do you work for? (If you are not working now, please answer about your LAST job.)

PLEASE FILL IN ONE BOX ONLY

Private sector firm or company (eg limited companies and plc's)

Nationalised industry or public corporation (eg Post Office, BBC)

Other public sector employer (eg Central Government, Civil Service, Local Authorities, Universities, LEA, NHS, Police, Armed Forces)

Charity/voluntary sector (eg charitable companies, churches, trade unions)

Other organisation (write in)

55. Are you self-employed, or do you work for someone else as an employee? (If you are not working now, please answer about your LAST job.)

PLEASE FILL IN ONE BOX ONLY

Self-employed

Employee

Never had a job

205

56. In your job, do you supervise, or are you responsible for the work of any other people? (Again if you are not working now, please answer in terms of your LAST job.)

Yes ☐   No ☐

57. If YES, how many people do you supervise?

Under 25 ☐

25 and over ☐

58. What is the title of your present job? (Again if you are not working now, please answer about your last job.) PLEASE WRITE IN

59. Would you describe in detail the type of work you do, being as specific as you can. PLEASE WRITE IN

60. Do you regard yourself as belonging to any one particular religion?

Yes ☐   No ☐

61. If YES, which denomination is that?

PLEASE FILL IN ONE BOX ONLY

Roman Catholic ☐

Church of England/Wales/Scotland/Anglican ☐

Methodist ☐

Muslim ☐

Jewish ☐

Other, please specify

62. How religious do you consider yourself to be? PLEASE FILL IN ONE BOX ONLY

Very religious ☐

Somewhat religious ☐

Not very religious ☐

Not at all religious ☐

63. Have you obtained any of the following qualifications?
PLEASE FILL IN AS MANY AS APPROPRIATE

CSE grades 2 to 5

CSE grade 1, GCE O level, GCSE, School Certificate

Scottish Ordinary/Lower Certificate

GCE A Level or Higher Certificate

Scottish Higher Certificate

Technical Qualification (eg City and Guilds, ONC/HNC, B.Tech)

University or CNAA degree

Post-graduate qualification, e.g. PGCE, Phd,

Other (please specify)

64. Do you ever think of yourself as belonging to any particular social class?

Yes _____ No _____

65. If YES, which class is that?
PLEASE FILL IN ONE BOX ONLY

Middle class

Working class

Other (please specify)

66. When you were young (i.e. a teenager) would you say that your family belonged to any particular social class?

Yes _____ No _____

67. If YES, which class was that?
PLEASE FILL IN ONE BOX ONLY

Middle class

Working class

Other (please specify)

68. How would you describe the level of party support of the following family members (including your parents when you were growing up)?

PLEASE FILL IN ONE BOX FOR EACH FAMILY MEMBER

	Your spouse/ partner	Your mother (when you were growing up)	Your father (when you were growing up)
Liberal Democrat (or Liberal) voter but not member			
Liberal Democrat (or Liberal) member not active			
Active Liberal Democrat (or Liberal) member			
Labour voter but not member			
Labour member			
Conservative voter but not member			
Conservative member			
Other/don't know			

69. What was your age last birthday? years

70. Please indicate your gender.

Male   Female

71. Please indicate your ethnic origins.   PLEASE FILL IN ONE BOX ONLY

White/European

Asian (for example Indian or Pakistani)

Black (for example West Indian)

Other (please specify)

72. Which of the following categories represents the total income of your household from ALL sources before tax?

PLEASE FILL IN ONE BOX

Under £5,000

£5,000 up to £10,000

£10,000 up to £20,000

£20,000 up to £30,000

£30,000 up to £40,000

£40,000 up to £50,000

£50,000 up to £60,000

£60,000 plus

POLITICAL THERMOMETER

 Please think for a moment of a thermometer scale that runs from zero to 100, where 50 is the neutral point.

If your feelings are warm and sympathetic towards something or someone, give them a score higher than 50, the warmer your feelings, the higher the score. If your feelings are cold and unsympathetic, give them a score less than 50, the colder your feelings the lower the score. Please mark a thermometer score for each of the following: -
(Leave a blank if you feel you don't know enough about the person or party to rate them).

	cold 0	10	20	30	40	neutral 50	60	70	80	90	warm 100
The Liberal Democrats											
The Labour Party											
The Conservative Party											
Plaid Cymru											
The Green Party											
Paddy Ashdown											
Tony Blair											
William Hague											
Alex Salmond											
Dafydd Wigley											
Menzies Campbell											
Charles Kennedy											
Nick Harvey											
Simon Hughes											
Malcolm Bruce											
Liz Lynne											
Don Foster											
Jim Wallace											
Jackie Ballard											
	0	10	20	30	40	50	60	70	80	90	100

POLITICAL ATTITUDES

74. Next there is another set of statements about important political issues. We would like to know if you agree or disagree with them.

PLEASE FILL IN ONE BOX FOR EACH STATEMENT

	Strongly agree	Agree	Neither	Disagree	Strongly disagree
The government should ban all experiments on animals.					
Coalition governments are the best form of government for Britain.					
Increasing income tax is no longer an acceptable way of reducing inequality.					
Further nuclear energy development is essential for the future prosperity of Britain.					

	Strongly agree	Agree	Neither	Disagree	Strongly disagree
Party members should be willing to compromise their political principles if the party is to achieve electoral success.					
Life sentences should mean life.					
Homosexual relations are always wrong.					
The government should establish a prices and incomes policy as a means of controlling inflation.					
The government should discourage the growth of one parent families.					
The central question of British politics is the class struggle between labour and capital.					
I would rather be a citizen of Britain than any other country of the world.					
The Single Transferable Vote is the only acceptable electoral system for Britain					
Britain should support harmonisation of taxation and spending as the next stage of European integration					
Prescription charges for medicines should be abolished even if this means higher taxes					
The only way to solve the housing crisis is to build on greenfield sites as much as brownfield sites					

75. Please indicate whether you think the government should or should not do the following things, or doesn't matter either way?
PLEASE FILL IN ONE BOX FOR EACH STATEMENT

	Definitely should	Probably should	Doesn't matter	Probably should not	Definitely should not
Get rid of private education					
Spend more money to get rid of poverty					
Encourage the growth of private medicine					
Put more money into the National Health Service					
Reduce government spending generally					
Introduce stricter laws to regulate trade unions					
Give workers more say in the places where they work					
Spend less on defence					

76. Do you think Britain's long term policy should be...
PLEASE FILL IN ONE BOX ONLY

..to leave the European Union

to stay in the EU and try to reduce the EU's powers

to leave things as they are

to stay in the EU and try to increase the EU's powers

or, to work for the formation of a single European government?

77. Next there is a final list of statements about various political issues. We would like to know if you agree or disagree with them. PLEASE FILL IN ONE BOX FOR EACH STATEMENT

	Strongly agree	Agree	Neither	Disagree	Strongly disagree
Britain should have nuclear weapons as part of a western defence system					
Only black and Asian MPs can properly represent the real interests of black and Asian people					
The government should pursue a foreign policy which maximises its independence from the United States					
The Liberal Democrat party should always stand by its principles even if this should lose an election					
The government should encourage grammar schools					
The English regions should have elected assemblies with taxing powers					
For the sake of the environment car users should pay higher taxes					
It is a good thing for schools to be made to compete against each other for pupils					
The government should make abortions more difficult to obtain					
People who break the law should be given stiffer sentences					
Local authorities should have greater independence from central government even if this produces big variations in the quality of services					
The public enterprises privatised by the Conservative Party should be returned to the public sector					
It would be a good thing to abolish the monarchy					
Everyone's taxes should go up to provide better old age pensions for all					
The only way to deal with the funding crisis in the NHS is to have a substantial increase in general taxation					
Labour politicians cannot be trusted and Liberal Democrats should keep their distance					
The use of cannabis should be legal for all citizens					

OFFICE USE ONLY

End of Questionnaire

Please check that you have answered all the questions.

THANK YOU VERY MUCH FOR YOUR HELP

If you would like to receive some feedback from our survey, please mark this box

211

References

Achen, Christopher H. (1975). 'Mass Political Attitudes and the Survey Response', *American Political Science Review*, 69: 1218–31.

Almond, Gabriel A and Sidney Verba (1963). *The Civic Culture: Political Attitudes and Democracy in Five Nations*. Princeton, NJ: Princeton University Press.

Barry, Brian (1970). *Sociologists, Economists and Democracy*. London: Collier-Macmillan.

Bennie, Lyn, John Curtice, and Wolfgang Rudig (1996). 'Party Members', in Don MacIver (ed.), *The Liberal Democrats*. London: Prentice-Hall.

Boothroyd, David (2001). *Politico's Guide to the History of British Political Parties*. London: Politico's.

Brennan, Geoffrey and James Buchanan (1984). 'Voter Choice: Evaluating Political Alternatives', *American Behavioral Scientist*, 28: 185–201.

British Election Study (1987). *Dataset*. University of Essex: ESRC Archive.

—— (1997). *Dataset*. University of Essex: ESRC Archive.

Budge, Ian et al. (2001). *Mapping Policy Preferences: Estimates for Parties, Electors, and Governments, 1945–1998*. Oxford: Oxford University Press.

Butler, David (1952). *The British General Election of 1951*. London: Macmillan.

—— and Gareth Butler (1994). *British Political Facts, 1900–1994*. Basingstoke: Macmillan.

—— and Dennis Kavanagh (1997). *The British General Election of 1997*. Basingstoke: Macmillan.

—— and Donald Stokes (1969). *Political Change in Britain: Forces Shaping Electoral Choice*. Basingstoke: Macmillan.

—— —— (1974). *Political change in Britain: The Evolution of Electoral Choice*, 2nd edn. London: Macmillan.

Cain, Bruce, John Ferejohn, and Morris Fiorina (1986). *The Personal Vote: Constituency Service and Electoral Independence*. Cambridge, MA: Harvard University Press.

Campbell, Angus, Philip E. Converse, Warren E. Miller, and Donald E. Stokes (1960). *The American Voter*. New York: Wiley.

Carter, John R. and Stephen D. Guerette (1992). 'An Experimental Study of Voting', *Public Choice*, 73: 251–60.

Clarke, Harold D., Marianne Stewart, and Paul Whiteley (1998). 'New Models for New Labour: The Political Economy of Labour Support, January 1992–April 1997', *American Political Science Review*, 92: 559–75.

—— David Sanders, Mariannce C. Stewart, and Paul Whiteley (2004). *Political Choice in Britain*. Oxford: Oxford University Press.

Clarke, P. F. (1971). *Lancashire and the New Liberalism*. Cambridge: Cambridge University Press.

Conover, Pamela and Stanley Feldman (1986). 'Emotional Reactions to the Economy: I'm Mad as Hell and I'm Not Going to Take It Any More', *American Journal of Political Science*, 30: 50–78.

Converse, Philip E. (1964). 'The Nature of Belief Systems', in David E. Apter (ed.), *Ideology and Discontents*. New York: Free Press. 206–61.

—— and Greg Markus (1979). 'Plus Ça Change... The New CPS Panel Study', *American Political Science Review*, 73: 32–49.

Cook, Chris (1998). *A Short History of the Liberal Party 1900–1997*. London: Macmillan.

Crewe, Ivor (1997). *New Statesman*. 12 December.

—— and Anthony King (1996). *SDP: The Birth, Life and Death of the Social Democratic Party*. Oxford: Oxford University Press.

Curtice, John and Michael Steed (1997). 'The Results Analyzed', in David Butler and Dennis Kavanagh (eds.), *The British General Election of 1997*. Basingstoke: Macmillan.

Dalton, Russell J. (2002). *Citizen Politics*. New York: Seven Bridges Press.

Dangerfield, George (1935). *The Strange Death of Liberal England*. New York: Capricorn Books.

Denver, David (1997). 'The Results: How Britain Voted', in Andrew Geddes and Jonathan Tonge (eds.), *Labour's Landslide*. Manchester: Manchester University Press.

—— (2003). *Elections and Voters in Britain*. London: Palgrave/Macmillan.

—— and Gordon Hands (1985). 'Marginality and Turnout in General Elections in the 1970s', *British Journal of Political Science*, 15: 381–98.

—— —— (1997). *Modern Constituency Electioneering*. London: Frank Cass.

Downs, Anthony (1957). *An Economic Theory of Democracy*. New York: Harper.

Dutton, David (2004). *A History of the Liberal Party*. London: Palgrave-Macmillan.

Duverger, Maurice (1964). *Political Parties, Their Organisation and Activities in the Modern State*. London: Methuen.

Elster (1989). *The Cement of Society: A Study of Social Order*. Cambridge: Cambridge University Press.

Erikson, Robert S. (1978). 'Analysing One Variable Three Wave Panel Data: A Comparison of Two Models', *Political Methodology*, 5: 151–61.

Evans, Geoffrey and Pippa Norris (1998). *Critical Elections: British Parties and Voters in Long Term Perspective*. London: Sage.

Festinger, Leon (1957). *A Theory of Cognitive Dissonance*. London: Tavistock Publications.

Finkel, Steven E., Edward N. Muller, and Karl-Dieter Opp (1989). 'Personal Influence, Collective Rationality, and Mass Political Action', *American Political Science Review*, 83: 885–903.

Frank, Robert H. (1988). *Passion within Reason: The Strategic Role of the Emotions*. New York: W. W. Norton.

Gallup (1997). *Gallup Political Index. Report 441*. London: Gallup Polls.

Goodhart, Charles A. E. and R. J. Bhansali (1970). 'Political Economy', *Political Studies*, 18: 43–106.

Granger, Clive W. J. (1990). *Modelling Economic Series: Readings in Econometric Methodology*. Oxford: Clarendon Press.

Greene, William H. (2003). *Econometric Analysis*. Upper Saddle River, NJ: Prentice-Hall.

Heath, Anthony, John Curtice, Geoff Evans, Roger Jowell, Julia Field, and Sharon Witherspoon (1991). *Understanding Political Change*. Oxford: Pergamon Press.

—— Roger M. Jowell, and John Curtice (2001). *The Rise of New Labour*. Oxford: Oxford University Press.

Himmelweit, Hilde T., Patrick Humphries, Marianne Jaeger, and Michael Katz (1981). *How Voters Decide: A Longitudinal Study of Political Attitudes and Voting Extending Over Fifteen Years*. New York: Academic Press.

Hirschman, Albert (1970). *Exit, Voice and Loyalty*. Cambridge, MA: Harvard University Press.

Inglehart, Ronald (1997). *Modernization and Postmodernization*. Princeton, NJ: Princeton University Press.

Johnston, Ronald and Charles Pattie (1995). 'The Impact of Spending on Party Constituency Campaigns at Recent General Election', *Party Politics*, 1, 261–73.

—— —— and Lucy Johnston (1989). 'The Impact of Constituency Spending on the Result of the 1987 British General Election', *Electoral Studies*, 8: 143–55.

Jordan, Grant and William A. Maloney (1997). *The Protest Business? Mobilizing Campaign Groups*. Manchester: Manchester University Press.

Kennedy, Peter (2003). *Guide to Econometrics*. Maldon, MA: Blackwell.

King, Anthony (1998). 'Why Labour Won—at Last', in Anthony King (ed.), *New Labour Triumphs: Britain at the Polls*. New Jersey: Chatham House.

Kitschelt, Herbert (1989). 'The Internal Politics of Parties: The Law of Curvilinear Disparity Revisited', *Political Studies*, 37: 400–21.

Luskin, Robert C. (1987). 'Measuring Political Sophistication', *American Journal of Political Science*. 31: 856–99.

Marcus, George E. (1988). 'The Structure of Emotional Response: 1984 Presidential Candidates', *American Political Science Review*, 83: 737–62.

Marshall, Paul and David Laws (eds.) (2004). *The Orange Book: Reclaiming Liberalism*. London: Profile Books.

May, J. (1973). 'Opinion Structure of Political Parties: The Special Law of Curvilinear Disparity', *Political Studies*, 21: 135–51.

References

Maynard, Geoffrey (1988). *The Economy Under Mrs Thatcher*. Oxford: Basil Blackwell.

McKenzie, Robert (1955). *British Political Parties: The Distribution of Power within the Conservative and Labour Parties*. London: Heinemann.

McKibbin, R. (1983). *The Evolution of the Labour Party, 1910–1924*. Oxford: Oxford University Press.

Miller, William L, Harold D. Clarke, Martin Harrop, Lawrence LeDuc, and Paul F. Whiteley (1990). *How Voters Change: The 1987 British Election Campaign in Perspective*. Oxford: Oxford University Press.

Morgan, Kenneth O. (1978). *The Age of Lloyd-George: The Liberal Party and British Politics, 1890–1929*. London: Allen & Unwin.

Muller, Edward and Karl-Dieter Opp (1986). 'Rational Choice and Rebellious Collective Action', *American Political Science Review*, 80: 471–89.

—— —— (1987). 'Rebellious Collective Action Revisited', *American Political Science Review*, 81: 561–4.

Nicholas, H. G. (1951). *The British General Election of 1950*. London: Macmillan.

Niemi, Richard (1976). 'Costs of Voting and Non-Voting', *Public Choice*, 27:115–19.

Olson, Mancur (1965). *The Logic of Collective Action*. Cambridge, MA: Harvard University Press.

Opp, Karl-Dieter (1990). 'Postmaterialism, Collective Action and Political Protest', *American Journal of Political Science*, 34: 212–35.

Pampel, Fred C. (2000). *Logistic Regression: A Primer*. Thousand Oaks, CA: Sage.

Panebianco, Angelo (1988). *Political Parties: Organization and Power*. Cambridge: Cambridge University Press.

Parry, Geraint, George Moyser, and Neil Day (1992). *Political Participation and Democracy in Britain*. Cambridge: Cambridge University Press.

Pattie, Charles, Ronald Johnston, and Edward Fieldhouse (1995). 'Winning the Local Vote: The Effectiveness of Constituency Campaign Spending in Great Britain 1983–1992', *American Political Science Review*, 89: 969–83.

—— Patrick Seyd, and Paul Whiteley (2004). *Citizenship in Britain: Values, Participation and Democracy*. Cambridge: Cambridge University Press.

Popkin, Samuel L. (1991). *The Reasoning Voter: Communication and Persuasion in Presidential Campaigns*. Chicago: University of Chicago Press.

Rallings and Thrasher (1997). *Local Elections in Britain*. London: Routledge.

Robinson, W. S. (1950). 'Ecological Correlations and the Behavior of Individuals', *American Sociological Review*, 15: 351–7.

Rose, Richard and Ian McAllister (1990). *The Loyalties of Voters: A Lifetime Learning Model*. London: Sage.

Rossiter, David, Ronald Johnston, Charles Pattie, Danny Dorling, Iain MacAllister, and H. Tunstall (1999). 'Changing Biases in the Operation of the UK's Electoral System, 1950–1997', *British Journal of Politics and International Relations*, 1: 133–64.

Russell, Andrew and Edward Fieldhouse (2005). *Neither Left Nor Right? The Liberal Democrats and the Electorate*. Manchester: Manchester University Press.

Samuelson, Paul (1954). 'The Pure Theory of Public Expenditure', *Review of Economics and Statistics*, 36: 387–9.

Sanders, David (1991). 'Government Popularity and the Next General Election', *Political Studies*, 62: 235–61.

—— (2005). 'Popularity Function Forecasts for the 2005 UK General Election', *The British Journal of Politics and International Relations*, 7: 174–90.

—— Harold D. Clarke, Marianne Stewart, and Paul Whiteley (2001). 'The Economy and Voting', in Pippa Norris (ed.), *Britain Votes 2001*. Oxford: Oxford University Press.

Sarlvik, Bo and Ivor Crewe (1983). *Decade of Dealignment: The Conservative Victory of 1970 and Electoral Trends in the 1970s*. Cambridge: Cambridge University Press.

Scarborough, Elinor (1984). *Political Ideology and Voting*. Oxford: Clarendon Press.

Scarrow, Susan (1996). *Parties and Their Members: Organizing for Victory in Britain and Germany*. New York: Oxford University Press.

Seyd, Patrick and Paul F. Whiteley (1992). *Labour's Grassroots: The Politics of Party Membership*. Oxford: Clarendon Press.

—— —— (2002). *New Labour's Grassroots*. Basingstoke: Palgrave.

Sniderman, Paul M., Richard A. Brody, and Philip E. Tetlock (eds.) (1991). *Reasoning and Choice: Explorations in Political Psychology*. Cambridge: Cambridge University Press.

Stuart, Mark (2005). *John Smith: A Life*. London: Politico's.

Times Newspapers (1997). *Times Guide to the House of Commons, 1997*. London: Times Newspapers.

Tomz, Michael, Jason Wittenberg, and Gary King (2001). *CLARIFY: Software for Interpreting and Presenting Statistical Results*. Cambridge, MA: Harvard University, Department of Government.

TSO (1998). *The Report of the Independent Commission on the Voting System*. Cmnd 4090. London: TSO.

Tullock, Gordon (1971). 'The Paradox of Revolution', *Public Choice*, 11: 89–99.

Verba, Sidney and Norman H. Nie (1972). *Participation in America*. Chicago: University of Chicago Press.

—— Kay Lehman Schlozman, and Henry E. Brady (1995). *Voice and Equality: Civic Voluntarism in American Politics*. Cambridge, MA: Harvard University Press.

Webb, Paul (2000). *The Modern British Party System*. London: Sage.

Whiteley, Paul (1986). *Political Control of the Macroeconomy*. London: Sage.

—— and Geoffrey Pridham (1986). 'Anatomy of the SDP: Is the Party Structurally Top Heavy?', *Government and Opposition*, 21: 205–17.

—— and Patrick Seyd (1998). 'The Dynamics of Party Activism in Britain—A Spiral of Demoblisation?', *British Journal of Political Science*, 8: 113–38.

—— —— (2002). *High-Intensity Participation: The Dynamics of Party Activism in Britain*. Ann Arbor, MI: University of Michigan Press.

Whiteley, Paul (2003). 'How to Win a Landslide by Really Trying: The Effects of Local Campaigning on Voting in the 1997 British General Election', *Electoral Studies*, 22: 301–24.

—— —— and Jeremy Richardson (1994). *True Blues: The Politics of Conservative Party Membership*. Oxford: Clarendon Press.

Wilson, Trevor (1966). *The Downfall of the Liberal Party 1914–1935*. London: Collins.

Index

Field, Julia 119, 128
Fieldhouse, Edward 116, 141, 164, 166
Finkel, Steven E. 80
Fiorina, Morris 128
First World War 4
Focus 21, 97
foreign aid 41, 41t;
  see also aid for developing countries
franchise 6
Frank, Robert H. 81
free enterprise 10, 63, 85, 86**f**
free markets 18, 29, 33, 35t, 49–50, 51,
    52, 53, 60, 63
  see also markets
free trade 6, 48, 51
free-riding 77–78, 80, 81
fund-raising 124
funding 73

Gallup 128
gender 38, 58, 109, 112, 163
  imbalance 22, 22t, 23, 33
general elections 113, 116–117, 128,
    130, 138, 145, 146, 149, 167, 176,
    182
  1918 173, 174
  1922 173
  1923 2
  1945 173
  1951 173
  1955 120
  1964 139
  1970 138
  1974 138, 139, 145
  1979 138, 145, 148
  1983 8, 138–139, 141
  1992 114–115, 117–118, 127, 139, 148
  1997 9, 114, 115, 116, 117, 120, 125f,
    126–126t, 127–135, 139, 145,
    148, 161, 168, 177
  2001 126, 148, 157, 158–163, 165, 168
  2005 1–2, 139–140, 141, 147, 157,
    163–168, 171, 177, 178n, 179

general incentives theory 18–19, 68,
    74–75, 76–82, 84–85, 85t,
    86–87t, 88, 89, 94, 102–107t,
    108t, 109, 109t, 110–113
geography 6, 7
Goodhart, Charles A. E. 145
government:
  lack of ability 184
  limited 26
  modern 184
  spending 29–30
Granger, Clive W. J. 154, 155
Granger causality test 154–155
grassroots campaigns 170–171
grassroots members 183, 184
  Conservative Party 136, 169
  Labour Party 136, 169
  Liberal Democrat Party 48, 169
  Liberal Party 7
Greene, William H. 150**n**, 152**n**
Greens 175
Grimond, Jo 10, 11
group benefits 80
group incentives 106, 109
Guerette, Stephen D. 81

Hague, William 159, 161, 163, 168
Hands, Gordon 116, 117, 118, 128, 132
Harrop, Martin 119, 128, 135
health 41, 50, 85
  state provision 29
Heath, Anthony 119, 127, 128
hierarchy 56
Himmelweit, Hilde T. 63
Hirschman, Albert 184
homosexuality 31, 31t, 50, 53, 57, 66
House of Commons 57
  majority 172
  representation 5, 114, 115, 139–140,
    182
  Labour Party 134–135
  seats 178
House of Lords, reform 26, 27, 38–39